CREATING FAMILY/SCHOOL PARTNERSHIPS

NATIONAL MIDDLE SCHOOL ASSOCIATION

Barry Rutherford, Editor
RMC Research Corporation

Studies of Education Reform, Office of Research
Office of Educational Research and Improvement
U.S. Department of Education

Published by National Middle School Association

National Middle School Association is dedicated to improving the educational experiences of young adolescents by providing vision, knowledge, and resources toall who serve them in order to develop healthy, productive, and ethical citizens.

Barry Rutherford is a Senior Research Associate with RMC Research Corporation in Denver, Colorado. A former public school teacher and administrator, Dr. Rutherford serves at RMC as project director and management team member. He is grateful for the contributions of his colleagues there, especially Dr. Pat Seppanen, for help in conceptualizing this volume.

National Middle School Association is pleased to publish these excellent and useful papers and extends its thanks to Dr. Rutherford.

Acknowledgements

RMC Research Corporation wishes to acknowledge the contributions of Dr. Thomas S. Dickinson of Indiana State University; Dr. John Lounsbury, National Middle School Association; Dr. Oliver C. Moles, Contracting Officer's Technical Representative, United States Department of Education, Office of Educational Research and Improvement; Ms. Marti Smith, former Project Director of the study, for providing leadership during the preparation of these papers; and April Tibbles, Katie Sullivan, and Cassandra Bonner of National Middle School Association for their conscientious work in designing and producing this book.

This work is part of the Studies of Education Reform program, supported by the U.S. Department of Education, Office of Educational Research and Improvement, under contract No. RR 91-1720.08. The program supports studies and disseminates practical information about implementing and sustaining successful innovations in American education. The opinions, findings, and conclusions in this document do not necessarily reflect the position or policy of the U.S. Department of Education, and no official endorsement should be inferred.

Preface

Overview

In 1991 the United States Department of Education, Office of Educational Research and Improvement (OERI) commissioned twelve studies that focus on evaluating nationally significant recent education reform and restructuring efforts across the country. The fundamental purpose of each of these studies is to document and analyze useful models and practices that others can learn from or emulate as they seek to reform American education. Key research questions include: What was expected of the reform? How did the initiative unfold? What has it accomplished? What lessons can be drawn from the study sites that are useful for others implementing similar reforms? Based on existing data, the studies examine the impact of the reforms, particularly the impact on students, and especially the impact on student learning. RMC Research Corporation was awarded the contract to study parent and community involvement in education, emphasizing programs at the middle grades (grades 6-8). Three aspects of parent and community involvement in education are the focus of this study: (1) comprehensive districtwide efforts to involve parents and community members in the education of all children; (2) parent and community involvement as either a strategy or outcome in the restructuring of middle grades education; and (3) the involvement of parents and families through interactive activities at home that support learning in school.

Scope of the work

The papers presented in this volume include two of the tasks accomplished in the study: a review of the research and practice literature on parent and community involvement related to the middle grades, and papers on related topics that were commissioned under the study and authored by nationally recognized researchers and practitioners. Although the literature base for parent and community involvement specifically related to the middle grades is not well-developed, this paper draws from the general literature and adapts information found there to the middle grades.

In June 1992 a national conference on middle grades parent and community involvement was held in the Washington, DC area for school administrators, teachers, and local, state, and national policymakers. The conference was sponsored by OERI; RMC Research Corporation; the Center on Families, Communities, Schools and Children's Learning; the Institute for Responsive Education; the National

Committee for Citizens in Education; and the National Education Association. This two-day working conference allowed over 150 conference participants to interact in small group sessions with commissioned paper authors and project staff. The conference was developed to enable each participant to hear a brief overview of the commissioned papers, to hear an expanded presentation on one paper, and an indepth presentation and discussion on two paper topics that were of greatest interest to them. As a result of the conference, participants' input was incorporated into the papers, and project staff revised the literature review.

Throughout the study, attention was paid to critical issues that shaped the research work. These issues are reviewed first, then an overview of each of the papers included in this volume is presented.

Issues that have shaped the work

A number of forces have focused recent attention on the connections among parents, communities, and the schools. One is the national concern with families and family life. A second is the quality and quantity of preparation prior to entering school for children and parents who are not proficient speakers of English. Another force is the recognition that schools and communities must join forces to provide resources for educational efforts. Finally, a new commitment to parent and community involvement in education and the strengthening of home learning for all parents is also becoming evident in legislation and calls for action.

There is great interest from many quarters in helping parents become more actively involved in their children's education—as a right, a responsibility, and an unfulfilled opportunity. Although many educators and schools and some school systems have developed programs and practices to strengthen parent involvement in education, not all programs have succeeded in involving low income, racial and ethnic minority, and limited-English-proficient parents. Many such programs come and go, are not studied systematically, and are not widely known. Most programs are concentrated in the lower grades, so that little is known about how schools can work with parents of older students.

In recent years, broadly representative studies have shown a strong interest on the part of parents, educators, and educational agencies in developing stronger relationships with parents concerning their children's education, particularly in terms of encouraging home learning activities. Many parents hold back, not from lack of interest, but from other considerations such as time conflicts, limited information, and feelings of estrangement and discomfort relating to educators and schools. How to involve these parents productively remains an open question, especially since few teachers and administrators have received training in working with parents.

Part I of this volume is a review of research and practice literature on parent and community involvement and literature related specifically to the middle grades. Five chapters focus on the context of parent and community involvement programs, the development and implementation of programs, the impact of programs, implications, conclusions and recommendations drawn from the review. The rich contextual environments of schools and school districts are influenced by both the larger environment—usually thought of as the historical, sociocultural and political conditions over which schools and school districts have little control—and the more immediate environment—conditions specific to the classroom, the school building, and the school district over which key players may have direct influence. School, district, state, and federal policies are key influences on parent and community involvement programs. The development and implementation of programs is shaped more by the diversity within systems and perceptions, attitudes and beliefs than by the organizational pattern of the school. Institutional settings and pre-adolescent/adolescent development are also found to have a direct influence on the middle grades.

This synthesis of the literature reveals three critical roles that parents and community members can play in the partnerships that are created in the development and implementation of parent and community involvement programs. The first role for parents is as the primary resource in the education of their own children, and is best exemplified in home learning. A second role is parents and community members as a resource in the formal education of their own children or other children in a specific school setting. For example, parents and community members may serve as volunteers, tutors, or share their expertise in specific subjects. The third role involves parents and community members as participants in the education of children in various schools throughout the community—most frequently, these programs are planned, designed, and implemented districtwide. Parents and community members may be involved though a variety of roles that can include volunteering in schools and classrooms, sitting on school governance and advisory boards, participating in parent/teacher organizations, and learning how to enrich the home learning environment. The review discusses the key program elements and strategies specific to parent and community involvement programs that are designed and implemented to enhance the partnership roles of parents, families, communities, and schools. Communication, key players, and resources are discussed as program elements that cut across all of the partnership roles and are critical factors in parent and community involvement programs at all levels of the education system.

The literature review explores the impact of parent and community involvement programs. Considerable research has been done which establishes an *associative link*, or correlation, between school efforts to create partnerships with parents, families and community members, and outcomes for students, parents, school personnel, and schools and school districts. Additionally, this review of the literature allows the authors to draw conclusions about successful programs and partnerships, and to discuss their implications.

Part II of this volume includes five papers that were commissioned by RMC

Research Corporation for the 1992 national conference. The first paper, *Comprehensive Districtwide Reforms in Parent and Community Involvement Programs*, by Nancy Feyl Chavkin, presents the definition and guiding questions that introduce the topic of districtwide reform along with a discussion of the importance of key people who share a common vision for change. The paper goes on to review the research about parent and community involvement, describe two key facilitating factors found in districts with promising parent and community involvement programs: policy and support for policy; and consider the critical issues of allocating budgets and resources, assessing outcomes, and the collaboration process for parent and community involvement programs. Using case studies from middle schools, the paper reviews ways districts can enhance parent involvement. The conclusions include a discussion of recommendations and further issues for improving parent and community involvement.

The second paper, *School Restructuring to Facilitate Parent and Community Involvement in the Middle Grades*, by Janet Chrispeels, addresses five major issues regarding how to change or restructure middle schools and middle grades education to involve parents and the community in student learning. First, a conceptual framework for thinking about the ways parents, community, and school staff must work together in partnership is presented. Second, several examples of how middle schools are changing and restructuring their parent and community programs to reach out to parents and the community are described. Third, emerging structures and instructional practices in middle school reform are discussed and ideas presented on how these restructuring efforts could be used to connect more fully students, their families, and communities with schools. Fourth, the paper discusses potential staff development needs that must be addressed if teachers and school staff are to be more actively involved and work with parents and community. Finally, the paper outlines further areas for research about family-school connections in the middle grades.

Joyce L. Epstein and Lori Connors address the question "What do we mean by 'parent involvement' in the middle grades?" in the third paper, *School and Family Partnerships in the Middle Grades*. They suggest that the term "school and family partnerships" better expresses the shared interests, responsibilities, and investments of families and schools in children's education.

How can we begin to understand and improve family and school connections when students become early adolescents?...when middle grades schools become more complex?...and when families become more confused about their children and their continuing influence in education in the middle grades? The design and organization of school and family partnerships in the middle grades must account for and respond to these factors. This paper addresses these questions with an overview of middle grades students, families, and schools; a framework to help build successful partnership; a brief review of research on partnerships at this level; and a discussion of pertinent issues for educators and researchers as they improve practice and conduct new studies to improve the knowledge base.

In the fourth paper, *Activities in the Home that Support School Learning in the Middle Grades*, author Diane Scott-Jones addresses the research on specific activities in homes that support school learning in the middle grades. With young children, these activities are more obvious and are closely related to children's play, games, and toys. Parents' reading to and with their children is an activity that supports the acquisition of early reading skills, but is also quite enjoyable to most parents and children. The change in activities in the home that support school learning in the middle grades is aptly denoted by the use of the word "work." No longer clearly in the realm of fun and play, "homework" is a serious enterprise, to be completed before turning to more pleasant activities.

Scott-Jones provides a conceptual framework for home learning that includes four roles parents may play: valuing, monitoring, helping, and doing. It is through the first three of these roles that parents foster effective learning in the home.

In the final paper, *Bringing Schools and Communities Together in Preparation for the 21st Century*, Patrick M. Shields explores the implication of the current reform agenda for governmental policies concerning the involvement of communities, families, and parents. The underlying questions addressed are: What are the most appropriate roles for parents and communities in the current efforts to improve schooling? What policies should federal, state, or local decisionmakers put in place to support this involvement? Where relevant, special attention is focused on policies related to the middle grades.

In responding to these questions Shields provides a brief review of the history of education reform and parent involvement policies over the past few decades. Next, the differences between the current wave of reform and previous efforts are discussed and implications for parent and community participation in the schools is provided. Then, based on this discussion, a set of policy recommendations for decision-makers at all levels of the educational system is outlined. Finally, promising directions for future research are given.

OERI and RMC Research published three practical products—the School/Family Partnership Series—that provide information, resources, and program descriptions to practitioners and parents on middle school conferences, resource programs, and seven themes that were drawn from the fieldwork of their study. Additionally, indepth fieldwork was conducted in nine sites across the country to study comprehensive districtwide parent and community involvement programs, parent and community involvement as a strategy or outcome of restructuring, and interactive activities at home that support school learning (three sites per area). As a result of the fieldwork, a three-volume technical report was written that details the research plan, methodology, findings, and implications from the study, as well as complete texts of the case studies.

Conclusion

This volume is intended to be used as a springboard to stimulate a much needed dialogue about parent and community involvement in middle grades education. It is our hope that both practitioners and policymakers will find it useful in framing their discussions and in planning, developing, and implementing school/family partnerships in the middle grades.

For further information about **Studies of Education Reform: Parent and Community Involvement in Education**, please call or write:

Barry Rutherford, Ph.D.
Project Director, Parent and Community Involvement
RMC Research Corporation
1512 Larimer St., Suite 540
Denver, Colorado 80202
1-303-825-3636

Table of Contents

Part I

A Review of the Research and Practice Literature on Parent and
Community Involvement

Barry Rutherford
Shelley H. Billig
Jim Kettering

Chapter 1

Introduction

The author of *Education Through Partnership* (1981) David Seeley has stated that genuine reform depends on working on relationships-with the home, community groups, politiciansand business. There is a rich history of schools and the public they serve working together toward a common goal: the education of America's youth. Existing partnerships between schools and parents, families, and communities are being sustained; new and exciting partnerships are being forged throughout the nation. This review of the literature on the current state-of-the-art in parent and community involvement looks at the programs, practices, and their effects in the research and practice literature, especially since 1980.

We explore past history and offer a contemporary view of the policies, trends, and factors that provide an understanding for the context of parent and community involvement programs. The discussion of the development and implementation of programs is framed within the roles that parents, families, and community members assume in the educational process. It is here that we focus on home learning, school restructuring, and districtwide programs as vehicles through which these roles are facilitated. We survey the literature on the impacts that parent and community involvement programs claim, especially on outcomes for students, parents, teachers, and schools. Finally, conclusions are drawn from the research and practice literature, implications of the literature are discussed and recommendations for further research are made. The literature on *middle grades* (i.e., grades 4 through 8) parent and community involvement programs and practices is highlighted throughout this review since activities in the middle grades are less well-developed and understood than those for earlier grades.

Purposes

This literature review of the current state-of-the-art serves two primary purposes:

- To assist researchers in the refinement of the plan for further research. As part of the national *Studies of Education Reform: Parent and Community Involvement in Education,* this review—in combination with information gained through commissioned papers and a national conference—will provide the basis for fieldwork.

- To inform practitioners, policymakers, and other interested parties of the current state-of-the-art in parent and community involvement programs. Where literature was available, the review focuses on those programs and practices targeted at *middle grades* populations.

Definitions

The conceptualization of parent and community involvement programs in Chapter 3 of this review involves the roles of parents, families, and community members as they are facilitated in schools and school districts. The roles of parents and families are well-established in the research and practice literature; the roles of community members in governance, as tutors, etc., are emerging as an important area for study.

In 1991 the United States Department of Education commissioned twelve studies of different aspects of national education reform. This study focuses on parent and community involvement in middle grades education. In the original Request for Proposals from the Department three areas were indicated for concentrated study. The three areas were: (1) home learning, (2) school restructuring, and (3) districtwide programs. Typologies and frameworks are important for understanding parent and community involvement (see, for example, Epstein & Connors, 1993; Chrispeels, 1993). These typologies and frameworks are important contributions to the conceptualization of parent and community involvement and include the roles of parents, families, and community members in home learning, school restructuring, and districtwide programs. However, for this review and anticipated field research RMC Research Corporation proposes a conceptual framework that includes the three broad areas outlined in the original Request for Proposals.

To provide clarity, we define the three areas as:

- **Home learning.** Parents can extend their children's school learning through home activities such as reading with their children; assisting them with homework; encouraging family games, activities, and discussions; promoting general study, learning skills and motives; and improving their own parenting skills. Parents are assisted by the classroom teacher or other school staff through workshops, seminars, and parent education courses, or more informally through suggestions from teachers for home learning activities to support the curriculum or assist with homework assignments.

- **School restructuring.** At the building level, schools may change their activities; relationships with parents, families, and community members; programs; practices and structure in significant ways to encourage more parent involvement. Examples include schools providing more time for staff to contact parents, hiring parent coordinators, adapting school meetings to parent needs and schedules, training staff to work more effectively with parents, or holding meetings in community gathering places. The emphasis is on school-initiated activities to promote contacts with all parents, to help parents learn more about their children's school programs and progress, to help them gain information on home learning activities and home supports for education, and to suggest other ways to help them help their children learn.

- **Districtwide programs.** The emphasis of comprehensive district programs is on the variety of roles for parents and community members, particularly in schools with many educationally at-risk students. It is in these districtwide programs that the roles of community members become most clear. These roles might include volunteering in classrooms and schools, serving on school governance and advisory boards, participating in parent/teacher organizations, and learning how to enrich the home learning environment. Collaboration with businesses and community service agencies such as flex-time for school conferences or other school-related activities may also be considered. Parents and community members are offered a variety of options for involvement from which to choose. Such comprehensive programs might use innovative methods of communicating with parents on various educational and child development issues; on recruiting and using volunteers in new, meaningful ways; and other ways to make the programs attractive to different kinds of parents and community members.

Criteria for Selection and Inclusion

There is an extensive body of literature on parent and community involvement. A determination of the sources to be selected and included was made according to the following criteria:

- **Timeliness.** Primarily, research and materials related to practice included in this review were conducted or developed after 1980. Some research that was conducted or materials that were developed prior to 1980 have been included if they were used as a foundation for later research or program development. It is worth noting that much research was done prior to 1980; the research climate, especially regarding funding for research, was more favorable during the 1970s.

- **Grade level appropriateness.** Every attempt was made to include literature and research on *middle grades* parent and community involvement programs. However, research and materials included in this review focus, primarily, on parent and community involvement programs *across all grade* *levels*. Items from other grades were included to provide an indication of the rich sources of information on parent and community involvement programs, and to illustrate the need for further research in the middle grades.

- **Focus on the roles of parents, families, and community members as facilitated in the areas of home learning, school restructuring, or districtwide programs.** The items included in this review focused primarily on one or more of the three topic areas mentioned above. Other items were included if they addressed the overall context of parent and community involvement in grades four through eight or if they laid the foundation for further research or material development in any of the three topic areas.

Limitations of the Review

This review of the literature is limited by the following factors:

- **Conceptualization.** There appears to be no uniform conceptualization of parent and community involvement evident in the literature. Neither researchers nor practitioners agree on common definitions.

- **Structure of schools.** Studies of parent and community involvement are rarely organized around middle grades (i.e., grades 4 through 8). It is often difficult to separate those aspects pertaining to the middle grades from studies that include the early elementary grades (K-3) and/or secondary school grades (9-12).

- **Overlap.** In our review of research and practices in the schools, we found considerable overlap among these topics. For example, a home learning initiative may be part of an overall effort to restructure the schools to facilitate parent involvement. As part of this restructuring effort, the school and/or district may be fostering new roles for parents and community members in the schools. When appropriate, we have indicated where issues under one topic are related to the other two.

- **Research base.** Although parent and community involvement literature is extensive it contains little research regarding the effects of parent and community involvement on student, parent, teacher, administrator, or other program outcomes. The one area where there is substantial research linking achievement outcomes with parent involvement is home learning. However, most studies that are available are generally descriptive in nature, or correlational, providing no strong evidence for cause-effect relationships.

Guiding Questions

The conceptual framework proposed for this study, and guidelines in the Request For Proposals indicated three areas of interest: the context of parent and community involvement programs; the roles that parents, families, and community members assume in the education of their children; and the effects of promising programs on parents, students, school staff, schools and school districts. From these areas of interest corresponding questions, and sub-questions of each, guided the review of the literature:

- What are the contexts within which parent and community involvement programs operate?

    How do these contextual factors influence those programs?

- What are the roles that parents, families, and community members assume in the education of their children?

    How are these roles facilitated?
    What key elements are specific to these areas?
    What key elements cut across all areas?
    What key resources are needed to design, develop, implement, and sustain these roles?

- What are the effects of promising programs on parents, students, school staff, schools, and/or school districts?

    How are these effects assessed or determined?

Overview of the Chapters

Chapters 2 through 4 contain a detailed discussion of parent and community involvement programs and practices. Chapter 5 draws conclusions, discusses implications, and recommends future research directions. The chapters parallel the guiding questions discussed above. The content of the chapters is described below:

- **Chapter 2.** The context within which parent and community involvement programs operate is discussed. The policy environment, factors that influence programs generally, and factors that are specific to middle grade programs are examined.

- **Chapter 3.** The roles of parents in three catagories are discussed: a primary resource in their children's education; parents as supporters and advocates for the education of their children in local programs; and parents as participants in the education of all children. How these roles are facilitated through home learning, school restructuring, and districtwide programs is reviewed;

the key elements specific to each area, and key elements that cut across all areas are explored.

- **Chapter 4.** The effects of parent and community involvement programs on outcomes for students, parents, school personnel, and schools and school districts are summarized.

- **Chapter 5.** Conclusions are drawn from the research and practice literature. Implications for schools and parents are considered. Future directions for research are also recommended.

Chapter 2

Creating Partnerships: The Context of Parent and Community
Involvement Programs

Overview

Context takes into account the conditions within which programs operate. Parent and community involvement programs operate in rich contextual environments: the environment of schools and school districts. The formulation and implementation of any policies and programs related to parent and community involvement will affect and be affected by forces external to any program. In identifying the set of actors and circumstances that are crucial for the development and implementation of parent and community involvement programs, it is helpful to distinguish between the larger environment and the more immediate environmental conditions. By the larger environment, we mean those historical, sociocultural, and political conditions that may have an indirect impact on the connections between the schools, parents, and the larger community. In contrast, the immediate environment includes the key players, issues, and conditions specific to classroom, the school building, and the school district. These elements have an immediate and/or direct influence on parent and community involvement in the schools. From the literature we see that these contextual factors serve to define the need to develop and sustain relationships between the home, school, and community while simultaneously serving as deterrents to any progress toward enhanced relationships.

Historically, it has been evident that local, state, and federal policies have either facilitated or inhibited the development and implementation of parent and community involvement programs. Four levels of policy are important to this discussion:

- **School policies** exist in two forms: as "stand-alone" documents (e.g., policies that address homework), or policies that are subsumed under a larger district policy framework.

- **District policies** designed to involve parents and communities in schooling are beginning to surface in light of state and federal initiatives.

- **State policies** reflect the urgency to use the resources of home and community to ensure student success. Forty-seven of fifty states responded to a survey about parent involvement policies and guidelines; over half had either policies or guidelines.

- **Federal policies** in education have a long and varied history. Parent involvement policies under Title I of the Elementary and Secondary Education Act (ESEA) were designed in response to social changes of the 1960s. Although these policies have changed through several reauthorizations, they nevertheless provide a template for other efforts that are intended to guarantee the involvement of parents in schooling.

A number of other trends and factors have been identified as either positively or negatively influencing parent and community involvement efforts, *regardless of the organizational structure of the school:*

- **Diversity within systems.** As families, communities, and cultural and economic systems change, so do the roles and responsibilities of parents, schools, and communities. A systems perspective provides a framework for understanding these changes.

- **Perceptions, attitudes, and beliefs.** It is a commonly held belief that parents, communities, and schools work toward a common goal—producing successful students. Research indicates that perceptions, attitudes, and beliefs differ dramatically among the constituents of schooling.

The literature reveals at least three factors directly affecting middle grades parent and community involvement:

- **Institutional settings.** Logistics, location, curriculum, and school size affect parent and community involvement at the middle grades. These institutional settings provide little encouragement, and are more often frightening, to parents.

- **Pre-adolescent/adolescent development.** The developmental stages of pre-adolescence and adolescence present particular challenges for parents, schools, and communities.

- **Expectations, attitudes, and beliefs.** What teachers and schools expect of middle grades students and parents changes as children mature and move into different academic settings. These expectations are often misperceived by both children and their parents.

An historical and contemporary view of the policies, trends, and factors that provides an understanding of the context of parent and community involvement is discussed in detail in the remainder of this chapter.

The Policy Environment

Historical influences provide an insight into the role of schools, and local, state, and federal agencies in the development of policies concerning parent and community involvement. The designers of the Constitution felt strongly that education should not be the domain of the federal government, and ultimately gave the right and responsibility for educating the nation's youth to the states. Snider's (1990a) historical review of the role of parents and community in school decision making portrays a long, and often embittered, struggle between politicians, practitioners, and parents/communities. Attempts to consolidate control over schools in the mid-1800s and a rising dissatisfaction in the 1960s with the quality of education in some of the nation's largest urban areas, often referred to as the "community-control movement," were two notable areas for disagreement.

Four contemporary policy levels are explored: school, district, state, and federal. This exploration lends understanding to the ways policy may facilitate and/or inhibit the involvement of parents and communities in educational processes, programs, and practices.

Generally, policies are not written explicitly for middle grades. Literature supporting the influences of policy on parent and community involvement in the middle grades is noted.

School Policies

Current school level policies and expectations tend to center on what parents can provide for teachers and schools rather than what *teachers and schools* can provide for *parents*. Studies of 171 teachers from Chapter 1 elementary and middle schools in Baltimore, for example, showed that teachers expect parents to fulfill a range of different responsibilities including teaching their children appropriate behaviors, knowing what children are supposed to learn at any given grade, and helping them with their homework. Few teachers could point to comprehensive programs in their classes or schools to help parents attain these skills (Dauber & Epstein, 1991).

There is evidence that policies and resource constraints in the schools themselves may inhibit parent involvement. For example, in the absence of a homework policy or failure by teachers to adhere to a homework policy consistently, parent involvement in home learning may be hindered. Conflicting expectations for the student may surface between parents and teachers. A similar problem occurs if there is a lack of materials or other resources for teachers to use to design or implement the home learning activities (Chrispeels, 1991b). Schools need to implement home learning policies that provide sufficient resources—funds, time, staff, and training—to enable teachers to be more effective in this area (Zeldin, 1989; Chrispeels, 1991a; Dauber & Epstein, 1991; McLaughlin & Shields, 1987).

District Policies

District level policy initiatives mirror federal and state initiatives. Chavkin and Williams (1987) surveyed educators, school board members, and parents in five southwestern states and found that parent involvement policies at the district level were virtually non-existent as of 1983. This condition existed in spite of the fact that educators and parents desired more school policies about parent involvement. Since that time, examples of successful district initiatives are beginning to surface.

In 1988 San Diego City Schools adopted a district parent involvement policy that closely paralleled the state policy. The policy addresses the roles of parents, communication, strategies and structures for effective parent involvement, supports for both teachers and parents, and the use of schools to connect families and students with community resources (Chrispeels, 1991b).

Indianapolis Public Schools view parent involvement "as an important component of the district's school improvement plan" (Warner, 1991, p. 373). The Parents in Touch program, the umbrella program for all parent involvement activities, emphasizes two-way communication on matters related to student success. Epstein's (1987a) model for comprehensive parent involvement includes: developing parenting skills, communication, the use of parent volunteers, home learning, and parental participation in decision making across the district. Using a wide variety of communication strategies, this model is operating in the Indianapolis schools.

State Policies

State education agencies develop policies because schools alone cannot ensure that all students are successful. They must also take into consideration the additional resources of home and community. Additionally, parent and community involvement policy may serve to provide state education administrators with evaluation information on educational practices (Nardine, Chapman, & Moles, 1989).

Nardine and Morris (1991) surveyed state legislation and guidelines concerning parent involvement and found that 20 states had enacted parent involvement legislation, six states had written guidelines, and 21 states had neither legislation nor written guidelines governing parent involvement. The authors reported that legislation on parent involvement was not a high priority and that a wide diversity exists from state to state in the decisions about policies and guidelines.

Federal Policies

The first active intervention in parent involvement by the federal government came with the passage of the Elementary and Secondary Education Act (ESEA) in 1965. Title I of the ESEA was created as much to empower poor communities to solve their own problems as to provide funding for the education of disadvantaged children (Snider, 1990b). Legislative requirements for the establishment of parent advisory councils at the district and local levels were enacted by 1978. With the 1981 reauthorization of Title I as Chapter 1 of the Education Consolidation and Improvement Act, parent advisory councils were no longer required and parents and community members were given minimal responsibility as "advisors" to Chapter 1 programs. Without federal regulation of parent involvement, most state and local education agencies chose to give little more than lip service to parent and community participation in schooling (Nardine & Morris, 1991).

The 1988 reauthorization of Chapter 1 included the Hawkins-Stafford Amendments to the Elementary and Secondary Education Act. Federal requirements concerning parent involvement were reinstated not in the form of parent advisory councils, but in the development of parent involvement policies. Parents and community members now have a role in developing policies and local educators can best decide how to use these resources in designing and implementing Chapter 1 programs.

Henderson and Marburger (1990) describe six federal educational programs, in addition to Chapter 1 legislation, that include policies pertaining to parent involvement: the Bilingual Education Act (Title VII of the Elementary and Secondary Education Act of 1965, as amended); the Education of the Handicapped Act, P.L. 94–142 (1974); the Family Educational Rights and Privacy Act (FERPA, 1974); Even Start (Part B of the Elementary and Secondary School Improvement Amendments of 1988); Head Start (1965); and FIRST (Fund for the Improvement and Reform of Schools and Teaching, authorized in the Elementary and Secondary School Improvement Amendments of 1988). Each of these programs target parent involvement as a necessary component for successful educational outcomes.

This review of the literature reveals the belief that school, district, state, and federal policies concerning parent involvement should exist, and researchers and policymakers argue that policy plays a critical role in parent involvement and should be a priority for policymakers (see, for example, Davies, 1987; and McLaughlin & Shields, 1986, 1987). Heath and McLaughlin (1987) suggest that a single policy solution is ineffective and call for the development of a national child resource policy. Oakes and Lipton (1990) believe that public commitment to education can be mobilized through the key role that policymakers can play.

Policies are not developed and implemented in the absence of other contextual elements. Various trends and factors may exert influence on the development and implementation of programs and their effects may be as powerful as the effects of the policy itself. The next section looks at trends and factors which influence, both positively and negatively, parent and community involvement in schooling.

Trends and Factors Influencing Parent and Community Involvement

Parent and community involvement programs are influenced, both positively and negatively, by trends and factors that define the immediate context for those programs. These trends and factors have a more direct, and often more immediate, impact on students, parents, school personnel and the larger community within which they operate.

First we focus on the trends and factors that impact parent and community involvement programs *regardless of the organizational structure of the school*. Next we look at the trends and factors that have a direct impact on parent and community involvement *at the middle grades*.

Diversity Within Systems

Parent and community involvement programs operate within complex sociocultural systems that define the more immediate environmental context. The diversity and interconnectedness of those systems make the task of addressing the individual needs of the client populations of schools increasingly difficult.

The focus of this section of the review is on the diversity of three systems that influence parent and community involvement in schools: families, communities, and economies. Although we attempt to delineate the relationships between trends and factors of each of these systems and their influence on programs, it is important to note that systems do not function in isolation. Changes in one system cause changes in other systems. An holistic approach to systems provides insight into ways schools can be restructured to facilitate parent and community involvement.

Families. In a seminal article on family diversity and school policy, Lindner (1987) analyzes three myths about families: the myth of the monolithic family form, the myth of the independent family, and the myth of parental determinism.

The monolithic family—the model of a "typical American family" with a working father, homemaker mother, and progeny solely from that relationship—does not exist. Instead, a myriad of family forms exist: single parents, blended families, dual career families, extended families and so on. In fact, a diversity of family forms has existed throughout American history.

Families, once considered to be independent both economically and educationally, are now expected to meet the challenges of fulfilling emotional needs, coordinating with outside agencies, and meeting the increasing demands of parenting. These challenges have lead to a dependence on experts outside the home. Kenniston (1987, p.9) states:

> ... parents today have a demanding new role choosing, meeting, talking with and coordinating the experts, the technology and the institutions that help bring up their children...No longer able to do it all themselves, parents are in some ways like the executives in a large firm—responsible for the smooth coordination of the many people and processes that must work together to produce the final product...

Early family experience is a critical factor in a child's life. It is unclear, however, just how critical these family experiences are. How much of a child's life experiences are determined by parents, or how much the child determines life experiences of the parents is vague.

"Encouraging the belief that children know nothing about the world except what the parents teach" (Lindner, 1987, p. 10), coupled with the myth of family independence often leads to a parent-blame approach. This is an underlying tension which exists throughout much of the literature on parent and community involvement— "the perception that those needing help are inadequate, rather than the system" (Lindner, 1987, p. 10). The solution to this willingness to blame parents is to "...look instead to the broader economic and social forces that shape the experience of children and parents" (Kenniston, 1987, p. 10). In short, changes within social and economic systems have a great impact on families: an impact which may be difficult to overcome.

Communities. Diversity within communities reflects the diversity of the families that comprise them. Prior to the twentieth century, much of the population was concentrated in rural, agrarian sections of the United States. With the onset of the industrial revolution, and the prospects of a "better life," large numbers of people migrated to these industrial centers. The early 1900s also brought immigrants from many nations to the United States. America became the "cultural melting pot."

Contemporary communities are difficult to characterize because of their diversity: there are large communities and small communities; there are communities that are culturally diverse and there are communities that are populated by persons of one culture; there are urban, suburban, and rural communities. Examples of population demographics illustrating the diversity in communities abound.

The age of the population is shifting. As a whole, the population of the U.S. is aging, but the "baby boom echo" has now reached the middle grades. As students get older, parent involvement tends to decrease. While there are still parents involved in the schooling of younger children, there are greater percentages of people who have no direct relationships with schools.

The elderly are also far less likely to support financial investment in educational institutions. Take, for example, Sun City, a suburb of Phoenix, Arizona. Sun City is a covenant-controlled community; residents can be *no younger* than 55 years old.

The residents of Sun City recently voted to rescind all property taxes supporting schools. Residents reasoned that they had raised their children, paid their taxes, and were no longer obligated to support education in their community. There are far-reaching consequences for such actions by older citizens in communities.

The number of citizens in the United States whose first language is not English is increasing. Educating non-English speakers presents particular challenges for parents, for teachers, and for schools and the community. In a review of the literature regarding limited English speaking populations, Bliss (1986) suggested several ways to enhance the involvement of these parents. These suggestions included:

- schools need to have more realistic expectations of parent capabilities;

- children in these families generally adapt more quickly to the language and culture than do their parents;

- there is a need to focus energy and programs at the middle school and junior high levels; and

- those professionals who deal with LEP students and parents must understand that those children with the greatest needs often do not have a parent available to become involved.

Cultural heritage, important to every citizen, is often overlooked in contemporary education. American Indian parents, educators, tribal leaders, and students present a clear message that they want: (1) direct control over the educational institutions educating their children, (2) implementation of a curriculum that takes their culture into account, and (3) development of community and educational partnerships among students, parents, educators, and community members (American Indian Science and Engineering Society, 1989). They see a need for the reform of American education to better meet their needs and to empower them to assist with reform measures that genuinely take their cultural heritage into account.

Economies. The economic system may have the greatest interactive effect on other systems. A strong economic system impacts families and communities in positive ways. A weak economic system can have devastating effects on both families and the communities in which they live.

As the distribution of wealth in the U.S. has become more skewed, there are increased numbers of impoverished children, families, and communities. Poverty, once thought to be the exclusive domain of urban centers with high concentrations of low socioeconomic populations, is now affecting urban, suburban, and rural areas alike. The perceptions of parents from low socioeconomic conditions can provide valuable lessons as educators seek to involve these parents.

Brantlinger (1985b) interviewed low-income parents and found that the majority of those parents felt that schools favor students from higher income families. While these parents were clearly concerned about their children's education, they generally felt powerless to change these perceived inequities. She also reported (Brantlinger, 1985a) that these same parents believed that high income schools were educationally superior with 94% of the parents favoring attendance of their children in such schools to receive a better education and preparation for social interaction in their adult lives.

Family, community, and economic systems are highly dependent on each other for survival. The adage that "the chain is only as strong as its weakest link" is appropriate when looking holistically at these systems. In restructuring parent involvement programs, each of these systems must be taken into account.

Perceptions, Attitudes, and Beliefs

There has been growing national concern with the relationship between parents and communities and the schools. There are two assumptions that underlie this concern. The first is the belief by the constituents of schools that there is a common goal: educating students to be successful socially, emotionally, and academically. The second assumption is that either parents or schools have somehow failed in reaching that common goal. The literature reveals that the perceptions of parents and school personnel concerning the purposes, goals, and outcomes of schooling may differ dramatically. Parent and community involvement programs, most often developed and implemented by educators, must take these perceptions, attitudes, and beliefs into account.

There is generally a strong interest on the part of parents, teachers, and administrators for developing more home-school collaborations than what currently exists in actual practice at the local school level (Moles, 1987; Williams, 1984; Herman & Yeh, 1983). One of the major difficulties, however, is the differing perceptions as to how to go about involving parents. Chavkin and Williams (1987) conducted surveys with elementary administrators and parents in five southwestern states. Both groups were asked about their attitudes and their school's policies and practices regarding parent involvement. The authors suggested that administrators need to envision a broader role for parent involvement and capitalize on parents as an educational resource. Parents, in turn, must capitalize on using administrators as an access point for further parent involvement. However, these parent/administrator partnerships do not automatically reduce the differences in values or the resultant tensions that may exist between the two groups.

The Parent Involvement Education Project (Williams, 1984) surveyed parents, teachers, principals and other school professionals on five aspects of parent involvement: (1) attitudes; (2) decisions; (3) roles; (4) activities; and (5) teacher training.

The results of the study showed a high degree of interest in home-school partnerships but suggest that parent interests extend beyond the involvement that has been typically sanctioned by schools. These and other studies suggest that educators typically do not welcome parent involvement in advisory or governance roles while parents indicate a strong interest in these activities (Williams & Stallworth, 1983; Ahlenius, 1983).

In general, when teachers and their students differ culturally or educationally or when teachers instruct large numbers of students, teachers are much less likely to know their students' parents, more likely to assume that these parents are disinterested, and much less likely to make efforts to involve the parents in learning activities (see review in Dauber & Epstein, 1991). The resulting pattern of interaction may give rise to parents and school personnel viewing each other with mutual mistrust and misunderstanding.

Some of the misperceptions stem from the attitudes and beliefs that teachers hold about the willingness of certain types of parents to help their children academically. One recurring theme in several studies and commentaries is that less educated, low income, single or dual career parents and families can not or do not want to become involved in the schools or in their children's education (Baker & Stephenson, 1986; Davies, 1987; Epstein & Dauber, 1989b; Lareau, 1987). Contributing to this is the fact that many teachers have been found to have a conventional middle class model of what constitutes a "good" family and a view that low income families are in some way deficient (Davies, 1988).

The reputed disinterest of low income and less educated families has been refuted by many researchers who have found that, in general, these parents do wish to become involved, but often lack the information needed to do so (Epstein & Becker, 1982; Clark, 1983; McLaughlin & Shields, 1987; Davies, 1988; Dauber & Epstein, 1991; Epstein, 1984a, 1986b, 1991a). In fact, Lightfoot (1975) found that not only do low income parents value education, but they view schooling as an avenue for economic and social success. Studies have also shown that single parents and dual career family members are also quite willing to help, even though they come to fewer school functions (Metropolitan Life Survey, 1987; Epstein, 1984a).

Diversity within family, community, and economic systems, and the perceptions, attitudes, and beliefs of the constituents of schooling, have direct effects on parent and community involvement programs regardless of the organizational structure of the school. There are also factors that influence the development of programs specifically *at the middle grades*. The next section of the review explores these factors.

Institutional Settings

The New York State School Board Association (1987) has identified four factors that inhibit parent involvement at the middle grades:

- **Logistics**—Departmentalization is often intimidating to parents. While their children had only one teacher in the elementary school, they have several teachers in middle schools.

- **Location**—The location of the school may present problems with transportation, or the school may be located in neighborhoods which are unfamiliar, unsafe, and/or frightening.

- **Curriculum**—If parents are expected to serve as primary reinforcers of what children are learning at school, then it is critical that they understand the subjects their children are exposed to on a daily basis. Some parents lack the skills necessary to provide homework assistance, nor are capable of serving as tutors.

- **School Size**—Secondary schools are constructed to house many more students than elementary schools. Parents may become confused, both mentally and physically, when confronted with a larger, unfamiliar building.

Recognizing that such barriers exist, the Committee for Economic Development, Research and Policy (1987, p. 54) strongly states, "We urge that these (junior high and middle) schools become the subject of new and comprehensive research and scrutiny. If not, it is doubtful that successful reform can be implemented."

Middle and junior high schools in particular present difficult challenges to involving parents in learning activities because they typically have a different structure than elementary schools. They are generally larger and more impersonal, with each student having as many as six teachers and each teacher instructing as many as 150 students a day.

Researchers have found some differences in parent involvement programs for children in middle grades according to type of classroom organization and academic subject. Epstein and Dauber (1989b), for example, found that teachers in self-contained classrooms are more likely to involve parents than teachers in teamed or departmentalized programs. Teachers of reading or English are also more likely to engage parents in home learning activities. Becker and Epstein (1982a) found that elementary school teachers who frequently involve parents in home learning activities are most likely to request parental assistance in reading or activities related to reading. Further, Dauber and Epstein (1991) reported that parents of sixth and seventh grade students are more likely to be involved with their children's education at home whereas parents of eighth grade students are more involved at the school building level.

Pre-Adolescent/Adolescent Development

Added to a sometimes confusing array of teachers and subject areas are the changing character and needs of children. Between the ages of 10 to 13, children change physically, mentally, and socially. They strive for more independence from their families at the same time that they require more support and reassurance (Berla, 1991; Carnegie Council on Adolescent Development, 1989). In addition, children of these ages increase their abilities to take on more responsibilities; gain greater understanding of abstractions and of themselves and others; build their memory, academic, and social skills; and add to their abilities to resolve conflicts (Epstein, 1987b; Ruble, 1980; Simmons, Blyth, Van Cleave, & Bush, 1979; Stipek, 1984).

While students are going through many biological changes, their adolescence is defined through their culture. Since the United States is a pluralist culture, there is a wide variety of ways that individuals experience adolescence (Atwater, 1983). In some cases, parents may exert too much pressure for intellectual achievement. Such children, called "hurried children" by David Elkind (1979), may suffer anxiety, especially if they perceive that parental affection and/or financial support are contingent on achievement. An implicit achievement-support contract can either push a student to excel or produce resentment, escapism, or acting out during the adolescent years.

Expectations, Attitudes, and Beliefs

Expectations of teachers and the socialization of students are also found to conflict, especially during the middle grades years. Black students, for example, who are socialized to demonstrate an overt sense of self-esteem and/or a relatively aggressive posture toward problem solving (Holliday, 1985; Bowman & Howard, 1985) are sometimes characterized as poor students when they are simply behaving according to subcultural norms (Zeldin, 1989). The opposite problem can arise for children particularly from lower income strata who have been taught to conform to authority. Helton and Oakland (1977) have shown that teachers view these children as less intelligent, and give the highest ratings of intelligence to boys who are perceived as nonconforming and independent. When the cultural expectations and beliefs of the school conflict with those of low income families, Black families, or families from linguistically diverse backgrounds, the child is not provided with the "maximum support for educational achievement that could be offered by home and school partnerships" (Zeldin, 1989, p. 27).

The relationship between parents and their children also changes as the children mature, as does parents' confidence in their own skills and knowledge (Maccoby, 1984; Sigel, Dreyer, & McGillicuddy-Delisi, 1984). While parents generally gain confidence in their abilities to guide and interact with their children, they lose confidence in their ability to help their children with their school work (Epstein, 1986a).

Teachers of middle grade students also increase their expectations for student achievement. Children are expected to consolidate previous learning, use their developing analytic abilities and read to learn. Greater expectations for conduct are also imposed. All of this is complicated by the fact that as students enter middle school or junior high school, report card grades tend to decline even as overall competence increases (Peterson, 1986). This occurs because middle school students are being compared with a new, larger group of students who also did well in elementary school and because the students are presented with more demanding tasks and more competition for grades (Epstein, 1987b).

Differences in academic expectations and classroom organization between the middle grades and the elementary grades caused some students and their families to misperceive their relationship when it came to schooling (Epstein, Jackson, Salinas, & Calverton & West Baltimore Middle School Teachers, 1990). Some children, for example, believed that their teachers did not want them to discuss or solicit help from their parents on their schoolwork. Many felt that all homework was designed to be done alone. Some parents may think that they should not try to help their children if they are not "experts" at the particular academic subject matter.

A study of inner city elementary and middle schools by Dauber and Epstein (1991) showed that the parent involvement programs in elementary schools are stronger, more positive, and more comprehensive than those for children in the middle grades. This is evident for a number of types of parent involvement, including learning activities. Useem (1990) found a similar pattern; parents of children in the middle grades received less information and guidance precisely at a time when they needed more in order to understand the larger and more complex schools, subjects, and schedules.

Low-income Black parents from two junior high schools in Washington, D.C. identified economic and educational differences between themselves and their children's teachers as barriers to home-school collaboration (Leitch & Tangri, 1988). While low socioeconomic status Black families often lack both human and material resources, their participation in their children's education enhances educational achievement (Slaughter & Epps, 1987).

Summary

Parent and community involvement is influenced by a variety of contextual factors. The school, district, state, and federal policy environments contribute both to the perception of the importance of parent and community involvement and to the way schools or districts define what the various roles and relationships should be. In the past, the policies that existed were primarily implicit and concentrated on what parents could do in the home to support the academic goals of the school. More recently policies on every level have become more explicit and have recognized the role of parents and community members as partners and decisionmakers.

The diversity within families, communities, cultures and economies, however, make uniform conceptualization of a school/parent/ community partnership difficult. With no "typical" family structure, no "typical" family culture and values, and no "typical" economic status, it is difficult for schools or districts to define realistic expectations for home learning, parent and community support, or even constellations of activities that will meet the needs and fall within the abilities of both partners. Given the inherent interdependence of such systems, however, the partners must find a way to accommodate both universal and local concerns.

Added to this challenge are the differing perceptions on the part of each group regarding the definition of appropriate roles and relationships. While school personnel and parents agree, for example, that more involvement is desirable, they do not agree on the role of parents in governance or on the degree to which parents are motivated and/or willing to help their children at home. In some cases, these disparate views are compounded by the differences in socioeconomic characteristics of school staff and families.

Factors within the school setting itself may also serve to inhibit involvement and skew perceptions. Schools that are departmentalized or are very large, that are located in areas that are not easily accessible or perceived to be unsafe, or that are confusing in their physical layout may, by their nature, discourage parents from coming on-site. Curriculum that surpasses the skills that parents have also discourages involvement.

Finally, the students themselves influence the nature and scope of the family/school partnership. During the middle grades years, children change physically, mentally, and socially. They tend to seek more independence from their families while at the same time needing more support as they face greater academic challenges. Student and teacher expectations for themselves and each other may also shift during this time.

All of these contextual variables make the definition of family/school partnership itself a complex undertaking. Examples of school, district, state, and federal roles in forging a positive relationship within this context will be addressed in later chapters.

Chapter 3

The Development and Implementation of Parent and Community Involvement Programs

Overview

The development and implementation of parent and community involvement programs encompasses activities and programs that promote strong partnerships between schools and the clients they serve—students, parents, families, and the larger community. It is expected that educational outcomes may be strengthened through these partnerships. Although these partnerships may assume various configurations, there are three critical roles that parents and community members may take in the education of their children. The first role, parents as a primary resource in their children's education, is exemplified through home learning activities. In this role, parents may have the most direct effect on student achievement. The second role, parents and community members as supporters and advocates is actualized through site-based school restructuring. The roles of parents and community are facilitated by the organizational structures of schools that have been changed to enable parents and families to better support the education of their children. Parent and community members as participants in the education of all children is the third role. This role broadens the scope of both the partnership and the effects of the partnership. Districtwide programs provide parents and community members the opportunity to be involved in a variety of decision-making roles; the effects of the partnership extend to all children in the district. In addition to the roles that parents and community members assume in the partnerships that are formed, we review program elements and strategies that effect roles in specific ways and other program elements that cut across all roles in the development and implementation process.

A synthesis of the literature reveals three critical roles that parents and community members can play in the partnerships that are created in the development and implementation of parent and community involvement programs. Each of these roles is actualized in very different ways in relationships in classrooms, schools, and school districts:

- **Parents as the primary resource in the education of their children** is best exemplified in *home learning*. Home learning is the activity, or set of activities, that parents and family members may engage in to help their children succeed academically. This partnership role between parents and/or family members and schools may have the greatest impact on achievement.

- **Parents and community members as supporters and advocates for the education of their children** is facilitated through site-based school restructuring. Restructuring schools to create parent and community partnerships with schools focuses on organizational structure. Changing activities; creating new relationships between parents, families, communities, and schools; and implementing innovative strategies are ways that schools can restructure to facilitate parent and community involvement in this role.

- **Parents and community members as participants in the education of all children** incorporates a broader vision in the partnership between schools and the populations they serve. Districtwide programs provide the vehicle for parents and community members to be involved in roles that reach beyond the immediate impact on an individual child to the impact on all children in the district.

There are key program elements and strategies that are specific to those programs that are designed and implemented to enhance the partnership roles of parents, families, communities, and schools. Successful parent and community involvement initiatives consider these program elements and strategies in design, development, and implementation.

- The key program elements specific to **home learning** are: well-developed local practices; a willingness of teachers to build on parent strengths; ongoing recruitment using multiple methods; effective strategies that promote home learning; and the home learning environment.

- **School restructuring** activities focus on the following key program elements: an emphasis on quality education; family participation; and site-based management.

- Development and implementation of policy; embracing the diversity of families and communities; and a focus on the linkages with the community and other agencies supporting education are key program elements in **districtwide programs** that seek to broaden the scope of the partnerships between schools and parents, families, and community members.

Several key program elements cut across all of the partnership roles and are critical factors in parent and community involvement programs *at all levels of the education system.* The literature reveals that successful programs give consideration to these elements as programs are designed and implemented:

- **Communication** is a primary building block in creating partnerships between parents, families, community members, and schools as programs are developed and implemented. Communication takes into account the equal participation by the partners in those relationships.

- **Key players,** including students, parents, families, and community members, are the primary focus in the development and implementation of parent and community involvement programs. Other key players may be teachers, counselors, site-based administrators, central administrators, and personnel from business and social agencies interested in the education of children.

- **Resources** are essential in the development and implementation of parent and community involvement programs. Funding, personnel, training, and coordination of effort are needed if these programs are to succeed.

The roles of parents, families, and communities and the partnerships that are created with schools speak to programs that are designed, developed, and implemented at any grade level. Where research literature on *middle grades* parent and community involvement roles and programs was found, it will be highlighted to avoid confusion for the reader. The synthesis that follows describes in detail the roles of parents as they are embedded within home learning, school restructuring, and district-wide programs; key elements that cut across all parent and community involvement programs; and elements and strategies specific to programs.

The Role of Parents, Families, and Community Members in the Development and Implementation of Programs

Parents, families, and community members can assume a variety of roles in developing and implementing partnerships and programs. They may serve as primary resources for children in providing achievement-related activities in the home or community to reinforce or extend the learning that takes place in school. They may serve as advocates for their children in the school setting by restructuring the relationship they have with the school to emphasize new roles, activities, or strategies to enhance partnerships. Finally, they may participate in the formulation of policies that affect all children. In this section, key elements of each of these roles will be discussed, along with those constructs, such as communication, key players and resources, that cut across all roles.

Parents as a Primary Resource in the Education of their Children

Parents, of course, serve as a primary resource in the education of their children. They establish a learning environment, complete with a set of normative expectations understood by their children. The research literature on enhancing parental roles in this regard generally focuses on how parents can help their children through home learning activities and the ways in which such activities can be optimized.

Home Learning

The involvement of parents in learning activities with their children at home has been characterized as the "meat and potatoes" of parent involvement (Rich, 1987a). It is the parents who provide the building blocks that make learning in school possible (Epstein, 1991b). Any time a student expends on academic activities in the home, increases the total amount of the learning time (Walberg, 1984). Involving parents in home learning activities thus vastly improves students' productivity. Programs and activities that may be called "home learning" take many forms, but most commonly include homework, leisure reading, family discussions, educational games, and enrichment activities (Moles, 1991).

Key Element: Well-developed local practices. Dauber and Epstein (1991, p. 11) asserted that "regardless of parent education, family size, student ability, or school level (elementary or middle school), parents are more likely to become partners in their children's education if they perceive that the schools have strong practices to involve parents at school, at home on homework, and at home on reading activities." Zeldin (1989) found that districts and schools play a key role in developing effective school-parent partnerships to encourage home learning. Birman, Orland, Jung, Anson, Garcia, Moore, Funkhouser, Morrison, Turnbull and Reisner (1987), for example, showed that local factors rather than federal requirements determined the success of Chapter 1 parent involvement programs. Hamilton and Cochran (1988), Comer (1988b) and others have shown that school policy revisions to promote home learning activities can be effective.

The most successful schools design home learning programs to fit the needs and expectations of families who intend to participate (Zeldin, 1989; Epstein, 1989). Planners can assess these needs in advance and work to design strategies that are suitable to the particular population (Rich, 1985; Epstein, 1989; Slaughter & Epps, 1987). Some researchers found that this worked best when parents are involved in planning the program (Chrispeels, 1991a). In addition, teachers or other service providers who received training in the best ways to work with families are more successful (Zeldin, 1989; Chrispeels, 1991a; Dauber & Epstein, 1991).

Epstein (1991a) has concluded that for teachers, parent involvement in students' home learning is largely an organizational problem. To manage parental assistance, "Teachers must have clear, easy, and reliable ways to (a) distribute learning activities to be completed at home, (b) receive and process messages from parents about the activities, (c) evaluate the help students obtain at home, and (d) continue to manage and evaluate the parent involvement practices" (Epstein, 1991a, p. 4).

Key Element: A willingness of teachers to build on parent strengths. One primary theme found throughout the research studies is that effective programs respect and utilize the strengths of all parents, regardless of parental income, education, or social status (Zeldin, 1989). Further, successful programs view even minor involvement as the basis for later, more active involvement (Eastman, 1988). Parent strengths such as their interest in their own child's education, interest in working with the schools, and informal literacy activities in the home, are a focal point for building a strong partnership between teachers and parents.

Research from the Johns Hopkins *Surveys of Schools and Family Connections* (Epstein & Becker, 1987) showed that teachers believe that parents' help is necessary if schools are to solve problems. About two-thirds of the teachers in these surveys frequently asked parents to engage in reading activities with their children at home. Teachers mainly requested that parents help their children with activities in reading and language arts (Epstein, 1991a). Requests usually took the form of asking parents to review or practice activities that were taught in class. Home learning activities were most likely to be promoted by teachers of younger students, those with advanced training, those who utilized some parent volunteers in their classrooms, and those who conducted at least three workshops for parents during the school year.

Some researchers have focused on how to increase teachers' understandings of the literacy practices that go on in any home (Brice-Heath, 1983; Cochran, 1987; Slaughter & Epps, 1987). This understanding has been shown to enhance teachers' effectiveness since they could use instructional styles consistent with those used in the home and they could write summaries so that parents could learn from other families. The use of differential strategies for various cultural groups, however, has been challenged by some researchers who question whether such treatment is either helpful individualization or detrimental bias (Cazden, 1986).

Key Element: Ongoing recruitment using multiple methods. Researchers found that specific recruitment practices to engage parents in home learning activities are a vital part of successful programs, especially for parents who are considered "hard to reach." The use of printed brochures and other school-generated print materials sent home with students are effective strategies for reaching middle class parents; however, they are not helpful in recruiting "at risk" parents (Pickarts & Fargo, 1975; McLaughlin & Shields, 1987). Instead, schools need to utilize alternative strategies such as home visits, employing parent liaisons, the use of the media and word-of-mouth to advertise efforts, and referrals of families by community agencies (Zeldin, 1989).

Rich (1985) offered several suggestions for convincing parents to become involved in home learning activities based on her research. Schools may want to initiate a bilingual media campaign and use respected community leaders to stress the importance of parents in the education of their children. Schools could establish family learning centers in schools, store fronts, or churches, and bilingual hotlines to help teach parents how to help their children to learn. Staff from individual schools can create many materials and learning activities for parents to use at home.

In her review of Thompson's *Family Math*, and Epstein's *Teachers Involve Parents in Schoolwork*, Chrispeels (1991a) found that home learning activities were most effective when parents received individual invitations to parent education workshops; follow-up phone calls were made to parents following the announcement of a parent education workshop; the school provided translation, transportation, and child care; small grade level groups were targeted; teachers connected family learning workshops with their regular classroom curriculum and instruction; and arrangements were made to accommodate students whose families could not attend.

Key Element: Effective strategies for promoting home learning. Many researchers found that parents need specific advice and strategies to enable them to engage in home learning activities. Others found that such programs needed to have sufficient flexibility to allow for time constraints and family initiatives (Zeldin, 1989; Barber, 1987). Personal support and one-on-one communication also were shown to enhance program effectiveness (Lightfoot, 1975; Chrispeels, 1987b).

Brown (1989) noted that teachers should not think of these activities in terms of worksheets or repetitions of what was learned in school. Parents tend to view this as "busywork." Instead, to be most beneficial, home learning activities need to be designed to be meaningful and interesting, such as on-going projects and integrated learning experiences (Brown, 1989; Epstein & Herrick, 1991).

The strongest effects on parent involvement at home and at school, according to Dauber and Epstein (1991, p. 13) were "demonstrated by parents who personally understand and act on teacher's practices that encourage their involvement." Further, Epstein (1991a) asserted that even when parents could not help their child on a specific assignment, they could listen and ask questions about the skill or topic. "These substantive conversations can be important motivating forces for the students and can help students 'tune in' to class work" (Epstein, 1991, p. 5).

Key Element: The home learning environment. Several researchers pointed to the importance of the home learning environment (Clark, 1983; Walberg, 1984; A. T., Henderson, 1987; de Kanter, Ginsburg, & Milne, 1986; Zeldin, 1989; Chrispeels, 1991a). Overt modeling of the importance of education and high expectations for student achievement were found to be important, as well as parents displaying an "authoritative" parenting style, interest and support for the child's schoolwork, and provision of youth enrichment activities. There are family process variables available to all parents that promote student learning. These behaviors and activities include an organized routine for the whole family; a limit to the amount of time children are allowed to watch television; reading, writing, listening, and conversing among family members; provision of a time and place for study; and books and other reading materials in the home.

Families, teachers, and schools each have a role to play. Families of middle grades students should structure household chores and other tasks that are challenging and appropriate to their children's age and engage children in conversations about school, current events, or even television shows (Epstein, 1986b; Rich, 1985). Parents should include children in family decision-making, as appropriate, and promote the development of problem solving skills. Parents can also encourage children to select friends who value school. Teachers can assist parents by providing information on learning objectives, testing and grading policies, and opportunities for remediation or enrichment. Finally, families and schools both can help students to manage time more appropriately. With adolescence, students' ability to work intensively increases. Families can adopt practices to assure that the student has the sustained time necessary to master school subjects. In general, to promote student motivation to learn, family and school structures need to be designed to support the developmental demands created by biological, cognitive, personal, and social growth of the child as he/she matures (Lipsitz, 1984).

Home learning in the middle grades. The major emphasis of activities that may be termed "home learning" in grades four through eight include helping parents:

- become partners with teachers in encouraging children with their schoolwork;

- interact with their children at home to support school goals and programs;

- understand early adolescence and middle grades programs; and

- assist children with decisions that affect their own and the families' futures (Epstein & Salinas, 1991).

Epstein and Herrick (1991) developed and evaluated a number of specific practices that teachers could use to increase parent involvement in the home. One such practice was the use of home learning packets in math and language arts which were used during the summer by parents of students who would enter grades seven and eight. The packets included a number of exercises and activities to help students review and practice useful skills. First year evaluations showed that while the packets served the function of communicating to parents and giving them specific suggestions to help their children academically, the packets needed to be reworked to fit the school curriculum more closely and to provide activities that students found more stimulating and fun. The packets were revised the second year and included activities in math, language arts, science, and health. Students were told they would be tested on the skills that were presented in the packets when they returned to school in the fall. Evaluations showed that students who worked with their parents completed a greater number of activities in the packets and that the packets had a moderate effect on student performance for some students, especially those who had marginal skills.

Parents and Community Members as Supporters and Advocates for the Education of Their Children

The focus of the review in this area is on practices that are implemented at the school building level to encourage the role of parents as supporters of their children's education: to promote contacts with all parents, to help parents learn more about their children's school programs and progress, to help them gain information on home learning activities and home supports for education, and to incorporate other ways to help parents help their children learn. As with home learning, schools must assume an active role to ensure that parents have a variety of ways to become involved, as advocates within the system, in their child's school. The larger community must also be given options for involvement and schools must listen to suggestions and input from parents and community members.

Key Element: A focus on quality education for all students. The effective schools research literature emphasizes the importance of developing the abilities of all children regardless of their current achievement level or their cultural, ethnic, or socioeconomic background. The concept of teaching the whole child has extended upward from the elementary level and has provided a balance to the historically heavy academic emphasis at the secondary level. The middle grades student is not just an intellect to be developed; educators must consider his or her social, emotional, and physical development as well (Davies, 1991).

This holistic and developmental approach to learning has implications for the involvement of families. Parents are hungry for information not only about how to help their children do well in school academically but how to help them with the social, emotional, and physical growth as their children face the problems of adolescence. Additionally, the changing structure of the family and its related needs must be considered in relationship to the school and its available resources (Epstein, 1988). Schools have begun to move beyond the informational phase with parents to modeling, guiding, and assisting them with becoming more effective in dealing with their children's development and learning. Thus, schools and families must work together to form high, yet realistic expectations that lead to success for all students as they restructure the school to meet their local needs (American Indian Science and Engineering Society, 1989; Bliss, 1986; Davies, 1991).

Key Element: Family participation in their children's education. Davies (1991) recommended that as we redefine parent involvement we are better served by the term "family involvement" as we deal with the current realities of the family structure. It may be that, for some children, it is the grandparents, aunts and uncles, brothers and sisters or even neighbors who make the most significant contribution in supporting the child's educational development outside of the school.

Family settings can provide a social and behavioral backdrop that helps ensure the success of their child in the school setting. They can also provide home learning activities that accelerate the process of acquiring skills and content that lead to higher student achievement. Schools must take the lead in helping families gain the knowledge and skills to provide this crucial support to their children (Bliss, 1986; Moles, 1990; Slaughter & Epps, 1987). This assistance may mean modified expectations by the school staff as well as changing school practices (Davies, 1991; Epstein, 1991b; Griswold, 1986). Teachers need training to become more effective in their communication with parents and to have specific practices to suggest to parents as they become more actively involved with their children's educational progress. Principals need to take the lead to ensure that parent and community involvement is a high priority for the school staff, parents, and the community (Purnell & Gotts, 1985).

Specific learning activities can be promoted by specific school practices. For example, completion of homework can be encouraged through providing homework hotlines, sponsoring after-school homework tutoring sessions, or assigning interactive projects that require parents to draw on their strengths or knowledge (Chrispeels, 1991a). Programs addressing homework were found to be most effective when the homework assigned was considered by parents and teachers to be clear and of an appropriate quantity (Walberg, 1984; Chrispeels, 1991a). Home learning activities designed to promote family learning (as opposed to independent practice or enrichment activities for students) were most effective when parents were given ideas and materials that fostered learning in the home, and teachers reinforced the activities by integrating the assignments into the classroom by having students share their progress in class or in school newsletters (Chrispeels, 1991a). Researchers also suggested that the school provide surrogate family members for students whose parents cannot participate (Davies, 1988).

Various practices have been implemented by schools to encourage greater parent involvement in school activities. The Quality Education Project, for example, encouraged parents to sign a pledge promising that they will help their children complete their homework; read to or with their children; provide their children with a quiet place to study; see that they get to school on time and to bed by nine o'clock;

and attend conferences, open houses, and other school events. Concomitantly, teachers signed documents promising to teach concepts necessary for academic achievement, be aware of individual student needs, provide a safe environment for learning, and communicate with parents about their children's progress.

Key Element: Site-based management. Site-based management has emphasized the importance of appropriate policies and local decision-making as it relates to the development of effective schools where parents are involved. In the early seventies, the changing demographics of many neighborhoods and communities across the country facilitated the site-based management process as a mean of addressing the unique needs of these changing communities. In the eighties, site-based approaches coupled with the research on effective schools led to pragmatic approaches to school improvement for all children. For example, the effective schools research highlighted the importance of involvement of the school staff and parents in the development and implementation of comprehensive school improvement plans. Without such staff and community involvement, both commitment and motivation to carry out these plans were often lacking (Taylor & Levine, 1991). This type of grass roots development of parent and community involvement is what Smith and O'Day (1990) characterize as the "second wave" of reform efforts that is bottom-up and is more effective than top-down ("first wave") changes.

One of the first reports to argue for this grassroots strategy for school improvement was *Investing in Our Children*, a report from the Committe for Economic Development (1987). In a 1989-90 survey of its members, the American Association of School Administrators (1990) found that almost one-fourth of the respondents had implemented school-based management and another quarter were considering this bottom-up management style.

Parent involvement in middle grades school restructuring. Berla, Henderson, and Kerewsky (1989) outlined the kinds of things that middle schools should be doing if an effective school/parent/family partnership is in place:

- a clear, welcoming parent involvement policy is published for all to see and posted in an obvious place;

- the school is organized so that at least one person knows each child well;

- the school office is friendly and open;

- the school sponsors parent-to-parent communication and events;

- a full-time parent contact person is responsible for bringing parents and school together;

- there is a parent room in the school building;

- parents and school staff work together to determine parents' needs and provide necessary service; and

- parents whose primary language is not English are made to feel welcome at the school and a translator is provided to help them communicate.

The Teachers Involve Parents In Schoolwork (TIPS) model (Epstein, 1987b) and the New Partnerships for Student Achievement (NPSA) program (Home and School Institute, 1988; Zeldin, 1989) provide elementary and middle school teachers with structured homework assignments in reading, language arts, math, science, and the arts that parents and students work together to complete. Megaskills (Rich, 1985), on the other hand, teaches parents more generic skills to use in everyday life to help them to motivate their children to succeed in school. School and Home (Zeldin, 1990) offers consistent learning activities for children and rewards them daily for completed homework.

Parents And Community Members as Participants in the Education of All Children

In this section, the broader roles of parents and communities in the education of all children are discussed. The focus is on districtwide programs as a vehicle for meeting both the common and diverse needs of children in the district's schools. This section addresses key elements and the types of linkages that foster positive interactions.

Districtwide Parent and Community Involvement Programs

Research on effective schools points to the importance of parent and community involvement in the reform/restructuring of schools. This critical relationship is often overlooked (Solomon, 1991). Parents and community members want to be heard concerning the education of their children. The 1989 Gallup Poll of the Public's Attitude Toward the Public Schools (Gallup & Elam, 1989) revealed that a majority of parents believed that they should be involved in tangible ways (e.g., in decisions on allocation of school funds and selection and hiring of school administrators) in the reform/restructuring of schools. Snider (1990c) reported on the powerful reform movement in Chicago, where parents gained a controlling majority on local school councils. Several other urban districts have explored this "Chicago-style" proposal, including Seattle, Boston, and Houston. In order to avert a teacher strike which threatened to close Denver Public Schools, Colorado Governor Roy Romer invoked a little known state statute and took control of the school district. He ordered the formation of 12-member school councils to supervise the running of the schools. Parents, community members, business leaders, and school personnel on these school councils have made decisions and changes that include: the setting of school goals and priorities, hiring and firing of administrators, and schoolwide exemptions from districtwide mandated standardized testing.

The school reform/restructuring movement has allowed parents and community members a greater share in how schools are operated. With this greater share, there are also high stakes; educators must be prepared to help parent/community groups who may have the zeal to reform but lack the knowledge base to make informed decisions. Sharing the wealth of knowledge and experience about issues such as curriculum and instruction, administration, and governance can only help to forge a strong bond between schools and the parents, families, and communities that they serve.

Key Element: Development and implementation of policy. As students leave elementary schools and progress to the middle grades, parents are less likely to become involved in their child's education (Henderson & Marburger, 1990). Federal, state, and local policies have been written in an attempt to bridge the gap which exists between these schools and parent and community involvement. Yet, it still usually falls to teachers or schools to involve parents, families, and communities in schooling. A key to school/family/community involvement is the presence and effective implementation of a districtwide policy.

The reform/restructuring of schools is a major undertaking and must involve parents and communities if the effort is to be successful. The need for parent/family/community partnership policies is well documented in the literature (Davies, 1987; Heath & McLaughlin, 1987; McLaughlin & Shields, 1987; National School Board Association, 1988; Williams & Chavkin, 1990). There is a strong indication that state initiatives are needed as guidance for district initiatives (Nardine and Morris, 1991; Chapman, 1991; Solomon, 1991; Council of Chief State School Officers, 1991), yet some studies indicate that the need or desire for policies does not ensure that they do, in fact, exist (Nardine & Morris, 1991; Chavkin & Williams, 1987). Rich (1985) and Oakes and Lipton (1990) posit that a single policy is no longer viable and that policymakers must consider schools and homes separately in making policy, as well as the connections between all agencies that serve children. Although a written policy may not guarantee parent involvement, McLaughlin and Shields (1987) argue that it is a necessary prerequisite.

The National Coalition for Parent Involvement in Education (1990) provided guidelines for policy development that includes input from teachers, administrators, parents, students, persons from youth-serving agencies, and the community. They contend that policies should contain the following concepts:

- opportunities for all parents to become informed about how the parent involvement program will be designed and carried out;

- participation of parents who lack literacy skills or who do not speak English;

- regular information for parents about their child's participation and progress in specific educational programs whose objectives are understood;

- opportunities for parents to assist in the instructional process at school and at home;

- professional development for teachers and staff to enhance their effectiveness with parents;

- linkages with social service agencies and community groups to address key family and community issues;

- involvement of parents of children at all ages and grade levels; and

- recognition of diverse family structures, circumstances, and responsibilities, including differences that might impede parent participation. The person(s) responsible for a child may not be the child's biological parent(s) and policies and programs should include participation by all persons interested in the child's educational progress.

Key Element: Embracing the diversity of families in the design of programs and practices. Zeldin's (1990) review of home/school partnership programs for at-risk students revealed that those programs should be designed and implemented with consideration of the special needs and challenges of at-risk families. Modifying institutional structures, including teacher training and administrative and supervisory support, recognizing the lifestyles of diverse parents and students, and implementing effective programs, including home learning components and active support to parents were suggested as the characteristics that should be incorporated into home/school partnership programs.

Districtwide programs must consider all families, including those considered by some schools to be hard to reach (Epstein, 1991b). The parent involvement program in McAllen, Texas, is exemplary in this area (D'Angelo & Adler, 1991). The McAllen community is predominantly Hispanic and due to large numbers of families that immigrate into the community, the parents' level of English-language proficiency is minimal. District leadership has encouraged parent and community involvement not only in federally-funded Chapter 1 or bilingual programs, but also districtwide. Workshops, materials, and information are presented in both English and Spanish, and staff are either bilingual or are making efforts toward becoming bilingual.

Key element: Focus on the linkages with the community and agencies supporting education. Businesses are recognizing the importance of quality education in the communities in which they are located. Quality schools help them to attract and retain competent employees who have children attending schools. The most common form of school-business partnerships is the "helping hand relationship" where businesses help to enhance existing school programs through donations, volunteers, equipment, and minigrants. Seventeen percent of the nation's schools were involved in such business relationships in 1984 and by 1990 this type of school-business involvement had grown to forty percent. These school-business partnerships increased the quality of education through better communication, enriched curriculum, and broader corporate support for education.

Volunteers from the business community working in schools to help motivate students and increase student achievement is not a new idea. The Fort Worth (Texas) Independent School District, for example, has had an active districtwide Adopt-A-School program for many years. Almost all of the district's schools have an "adopted partner." These volunteers give support to the schools in terms of additional funding, tutoring services, and special presentations. Both community/business volunteers and schools reported positive relationships had been formed through participation in the program.

Cohen (1990) reported that approximately 1,000 companies are now making efforts to help families balance responsibilities between home and work. U.S. West Telecommunications, for example, has established an educational foundation for the purposes of providing parents with tools to help their children thrive academically, and strengthening home/school involvement through the workplace.

Community agencies and institutions that serve families can also be brought into this support system to nurture the development of the whole child, thus supporting his or her educational success as well (Epstein, 1991b; Griswold, 1986). The home-school connection for facilitating broader parent and community involvement requires that members of the community be involved in teaching, supporting, learning, and making decisions along with school personnel. The broader the involvement of the community, the more likely it is that schools will move toward realizing their full potential in the effort to educate all children (Chrispeels, 1991b; Henderson, 1986; Jones, 1991).

Cities-in-Schools is a long-standing effort to align human services and businesses with schools to increase student attendance and academic achievement, as well as address family health issues and increase parent involvement. The program is currently operating in fourteen states, nine of which have adopted it as a statewide model. Individual schools using this model often become the site for the delivery of much broader human services such as health and child care, social services, and adult literacy and education efforts.

Key Elements That Cut Across Programs at All Levels

Certain elements operate at all levels of the educational system. No matter what character the organization or relationship assumes, schools and districts must develop positive communication patterns with families and communities. They must recognize the value in the roles assumed by teachers, counselors, administrators, business persons, and other key players. They must access and provide sufficient resources for programs to be successful. These common elements will be addressed in the following sections.

Key Element: Communication. Healthy communication is a key attribute in any partnership. The nature, amount and mutuality of communication affects the success of any relationship between schools and homes or communities. This section reviews the role of communication in the context of home learning, restructuring and district programs, and offers guidance from the research on improving communication patterns.

Communication and home learning. Several researchers have studied the need for mutuality between the home and the school to promote home learning activities. Leler (1983), for example, examined 65 studies to determine whether one- or two-way communication between the home and the school resulted in increased participation of parents. She found that the two-way communication projects all showed positive results, and that the best of all programs are the ones that have somewhat structured programs that trained parents to tutor their children. Cole and Griffin (1987) confirmed this need in their summary of evidence from a number of studies. They noted that the "school-to-home pathway . . . is more likely to be effective if the two-way nature of the path is explicitly recognized by educators" (Cole & Griffin, 1987, p. 78).

Communication and school restructuring. The issue of communication between the home and the school is addressed repeatedly in the literature. At the building level, parents need basic information regarding school goals, programs, and policies if they are to be effective in supporting and enhancing their children's education. Schools must listen to what parents have to say about their involvement in the schools and then develop programs to meet identified parent needs (Chrispeels, 1987a). Historically, the written word in the form of notes, calendars, newsletters, and handbooks has been the primary means of communication between the school and the home. Face-to-face communication such as home visits, parent/teacher conferences, meetings, and workshops are viewed as the most effective means of communication and these are the type of activities over which the schools have the most control. More recently, the use of radio and television, as well as audio and video tapes have been used to inform parents and community members about the school (D'Angelo & Adler, 1991). While much can be accomplished by individual schools using the media, district support is often a necessity.

Gotts and Purnell (1984) recommended that researchers link additional research to communication issues related to: (1) academics, (2) the locus of communication, (3) the intended audience, (4) school-to-home and home-to-school, (5) specific topics, and (6) methods of communication. By linking the research to these topics, better practices leading to increased school effectiveness are predicted. In a later study, the authors surveyed teachers on the topic of family-school relations and found that the teachers overwhelmingly favored parent involvement, but that they generally were not interested in training that could increase their effectiveness in communicating and working with parents.

In interviews with administrators, teachers, social agency personnel, and low income parents, in Boston, Liverpool, and several cities in Portugal, Davies (1988) found there was little contact between the schools and the parents, and that the communication that did exist was primarily negative, focusing on academic or behavioral problems of the students. Teachers and administrators tended to dwell on family problems and conditions, and generally considered the parents to be "hard to reach." They believed that the problem was the parents' apathy (i.e., that these family members did not have the time, interest, or competence to be involved). They felt that the parents did not value education. While expressing strong interest in their children's education, the parents in this study had a low assessment of their abilities to help their children. They saw themselves as being academic failures. Davies concluded that these parents were "reachable," but that schools were either not trying to reach them, insensitive, or not knowledgeable about how to overcome social class, linguistic, or cultural barriers.

Several researchers discussed the tendency for teachers to contact parents more frequently for negative messages (Chrispeels, 1987b; Lightfoot, 1975; Seginor, 1983). This activity contributes to a pattern of mistrust and misunderstanding from the points of view of parents and has resulted in some parents viewing schools as a "threatening monolith unwilling or unable to develop the strengths of the child or accurately measure achievement" (Zeldin, 1989, p. 17).

Communication and district programs. D'Angelo and Adler (1991) illustrated districtwide programs from various regions of the country and, using successful strategies of Chapter 1 parent/community involvement programs, described effective communication in three areas: face-to-face communication, the use of technology, and written communication.

Districts in Lima, Ohio; Buffalo, New York; Natchez/Adams, Mississippi; and the Migrant Education State Parent Advisory Council in New York have made communication with parents and community a focal point of their parent/community involvement programs. These agencies have used parent conferencing techniques and the establishment of parenting centers within schools as vehicles for communication.

The use of various forms of electronic media (e.g., television, videotape, telephone) are used in district programs to facilitate communication between schools and families/communities. Efforts in McAllen, Texas; Poudre School District (Fort Collins), Colorado; San Diego, California; Indianapolis, Indiana; Casey County, Kentucky; and Omaha, Nebraska have successfully integrated technology into their parent/family/community programs.

Written communication has been used effectively in parent involvement programs in Omaha, Nebraska; Cahokia, Illinois; and Palatine, Illinois. Most frequently mentioned written methods include newsletters, calendars, and handbooks to help parents help their children at home.

D'Angelo and Adler (1991) provided four caveats for improving communication:

- Communication strategies for individual schools should be adapted to match the needs of families.

- Materials must reach the intended audience.

- If a meeting, workshop, presentation, assembly, or other event presents information deemed essential for parents, then the schools must find other ways to get that information to those who cannot be there.

- Do not wait for a problem to arise before contacting parents.

Key Players

Leadership is a key characteristic that contributes to the effectiveness of parent and community involvement at the school level. Procedures for involving community members must be clearly communicated and applied consistently. Parents need to know that their involvement does make a difference and that the school honestly welcomes their participation (Northwest Regional Education Laboratory, 1990). The responsibility for effective involvement must begin with building administrators and teachers (Center for Evaluation, Development and Research, 1990). They are the ones having direct contact with parents and community members, and it is their leadership that sets both the tone and the standards. Training may be necessary for the school staff and parents to optimize the activities, procedures, and practices.

Key Player: Principals. The principal, in particular, must ensure that there is adequate money, time, personnel, and space to address the needs of parent and community involvement within the school (Chrispeels, 1991b). This leadership role of the principal is particularly important beyond the elementary school because of the decrease in parent involvement with each passing grade. By making involvement a focal point of both spoken and written communications, the principal regularly can emphasize involvement opportunities to the parents in school newsletters and at meetings. It is important that the principal have an understanding of, and be able to work with, all types of families and appropriately apply parent involvement strategies with attention to family differences. In addition, the principal must ensure that parent and community involvement in the school is well planned, comprehensive, and systematic (Chrispeels, Bourta, & Daugherty, 1988; Henderson & Marburger, 1990; Northwest Regional Education Laboratory, 1990). Chrispeels (1991a) and Henderson (1986) provide assessment and planning checklists to facilitate effective parent and community involvement.

Key Player: Teachers. Teachers can reach out to parents to form partnerships that benefit families and enhance the educational progress of their students. Teachers can share insights with parents regarding the school as a whole and their individual classrooms. They can provide tips on academic subjects and how parents can help with homework. They can encourage parents to volunteer in the school and share their knowledge, skills, and perceptions to continuously improve the educational program. Teachers who take such initiatives tend to have higher student achievement gains and feel better supported by parents (Epstein & Becker, 1982; Epstein, 1987c; Tangri & Moles, 1987).

Key Player: District leadership. District leadership is necessary to provide a comprehensive and coordinated effort for creating and sustaining effective parent and community involvement. By aligning district policy with practice, districts are better able to fulfill the promise that parent and community involvement offers in the development of quality education for all students.

Resources Needed to Develop, Implement, and Sustain Parent and Community Involvement Programs

To be successful, parent and community involvement programs need to garner sufficient resources including financial, human, staff development, and time to coordinate. This section addresses each of these areas, with attention to how each contributes to the effectiveness of the partnership.

Key Resource: Funding. Currently across the United States, funding for program development and evaluation at the state level is lacking (Nardine & Morris, 1991). Epstein (1991b) estimated that a district commitment to parent involvement should be approximately $10 per student. Combined with school- and state-level funds, this amount would provide a supportive structure for ensuring successful school/home partnerships. She also pointed out that grant monies can be used as a motivator for school leaders—and ultimately result in positive support for parent/community programs and schoolwide change. Chavkin and Williams (1987) suggested that school districts need to provide monetary resources for the implementation of effective programs. The provision of resources, they argue, helps emphasize the importance of parent involvement in education and demonstrates a commitment to its success.

Key Resource: Personnel. Sufficient staff are needed to operate effective programs (Williams & Chavkin, 1990). Epstein (1991b) recommended that a family/school coordinator be hired to coordinate and link school, district, and state efforts. She underscored the important role of the coordinator to guide school staffs, provide inservice training for educators, offer services to parents, and perform other tasks that promote partnerships. Both Berla (1991) and Earle (1990) recommended that a full-time parent/school partnership position be created on each middle school campus. The responsibilities of this staff person would be to work with families and school personnel (such as counselors, administrators, teachers) in assuring the success of students at risk of failure or dropping out. Aggressive, ongoing outreach efforts may be needed to procure the participation of "hard to reach" parents (Zeldin, 1989; Dauber & Epstein, 1991). These families may also need to be acculturated to the new school norms of parent involvement, particularly if they had viewed parent involvement as unwelcome (Simich-Dudgeon, 1986).

Key Resource: Training. Not all professionals place a high value on parent involvement (Dauber & Epstein, 1991). Teachers should receive preservice and inservice training if they are to implement a successful parent involvement program (Zeldin, 1990; Chrispeels, 1991b; Dauber & Epstein, 1991; Comer 1988a). For example, teachers may need training to develop new means of communicating with parents, effective communication skills such as active listening and showing empathy, interpersonal skills such as perspective-taking and conflict resolution, and skills for working with parents from a variety of backgrounds and life styles. Epstein and Dauber (1989a) pointed out that math, science, and social studies teachers may require more assistance than reading and language arts teachers since they currently do not place as much value on parent involvement.

Planners of home-based parent involvement, especially those in schools serving low income or minority students, need to take care that they reach those parents who most need to be involved and teach skills that parents want to learn. They should not imply that school success is only for children whose parents are willing to conform to established middle class norms (Flaxman & Inger, 1991). If teachers and administrators are not aware of these pitfalls, they are likely to reinforce existing home-school barriers.

Effective districtwide parent involvement programs reveal that a key component is training for practitioners (see, for example the Indianapolis "Parents In Touch" program described by Warner [1991], or the efforts in San Diego described by Chrispeels [1991b]). Oakes and Lipton (1990) argue against top-down authority and point out that teachers need to be provided with resources and technical assistance, particularly related to finding creative ways to increase learning in the classroom and at home. The Williams and Chavkin (1990) study of promising programs in the southwestern United States indicated that training was essential for an effective parent involvement program.

Training for school/family/community partnerships should also include parent training, especially related to helping parents acquire parenting ideas and leadership strategies for helping their children achieve literacy skills (Clark, 1989). The section of this literature review on Home Learning examines the relationships between effective parenting, home learning and the need for parent and school staff training on how to reach these positive outcomes.

Key Resource: Coordination. Davies (1985) wrote that "co-production," (i.e., individual and collective activities in the school or home that contribute to more effective instruction and school achievement) should be *initiated* by teachers and principals and *coordinated* with all school personnel. Co-production includes home tutoring programs, homework assistance and hotlines, frequent reporting of student progress, and specific suggestions for reinforcement and enrichment activities. Co-production can be initiated by teachers with parents through a variety of activities. These activities include: parent education programs to inform families of school and class learning objectives; home visitor programs for those needing specific guidance; and the involvement of low income and immigrant families and parent volunteers to help teachers in the classroom and to help develop home learning activities. The implementation of such a project would require a significant investment of time and funds for development and promotion of materials and for appropriate teacher and parent training. Additional funds and arrangements would also be required to provide surrogate families for students whose families are not able to participate. Churches, social agencies, and community organizations could be contacted to provide the surrogate families.

McLaughlin and Shields (1987) suggested a combination of norm-based pressure and support to encourage educators to implement a home learning parent involvement program. Included were such things as providing incentives to teachers to try new practices, disseminating information about the nature and effect of parent involvement programs, and providing specific models of parent involvement that have proven to be effective. If these efforts were successful, teachers would require materials, training, networks, and mini-grants to help them implement the practices. Chrispeels (1991b) goes further by saying that additional resources will be needed for recognition and reinforcement of staff, parents, and students who participate.

While some recent research has focused on methods for creating positive learning environments in the home (for example Walberg, 1984), others emphasize programs for increasing teachers' and administrators' understandings of the 'natural' learning that occurs with the home (Brice & Heath, 1983; Cochran & Henderson, 1986). Rich (1985) advocates community outreach efforts, noting that the greater the continuity and contact, the greater the benefit for the child.

Summary

Parents and community members can adopt a variety of roles and relationships with schools. Three of the most critical roles they can assume are:

- becoming primary educational resources for their children;

- becoming supporters and/or advocates for children through site-based school restructuring efforts; and

- participating in the development and implementation of district programs that support partnerships.

Home learning activities present the most common vehicles through which parents and community members assume primary educational roles for middle grades children. The most successful of these activities incorporate practices that take local factors into account and that build on parent strengths. Promotion of home learning is best accomplished by using multiple methods and by being both sufficiently clear and sufficiently flexible about expectations being made of parents. Home learning activities often take the form of modeling high expectations, supporting schoolwork and homework, and providing a positive learning climate in the home. Specific activities benefit from being more stimulating and fun.

By focusing on quality education for all students, parents and community members can be effective supporters and advocates for their children in programs developed and implemented at local sites. This approach assumes that all families, no matter what their structure, economic background or culture, will be encouraged to help children acquire skills and content that lead to greater achievement. Home practices to be encouraged include modeling, setting high but realistic expectations for student learning, facilitating the completion of homework and other school assignments, attending conferences and actively communicating with the school. School practices that make positive contributions to this relationship include site-based management, clear and welcoming policies and communications, an identified liaison person, physical accommodations, and planning geared toward determining and meeting families' needs.

Districtwide parent and community involvement programs also need to embrace the diversity of families in the design of policies, programs, and practices. While the literature is not clear as to the optimal separate and joint roles of state and local policies, research does show that both can be effective, particularly in written form. Policies at any level should contain methods by which all parents, regardless of socioeconomic, linguistic, or literacy backgrounds, can be informed about programs and the progress of their children. Professional development opportunities for staff on the various aspects of parent involvement enhance the effectiveness of any program. Recognizing and valuing diversity in family structures, circumstances, and responsibilities is also a key feature of effective policies. Finally, linking the various groups and agencies that support education with both schools and families strengthens the overall partnership.

The research literature reveals overarching elements that affect the home/school connection in whatever form it takes. Two-way communication surfaces repeatedly as a key to successful partnerships. The valence of the communication is also important with researchers concluding that negative communication is often the norm, sometimes with reverberating negative effects. To improve communication, schools must become more inclusive and creative, taking advantage of electronic media, new parent conferencing techniques, and a knowledge of the local community.

Key players in the partnerships include principals, teachers, and district administrators. Each should assume responsibilities within the home/school relationship and adopt facilitative roles. Finally, adequate resources must be available to enable the development and implementation of programs. These resources include funding, but also emphasize sufficient numbers of staff, training for all partners, and close coordination of all activities and interested parties. More linkages benefit all constituents, including the children.

Chapter 4

The Impact of Parent and Community Involvement Programs

Overview

A primary dilemma faced by policymakers and practitioners is establishing strong claims about the outcomes of any program. Typical experimental designs include random assignment of subjects. While the application of these designs is possible in other situations and circumstances, they are not often accepted in studies of educational programs. Without random assignment a direct link between cause and effect cannot be established. In other words, without random assignment it is impossible to determine if the outcomes of a program are the direct result of the program itself.

Studies of educational programs seek to explain why, how, and whether programs work. Their designs attempt to "partition out" the effects of a variable, or set of variables, in order to determine the contribution of certain features to overall program outcomes.

Most often the outcomes of educational programs are the result of the interaction of many complex variables. The interactive nature of these variables is elusive and the ability to make **definitive** statements about their effects on outcomes is problematic. However, considerable research has been done which establishes an **associative link**, or correlation, between school efforts to create partnerships with parents, families, and community members and outcomes for students, parents, school personnel, and schools and school districts:

- School and parent/family/community partnerships are associated with positive effects on **student outcomes** (e.g., higher levels of achievement as measured by standardized test scores; factual, conceptual, critical, and attitudinal aspects of learning).

- Acquisition of new skills; increased involvement, interaction with their children, and positive self-concept are examples of **parent outcomes** associated with school/family partnerships.

- **Teacher outcomes** associated with partnerships included positive attitudes, the use of varied strategies, and an increased sense of self-efficacy.

- Positive effects for **schools and school districts** were found through the partnerships schools forge with parents/families/communities. An increase in student attendance rates; reductions in dropout, delinquency, and pregnancy rates; and improved discipline practices were associated with these partnerships.

The remainder of this chapter focuses on the research related to the outcomes claimed by programs that involve school, parent, family, and community partnerships. As a cautionary note, readers should be aware that the research cited pertains to general outcomes at all levels, not specifically to the middle grades.

The Impact of Parent and Community Involvement Programs

Involving parents in the education of their children has been found to have an associated link not only with students but also with parents, teachers, schools, and districts (Becker & Epstein, 1982b; Comer, 1986; Epstein, 1991a). These outcomes include increased student achievement, increased student attendance, lower dropout rates, increased interactions between parents and their children at home and increased positive attitudes by teachers toward parents being involved. This section on the associated effects of parent involvement in the middle grades examines student, teacher, parent, school, and district outcomes.

In general, the research demonstrates that parents can be powerful contributors to their children's education, both stimulating and reinforcing their children's learning. However, parent involvement should not be viewed as an educational panacea (Ascher, 1987; Brown, 1989). As Ascher, (1987, p. 17-18) warns: "Although the problem for schools in the next period will be to give some priority to parent involvement efforts, educators should not demand more from this strategy than it can deliver. Nothing would be gained by subjecting parents to another round of blame when home learning does not yield hoped for improvements."

Student Outcomes

Studies of the effects of parent involvement were almost always measured in terms of student achievement as indicated by grades or even more commonly, by standardized test scores. Most of the studies on the influence of parent involvement have focused on elementary schools. In most cases, it is difficult to establish causality. It is also impossible to compare results from one study to another to determine which of the activities have had the greatest impact (Zeldin, 1989). As Clarke-Stewart (1983) pointed out, these family behaviors probably interact, and these interactions have not been examined.

Shields and McLaughlin (1987) reported that there are two facts that are "fairly well settled" in the literature regarding the link between parent involvement and student achievement. First, students, including students from low SES whose parents are involved in their schools, do better in their academic subjects than those students whose parents are less involved (Stevenson & Baker, 1987; Rood, 1988; A. T., Henderson, 1987; Jacob, 1983; Comer, 1984; Walberg, 1984; McCormick, 1989). Second, those schools where parents are well informed and highly involved are most likely to be effective schools (Brandt, 1986; Chubb, 1988; Comer, 1984; Henderson, 1988b; Jacob, 1983; Purkey & Smith, 1983; Walberg, 1984). Other studies have indicated that students are less likely to drop out of schools when parents are involved (Henderson, 1988a; McCormick, 1989).

Research on the effects of specific home learning activities has also been conducted. The assignment and completion of homework that is consistent with a student's ability, for example, was found to have uniformly positive effects on factual, conceptual, critical, and attitudinal aspects of learning (Zeldin, 1989; Chrispeels, 1991a; Walberg, 1984). Similarly, monitoring of television viewing, structuring home routines, and offering verbal praise were associated with student achievement. Students also were found to have developed better study habits and social skills (Zeldin, 1989).

Nearly all of the research reviewed showed that increased parent involvement was consistently associated with positive results, although "nothing so dramatic as to suggest a revolution in the educational process" (Ascher, 1987, p. 17). Many researchers found that students whose parents were involved scored higher on achievement tests (Epstein, 1991a; de Kanter, et al., 1986; Epstein & Dauber, 1989a; Henderson, 1988a; Benson, Buckley, & Medrich, 1980). However, in one study of fifth graders, Epstein (1991a) found that while parent involvement was related to positive achievement in reading, it was not found to be related to achievement in math.

Parent outcomes

Parents involved in their children's schools acquire new skills, gain confidence, and improve employment opportunities (Comer, 1984). Further, parents are more likely to increase their involvement over time (Herman & Yeh, 1983) and spend more time working with their children at home on school-related tasks (Becker & Epstein, 1981). In addition, participating parents who are involved are likely to have more positive attitudes about themselves, including more self-confidence.

Becker and Epstein (1982b), Dauber and Epstein (1991), Epstein and Dauber (1989a, 1989b), and Epstein (1986b, 1991a) found that parents who were involved in their children's learning increased their interactions with children at home, felt more positively about their abilities to help their elementary school-aged children, and rated their children's teachers as better instructors.

Chrispeels (1991b) noted that schools implementing programs to encourage home learning may encounter several dilemmas. They must determine both how to implement programs that do not favor children who are already doing well and how to evaluate the programs effectively in order to make resource allocation decisions. School staff need to communicate in such a way that teachers and parents together can determine what specific activities will suit individual children best, finding a way to balance creativity and individualized attention with the need for consistent guidelines and practices. The schools also need to create safety nets for children whose parents are unable or unwilling to respond.

Research also indicated that home learning programs should not necessarily be limited to parents helping children with academic tasks. Epstein (1987a) has shown that it is important for parents to promote the development of children's curiosity or self-esteem as motivators for learning.

Teacher outcomes

Teachers' attitudes and behaviors influence whether attempts are made to involve parents. Teachers who do involve parents are much less likely to make stereotypical judgments about the willingness and abilities of parents to help (Becker & Epstein, 1982a; Epstein, 1986b). Involving parents more often and more productively necessitates more than a change of attitudes, however. According to Epstein, it "requires changing the major location of parent involvement from the school to the home, changing the major emphasis from general policies to specific skills, and changing the major target from the general population of students or school staff to the individual child at home" (Jennings, 1990, p. 23).

The more frequently teachers were engaged in parent involvement activities, the more positive their attitudes became about parents and the more likely they included parent input in decisions about curriculum development and instructional strategies (Epstein & Becker, 1987). Teachers' attitudes toward parents also improved as a result of parent involvement. Teachers who promoted parent involvement saw more value in holding conferences and communicating with parents about school programs and student progress (Epstein & Dauber, 1989b).

Teachers who acknowledge the benefits of parent involvement were found to be more likely to overcome obstacles through the use of a variety of parent involvement strategies. They were also more likely to seek training to improve their skills for involving parents in the schools (Becker & Epstein, 1982b; Purnell & Gotts, 1985).

In a study of elementary schools, Hoover-Dempsey, Bassler, and Brissie, (1987) found that teacher efficacy was also related to the strength of parent involvement programs. Teachers who felt that they were capable and effective were more likely to conduct conferences with parents and to assign interactive homework activities.

While individual teachers' practices were a key factor in building parent involvement programs, they were not the only factor. In schools where teachers perceived that they, their colleagues, and parents supported parent involvement, programs and practices were stronger (Dauber & Epstein, 1991).

School and district outcomes

Comer (1984) found that those schools with parent involvement have an improved school climate. He reported that the parent involvement programs established in elementary schools in New Haven, Connecticut decreased conflict and apathy in the school and produced a more positive climate for teaching and learning. Further, he asserted that parent involvement in a well-structured and well-managed program helped to eliminate harmful stereotypes that teachers held about the families of the students they taught. Peterson (1989) noted that parent involvement also produced long-term effects. Citing a number of studies, he found that increased parent involvement positively affected student attendance rates and was associated with reductions in dropout, delinquency, and pregnancy rates. Students' citizenship and social values were also found to be more positive. Zeldin (1989) cited research that showed improved discipline practices and increased support for students' educational activities.

Armor, Conny-Osegura, Cox, King, McDonnell, Pascal, Pauly, and Zellman (1976) showed that while efforts to involve parents of Black children in their sixth grade students' education were successful, efforts to involve Mexican American parents and community members were not. The authors attributed this difference to language barriers and to the differential content of the school's outreach effort.

The positive effects of parent involvement may help to counterbalance the effects of economic disadvantagement. While many researchers (Henderson, 1987) found this to be the case, several others refuted this claim. Benson et al. (1980), for example, found that while parent involvement made a difference in middle class families, it did little to affect achievement in either high or low socioeconomic groups.

A few studies examined the differences in effect between school-based and home-based parent involvement. Toomey (1986) found that programs for low income parents that featured home visits were more successful in generating involvement than those requiring school visits, though the latter yielded greater reading gains.

It is obvious that a more concerted effort to document the effects of parent and community involvement will yield information and research for increasing the effectiveness of such programs. By better defining the outcomes that are being sought, the research can be fine-tuned to provide a more detailed analysis regarding those practices that are truly effective.

Summary

While the research on the impact of parent and community involvement programs does not show a definitive causal link, many studies demonstrate a correlation between programs and outcomes. Nearly all of the research shows that these programs are associated with positive student outcomes, including increased student achievement. Parents who participate in these programs were found to have more interactions with their children in their homes and in some cases, to acquire new skills and more positive attitudes toward teachers and schools. Teachers also developed more positive attitudes toward parents, especially as they engaged more often and more directly in the parent involvement activities. School climate also improves.

Long-term effects are more difficult to demonstrate. Some researchers suggest a relationship between parent involvement and reduction in dropout, delinquency, and pregnancy rates. Others show a relationship to improved attendance, discipline, and long-term student achievement. Several researchers caution that the effects of parent involvement may vary based on family socioeconomic status and ethnicity. Much more research is needed in this area to determine exactly what outcomes are produced, under what condition, and what the longer term effects of particular programs and practices are.

Chapter 5

Conclusions, Implications, and Recommendations

Overview

As educators continue to struggle with the question of how to design the best structures, programs, and practices to meet students' and society's needs, they must consider the most effective ways to create and use partnerships with parents and communities to help accomplish this task. The research literature on parent and community involvement in the middle grades is sparse, but what does exist illuminates some of the challenges and some ways that schools and parents can forge relationships to meet those challenges and produce positive outcomes for students, parents, schools, and society as a whole.

This review of the literature on parent and community involvement and literature related specifically to the middle grades was guided by three questions:

- What are the contexts within which parent and community involvement programs operate?

    Context refers to the policy environment; trends and factors influencing parent and community involvement that include: diversity within systems, families, communities and economies; perceptions, attitudes, and beliefs; institutional settings; pre-adolescent and adolescent development; and expectations, attitudes, and beliefs.

- What are the roles that parents, families, and community members assume in the education of their children?

    Roles of parents and/or community members are described as: a primary resource in the education of their children through participation in home learning activities; supporters and advocates for the education of their children through site-based restructuring efforts at the local level; and participants in the education of all children through districtwide parent involvement programs.

- What are the effects of promising programs on parents, students, school staff, schools, and/or school districts?

Effects of parent involvement programs relate to the outcomes for students, parents, teachers, and schools and school districts.

It is around these questions that the conclusions, implications and recommendations for future research directions are made.

Conclusions

This review of the literature on parent involvement, and literature related specifically to the middle grades has indicated that the following conclusions appear to be warranted. The conclusions are stated in terms of the findings about successful middle grades school/family partnerships and parent involvement efforts.

Successful middle grades school/family partnerships:

- are supported through well-developed policies at the school, district, state, and federal levels;

- consider the highly-related trends and factors that influence all school/family partnerships and parent and community involvement programs in the design, plan, and implementation of these programs; trends and factors specific to the middle grades are given priority;

- use parents, families, and community members in appropriate roles through home learning, school restructuring activities, and districtwide involvement programs;

- employ frequent, varied, two-way communication;

- value the roles of key players, such as parents, teachers, school personnel, and community members;

- provide sufficient physical, human, and fiscal resources and training; and

- attempt to measure student, parent, teacher, school and school district outcomes through both formative and summative evaluation methods.

Implications: Policies at various levels can help to inform and institutionalize effective practices. At the school level, policies can suggest the need for reciprocity, local decision-making that is responsive to school/community needs, and specific practices such as homework completion standards that may be uniformly required or encouraged. Site-based management practices lead to an even greater need for partnerships and parent involvement based on common goals and understandings. Such policies can also serve to guarantee or at least recommend that sufficient resources are allocated to the programs that have been jointly designed. Schools should be careful to design policies that reflect partnerships and avoid those based on a "deficit model" of parenting where the focus is on improving parents.

District policies serve many of the same functions and can also be used to promote equity across schools. Effective district policies may address roles of key players, communication strategies, particular practices or program structures, content areas, and community outreach.

State and federal policies tend to serve other functions. They may encourage or require particular forms of parent involvement, may lay out specific parameters for that involvement, and even provide for funding. However, because such policies are "top-down," their ability to assure the effectiveness of local implementation strategies is limited. However, they serve an important motivating role through both the symbolic and real commitment to the partnership that they make.

The first step in understanding how trends and factors are related involves the development of a knowledge base. Through this knowledge base all key players (parents, teachers, administrators and interested community members) can develop an understanding of the rich context in which successful parent involvement programs operate. This includes understanding pre-adolescent and adolescent development and how this impacts a child's relationship with peers, teachers, authority figures and motives to succeed; the variety of ways in which adolescents express their needs and feelings; and ways to capitalize on the newly emerging quests for independence, connectedness, and identity. Key players need to understand how various school structures affect partnerships. How schools are organized, how curriculum is delivered, where schools are located and the sheer size of classes and schools all impact the ways that parent and community programs should be designed and delivered.

Other features of the context must also be understood. All involved parties should seek to understand and value the diversity that exists within and between them. Varying economic, cultural, and social backgrounds should be used to shed light on circumstances affecting behaviors, beliefs, and attitudes of students and home/community/school partners. Differences should be viewed as potential assets in seeking to expand options and opportunities for program design.

The partnership itself should be viewed strategically, with constituents engaging in discussions designed to achieve consensus on valued goals and student outcomes. Parent and community members should be viewed as co-equals who bring valued expertise on their own to children, family, and community needs; teachers and administrators should be viewed as co-equals who bring valued expertise on educational practices and strategies. Together, these groups can work toward achieving the same ends, that is, increased student achievement, positive climate, and other desired goals.

A variety of different practices, programs and partnerships can be developed and implemented. One of the most promising is the creation of a home learning program.

Such programs can be designed in the same way any successful program is designed: initially conducting a needs assessment with all affected parties, analyzing the challenges presented and engaging in problem-solving techniques to meet the challenges. The research suggests that effective home learning programs use multiple methods for recruitment, understand local conditions and practices, and build on parent/family/community strengths. Clear communication that features specific advice and strategies, meaningful, interesting, and flexible activities and guidance as to appropriate student and parent roles are most successful. Information on parenting styles, household routines, adolescent behavior and other related topics has been found to be useful. Finally, being clear on expectations, learning objectives and student progress helps partners to understand the rationale underlying the activities and the motivation to complete them.

As parents and family members assume a broader role in education, either by serving as advocates or partners in education or through decision-making for restructuring, their information needs increase. In addition to understanding the context that affect their own children, they need to gain insight into the entire community of children. They also need to familiarize themselves with many other aspects of schooling, including the literature on effective organization, instruction, and assessment and legislative, financial and other constraints.

A promising area here is to develop partnerships around the concept of quality education, using tools such as Total Quality Management (TQM). Discussions can center around, for example, holistic and developmental approaches to learning, determining outcomes in the form of what children should know and be able to do, and jointly determining the best definitions of roles and relationships to accomplish these ends for all children.

Any parent/community involvement program must have sufficient staff, funding, training, and planning to be successful. Their effectiveness is likely to be enhanced if these programs are well-coordinated with other community efforts. Linkage to other schools, recreational centers, social service agencies, health agencies and other community groups serves a synergistic function, with the children as ultimate beneficiaries.

The paucity of research on parent involvement in the middle grades illustrates what little is known about programs and practices that specifically benefit children during these crucial years in their development. Most of the research is descriptive in nature, so little can be concluded about direct effects. While it is clear that there is an association between parent involvement and student achievement, for example, there is not enough research to identify optimal practices, to reveal the conditions under which programs are more or less effective, to understand how and why the relationship works, and to know whether replication in other sites produces similar results. Some researchers are making strides in this direction, but a much greater effort is needed, along with sufficient funding to make the research possible.

Recommendations for Future Research

Future research on school/family partnerships and parent involvement in education should be directed toward:

- middle grades education, based on specific roles as schools/families/communities join together to benefit students;

  > Although more attention is being devoted to middle grades education, the knowledge base in both research and practice needs to be expanded. This knowledge base should include a broad range of possibilities that school personnel, parents, families and community members can play in working together. Research and practice should focus on how these roles are facilitated within education and community organizational structures, and how different groups will depend on each other as their members play various roles in building partnerships.

- both quantitative and qualitative analyses of the context and processes of developing, planning, and implementing and middle grades school/family partnerships and parent involvement programs;

  > The sheer variety of family and community systems presents a challenge to partnership building, as do economic differences among the populations served by middle grades schools. Research should give us greater insights into these and other factors affecting partnerships: group culture and beliefs that influence individuals' perceptions of the schooling situation and their attitudes toward it; organizational barriers or supports to active involvement; attitudes of key players toward school/family partnerships; and possible resources, including training strategies and practice. Applied research can be directed to assist in choices of action that take these factors into account. Such action might include targeting specific resources and training toward parents, families, community members or school personnel; improving communication skills among participants or using various media as channels for communication; assigning additional school personnel to link schools more directly with parents, families, and community members, and coordinating services with other community organizations or agencies that work with children, families, and neighborhoods.

- the challenges to forming middle grades school/family partnerships, and the strategies used to meet those challenges;

  > Research should focus on the challenges of diversity within family, community and economic systems as they affect partnerships; the perceptions, attitudes and beliefs of key players; the institutional setting as

a challenge to active involvement; the attitudes and beliefs of key players toward school/family partnerships; and resources and training. Strategies to meet these challenges are a worthwhile area for future study. These might include: dedicated resources and training for parents, families, community members and school personnel; communication; additional school personnel to directly link schools with parents, families, and community members; and coordination of services.

• short and long-term potential outcomes of the partnership on students, teachers, schools, school districts and communities.

Short-term potential outcomes worthy of study include: higher levels of achievement as measured by standardized test scores; factual, conceptual and critical aspects of learning; acquisition of new skills, increased involvement; the use of varied strategies; increased student attendance rates, reductions in dropout, delinquency, and pregnancy rates; and improved discipline practices. Long-term potential outcomes that merit attention include: improved attitudes about schooling for all participants; empowerment and increased self-efficacy of parents, families, teachers and other school personnel, and community members; and increased family interactions.

This research review shows that creating partnerships between school, parents, families and communities can provide a promising avenue through which education can be more effective in achieving its goals. As reform efforts continue to grow the education community should be encouraged to explore this potential to its fullest.

Ahlenius, M. (1983). *Colorado families and schools project: A study of school policy and its impact on families*. Final report. Denver, CO: Colorado Congress of Parents, Teachers, and Students.

American Association of School Administrators. (1990). *Leadership News, 61*, 3.

American Indian Science and Engineering Society. (1989). *Our voices, our vision: American Indians speak out for educational excellence*. Boulder, CO: Author.

Armor, D., Conny-Osegura, P., Cox, M., King, N., McDonnell, L., Pascal, A., Pauly, E., & Zellman, G. (1976). *Analysis of the school preferred reading program in selected Los Angeles minority schools*. Santa Monica, CA: The Rand Coporation. (ED 130243)

Ascher, C. (1987). *Improving the home-school connection for poor and minority urban students*. (ERIC/CUE Trends and Issues, 8.) New York: Columbia University. ERIC Clearinghouse on Urban Education. (EJ No. 381 241)

Atwater, E. (1983). *Adolescence*. Englewood Cliffs, NJ: Prentice-Hall.

Baker, D.P., & Stevenson, D.L. (1986). Mothers' strategies for children's school achievement: Managing the transition to high school. *Sociology of Education, 59*, 156-166.

Barber, G.M. (1987). *Increasing parental involvement in helping fourth grade children to learn through home curriculum to improve homework habits*. (Practicum Report). Miami, FL: Nova University. (ERIC Document Reproduction Service No. ED 291 520)

Becker, H.J., & Epstein, J.L. (1981). *Parent involvement: Teacher practices and judgments*. Baltimore, MD: The Johns Hopkins University, Center for Social Organization of Schools.

Becker, H.J., & Epstein, J.L. (1982a). Parent involvement: A study of teacher practices. *Elementary School Journal, 83*, 85-102.

Becker, H.J., & Epstein, J.L. (1982b). *Influence on teachers' use of parent involvement at home*. (Report No. 324). Baltimore, MD: The Johns Hopkins University, Center for Social Organization of Schools.

Benson, C.S., Buckley, S., & Medrich, E.A. (1980). Families as educators: Time use contributions to school achievement. In J. Guthrie (Ed.), *School finance policies and practices: The 1980s, a decade of conflict* (pp. 162-206). Cambridge, MA: Ballinger.

Berla, N. (1991). Parent involvement at the middle school level. *The ERIC Review*. Washington, DC: U.S. Department of Education.

Berla, N., Henderson, A.T., & Kerewsky, W. (1989). *The middle school years: A parents' handbook*. Columbia, MD: National Committee for Citizens in Education.

Birman, B.F., Orland, M.E., Jung, R.K., Anson, R., Garcia, G.N., Moore, M.T., Funkhouser, J.E., Morrison, D.R., Turnbull, B.J., & Reisner, E. (1987). *The current operation of the Chapter 1 program: Final report from the National Assessment of Chapter 1*. Washington, DC: U.S. Department of Education.

Bowman, P. & Howard, C. (1985). Race-related socialization, motivation, and academic achievement: A study of black youth in three generation families. *Journal of the American Academy of Child Psychiatry, 24*(2), 134-141.

Brandt, R. (1986). On improving achievement of minority children: A conversation with James Comer.

Educational Leadership, 43(5), 13-17.

Brantlinger, E. (1985a). Low income parents' opinions about the social class composition of schools. *American Journal of Education, 93*, 389-408.

Brantlinger, E. (1985b). Low income parents' perceptions of favoritism in the schools. *Urban Education, 20*(1), 82-102.

Brice-Heath, S. (1983). *Way with words.* New York: Cambridge University Press.

Brown, P.C. (1989). Involving parents in the education of their children. *ERIC Digest.* Urbana, IL:ERIC Clearinghouse on Elementary and Early Childhood Education.

Carnegie Council on Adolescent Development. (1987). *Turning points: Preparing American youth for the 21st century.* New York: Carnegie Corporation.

Cazden, C.B. (1986). Classroom discourse. In M.C. Wittrock (Ed.), *Handbook of Research on Teaching* (3rd ed.). (pp. 432-463). New York: MacMillan.

Center for Evaluation, Development, and Research. (1990). *Parent involvement in the schools.* Bloomington, IN: Phi Delta Kappa

Chapman, W.K. (1991). Can a state school/home/community initiative make a difference: The Illinois Urban Partnership for at-risk students. *Phi Delta Kappan, 72*, 355-358.

Chavkin, N.F., & Williams D.L., Jr. (1987). Enhancing parent involvement: Guidelines for access to an important resource for school administrators. *Education and Urban Society, 19*, 164-184.

Chrispeels, J.A. (1987a). *Home-school partnership planner.* San Diego, CA: San Diego County Office of Education.

Chrispeels, J.A. (1987b). The family as an educational resource. *Community Education Journal, 14*(3), 10-17.

Chrispeels, J., Bourta, M., & Daugherty, M. (1988). *Communicating with parents.* San Diego, CA: San Diego Public Schools.

Chrispeels, J. (1991a). *School building practices that foster home learning. Presenter's guide.* San Diegoe, CA: San Diego Public Schools.

Chrispeels, J. (1991b). District leadership in parent involvement: Policies and actions in San Diego. *Phi Delta Kappan, 72*, 367-371.

Chrispeels, J. (1993). *School restructuring to facilitate parent and community involvement in the middle grades.* (Contract No. RR-91-1720.08). Denver, CO: RMC Research Corporation.

Chubb, J.E. (1988). Why the current wave of school reform will fail. *The Public Interest, 90*, 28-49.

Clark, R. (1983). *Family life and school achievement: Why poor black children succeed and fail.* Chicago, IL: University of Chicago Press.

Clark, R.M. (1989). *The role of parents in ensuring education success in school restructuring efforts.* Washington, DC: Council of Chief State School Officers.

Clarke-Stewart, K.A. (1983). Exploring the assumptions of parent education. In R. Haskin & D. Adams (Eds.), *Parent education and public policy,* (pp. 257-276). Norwood, NJ: Ablex.

Cochran, M. (1987). The parental empowerment process: Building on family stregths. *Equity and Choice, 4*(1), 9-24.

Cochran, M. & Henderson, C. R. (1986). *Family matters: Evaluation of the parental empowerment program.* Final report summary . Washington, DC:National Institute of Education.

Cohen, D. (1990, May 9). Parents as partners: Helping families build a foundation for learning. *Education Week, 9*(33), pp. 13-20.

Cole, M., & Griffin, P. (1987). *Contextual factors in education: Improving science and mathematics education for women.* Madison, WI: Wisconsin Center for Educational Research.

Comer, J.P. (1984). Home-school relationships as they affect the academic success of children. *Education and Urban Society, 71*, 323-337.

Comer, J.P. (1986). Parent participation in the schools. *Phi Delta Kappan, 67*, 442-446.

Comer, J.P. (1988a). Educating poor minority children. *Scientific American, 259*(5), 42-48.

Comer, J.P. (1988b). Is parenting essential to good teaching? *National Education Association Today, 6*(6), 34-40.

Committee for Economic Development. (1987). *Children in need-Investment strategies for the educationally disadvantaged.* New York: Author.

D'Angelo, D., & Adler, C. (1991). Chapter 1: A catalyst for improving parent involvement. *Phi Delta Kappan, 72,* 350-354.

Dauber, S.L., & Epstein, J.L. (1991). Parent attitudes and practices of involvement in inner-city elementary and middle schools. In N. Chavkin (Ed.), *Minority parent involvement in education* (pp. 53-71). Albany, NY: State University of New York Press.

Davies, D. (1985, May). *Parent involvement in the public schools in the 1980s: Proposals, issues, opportunities.* Paper presented at the Research for Better Schools Conference, Philadelphia, PA.

Davies, D. (1987). Parent involvement in the public schools: Opportunities for administrators. *Education and Urban Society, 19,* 147-163.

Davies, D. (1988, April). *Hard to reach parents in three countries: Perspectives on how schools relate to low-status families.* Paper presented at the annual meeting of the American Educational Research Association, New Orleans, LA.

Davies, D. (1991). Schools reaching out: Family, school and community partnerships for students' success. *Phi Delta Kappan, 72,* 376-382.

de Kanter, A., Ginsburg, A.L., & Milne, A.M. (1986, June). *Parent involvement strategies: A new emphasis on traditional parent roles.* Paper presented at the Conference on Effects of Alternative Designs in Compensatory Education, Washington, DC. (ERIC Document Reproduction Service No. ED 293 919)

Earle, J. (1990). *The steps to restructuring: Changing Seattle's middle schools.* Alexandria, VA: National Association of State Boards of Education.

Eastman, G. (1988). *Family involvement in education.* Madison, WI: Department of Public Instruction.

Elkind, D. (1979). Growing up faster. *Psychology Today, 60,* 180-186.

Epstein, J.L. (1984, April). *Effects of teacher practices of parent involvement change in student achievement in reading and math.* Paper presented at the annual meeting of the American Educational Research Association, Baltimore, MD. (ERIC Document Reproduction Service No. ED 256 863)

Epstein, J.L. (1986a). Parent involvement: Implications for limited-English-proficient parents. In C. Simich-Dudgeon (Ed.), *Issues of parent involvement and literacy* (pp. 4-5). Proceedings of the symposium held at Trinity College, Washington, DC.

Epstein, J.L. (1986b). Parents' reactions to teacher practices of parent involvement. *Elementary School Journal, 86,* 277-294.

Epstein, J.L. (1987a). Parent involvement: What research says to administrators. *Education and Urban Society, 19,* 119-136.

Epstein, J.L. (1987b). *Teacher's manual: Teachers Involve Parents in Schoolwork* (TIPS). (Report P 61). Baltimore, MD: The Johns Hopkins University, Center for Research on Elementary and Middle Schools.

Epstein, J.L. (1987c). Toward a theory of family-school connections: Teacher practices and parent involvement. In K. Hurrelmann, F. Kaufmann, & F. Losel (Eds.), *Social intervention: Potential and constraints* (pp. 121-136). New York: DeGruyter.

Epstein, J.L. (1988). How do we improve programs for parent involvement? *Educational Horizons, 66*(2), 58-59.

Epstein, J.L. (1989). Family structures and student motivation: A developmental perspective. In C. Ames & R. Ames (Eds.), *Research on motivation in education: Goals and cognitions* (pp. 259-

295). San Diego, CA: Academic Press.

Epstein, J.L. (1991a). Effects on student achievement of teachers' practices of parent involvement. In S. Silbern (Ed.), *Advances in reading/language research, 5,* 261-276.

Epstein, J.L. (1991b). Paths to partnerships: What we can learn from federal, state, district, and school initiatives. *Phi Delta Kappan, 72,* 344-349.

Epstein, J.L., & Becker, H.J. (1982). Teachers' reported practices of parent involvement: Problems and possibilities. *Elementary School Journal, 83,* 103-113.

Epstein, J.L., & Becker, H.J. (1987). *Hopkins surveys of schools and family connections: Questionnaires for teachers, parents, and students.* (Report P 81). Baltimore, MD: The Johns Hopkins University, Center for Research on Elementary and Middle Schools.

Epstein, J.L., & Connors, L.J. (1993). *School and family partnerships in the middle grades.* (Contract No. RR-91-1720.08). Denver, CO: RMC Research Corporation.

Epstein, J.L., & Dauber, S.L. (1989a). *Evaluation of students' knowledge and attitudes in the Teachers Involve Parents in Schoolwork (TIPS) social studies and art program.* (CREMS Report No. 41). Baltimore, MD: The Johns Hopkins University, Center for Research on Elementary and Middle Schools.

Epstein J.L., & Dauber, S.L. (1989b). *Teachers' attitudes and practices of parent involvement in inner-city elementary and middle schools.* Baltimore, MD: The Johns Hopkins University, Center for Research on Elementary and Middle Schools.

Epstein, J.L., & Herrick, S.C. (1991). *Reactions of parents and students to summer home learning packets in the middle grades.* (CDS Report 21). Baltimore, MD: The Johns Hopkins University, Center for Effective Schooling for Disadvantaged Students.

Epstein, J.L., & Salinas, K.C. (1991). *Promising practices in major academic subjects in the middle grades.* Reston, VA: National Association of Secondary School Principals.

Epstein, J.L., Jackson, V., Salinas, K.C., & Calverton & West Baltimore Middle School Teachers. (1990). *Teachers Involve Parents in Schoolwork (TIPS) language arts and science/health interactive homework in the middle grades.* (Draft document). Baltimore, MD: The Johns Hopkins University, Center for Effective Schooling for Disadvantaged Students.

Flaxman, E., & Inger, M. (1991). Parents and schooling in the 1990s. *ERIC Review, 1*(3), 2-6.

Gallup, A.M., & Elam, S.M. (1989). The 1989 Gallup poll of the public's attitude toward the public schools. *Phi Delta Kappan, 71,* 41.

Gotts, E.E., & Purnell, R.F. (1984, April). *Evaluation of home-school communication strategies.* Paper presented at the annual meeting of the American Education Research Association, New Orleans, LA. (ERIC Document Reproduction Service No. ED 244 376)

Griswold, P.A. (1986). *Parent involvement in unusually successful compensatory education.* Portland, OR: Northwest Regional Educational Laboratory. (ERIC Document Reproduction Service No. ED 279 428)

Hamilton, M.A., & Cochran, M. (1988). *Parents, teachers, and the community: Building partnerships for the child.* Ithaca, NY: New York State College of Human Ecology.

Heath, S.B., & McLaughlin, M.W. (1987). A child resource policy: Moving beyond dependence on school and family. *Phi Delta Kappan, 68,* 576-580.

Helton, G.B., & Oakland, T.D. (1977). Teachers' attitudinal responses to differing characteristics of elementary school students. *Journal of Educational Psychology, 69,* 261-266.

Henderson, A.T. (1986). *Beyond the bake sale: An educator's guide to working with parents.* Columbia, MD: National Committee for Citizens in Education.

Henderson, A.T. (1987). *The evidence continues to grow: Parent involvement improves student achievement.* Columbia, MD: National Committee for Citizens in Education.

Henderson, A.T. (1988a). Good news: An ecologically balanced approach to academic improvement.

Educational Horizons, 66(2), 60-62.

Henderson, A.T. (1988b). Parents are a school's best friend. *Phi Delta Kappan, 69,* 148-153.

Henderson, A.T., & Marburger, C.L. (1990). *A workbook on parent involvement for district leaders.* Columbia, MD: The National Committee for Citizens in Education.

Henderson, P. (1987). *Parental involvement (Los Padres Participan): Encouraging parent involvement through ESL, bilingual parent-teacher workshops, computer literacy classes, and the bilingual adult evening school program.* New York: New York City Board of Education Office of Bilingual Education. (ERIC Document Reproduction Service No. ED 285 400)

Herman, J.L., & Yeh, J.P. (1983). Some effects of parent involvement in schools. *Urban Review, 15*(1), 11-17.

Home and School Institute. (1988). *New partnerships in student achievement.* Washington, DC: Author.

Hoover-Dempsey, K.V., Bassler, O.C., & Brissie, J.S. (1987). Parent involvement: Contributions of teacher efficacy, school socioeconomic status, and other school characteristics. *American Educational Research Journal, 24,* 417-435.

Jacob, J. (1983, December). *Parent involvement. Remarks.* Paper presented at the meeting of the National Forum on Excellence in Education, Indianapolis, IN. (ERIC Document Reproduction Service No. ED 241 175)

Jennings, L. (1990, August 1). Parents as partners: Reaching out to families to help students learn. *Education Week, 9*(40), 23-25.

Jones, L.T. (1991). *Strategies for involving parents in their child's education.* Bloomington, IN: Phi Delta Kappa Educational Foundation.

Lareau, A. (1987). Social class differences in family-school relationships: The importance of cultural capital. *Sociology of Education, 60*(2), 73-85.

Leitch, M.L., & Tangri, S.S. (1988). Barriers to home-school collaboration. *Educational Horizons, 66*(2), 70-74.

Lightfoot, S.L. (1975). Families and schools: Creative conflict or negative dissonance. *Journal of Research and Development in Education, 9*(1), 34-43.

Lindner, B. (1987). *Family diversity and school policy.* Denver, CO: Education Commission of the States.

Lipsitz, J. (1984). *Successful schools for young adolescents.* New Brunswick, NJ: Transaction Books.

Maccoby, E. (1984). Middle childhood in the contest of the family. In W.A. Collins (Ed.), *Development during middle childhood: The years from 6-12*(pp. 184-239). Washington, DC: National Academy Press.

McCormick, K. (1989). *An equal chance: Educating at-risk children to succeed.* Alexandria, VA: National School Boards Association.

McLaughlin, M.W., & Shields, P.M. (1986). *Involving parents in the schools: Lessons for policy.* Washington, DC: Designs for Compensatory Education, Conference Proceedings and Papers. (ERIC Document Reproduction Service No. ED 293 290)

McLaughlin, M.W., & Shields, P.M. (1987). Involving low-income parents in the schools: A role for policy? *Phi Delta Kappan, 69,* 156-160.

Metropolitan Life Insurance Company. (1987). *The American teacher, 1987: Strengthening links between home and school.* New York: Louis Harris and Associates, Inc.

Moles, O. (1987). Who wants parent involvement? Interest, skills, and opportunities among parents and educators. *Education and Urban Society, 19,* 137-145.

Moles, O.C. (1990). Effective parent outreach strategies. Paper prepared for parent involvement seminars, California State Department of Education.

Moles, O.C. (1991). School performance of children from one-parent families. In M. Bloom (Ed.), *Changing lives* (pp. 110-118). Columbia, SC: University of South Carolina Press.

Nardine, F.E., Chapman, W.K, & Moles, O.C. (1989). *How involved are state education agencies in parent involvement?* (Report No. 17). Boston, MA: Institute for Responsive Education.

Nardine, F.E., & Morris, R.D. (1991). Parent involvement in the states: How firm is the commitment? *Phi Delta Kappan, 72,* 363-366.

National Coalition for Parent Involvement in Education. (1990). *Developing family/school partnerships: Guidelines for schools and school districts.* Washington, DC: National Education Association.

New York School Boards Association. (1987). *Home school partnership: School boards and parents. A position paper.* Albany, NY: Author. (ERIC Document Reproduction Service No. ED 290 206)

Northwest Regional Educational Laboratory. (1990). *Effective schooling practices: A research synthesis, 1990 update.* Portland, OR: Author.

Oakes, J., & Lipton, M. (1990). *Making the best of schools: A handbook for parents, teachers, and policymakers.* New Haven, CT: Yale University Press.

Peterson, A.C. (1986, April). *Early adolescence: A critical developmental transition?* Paper presented at the annual meeting of the American Educational Research Association, Miami, FL.

Peterson, D. (1989). *Parent involvement in the educational process.* Urbana, IL: ERIC Clearinghouse on Educational Management.

Pickarts, E., & Fargo, J. (1975). *Parent education: Toward parental competence.* New York: Meredith Corporation.

Purkey, S.C., & Smith, M.S. (1983). Effective schools—A review. *Elementary School Journal, 83,* 427-452.

Purnell, R.F., & Gotts, E.E. (1985, April). *Preparation and role of school personnel for effective school-family relations.* Paper presented at the annual meeting of the American Educational Research Association, Chicago, IL. (ERIC Document Reproduction Service No. ED 262 000)

Rich, D. (1985). *The forgotten factor in school success: The family.* Washington, DC: Home and School Institute.

Rich, D. (1987). *Schools and families: Issues and actions.* Washington, DC: National Education Association.

Rood, M. (1988). *A new look at student achievement: Critical issues in student achievement.* Paper #2. Austin, TX: Southwest Educational Development Laboratory.

Ruble, D.N. (1980). A developmental perspective on theories of motivation. In L.J. Fyans, Jr. (Ed.), *Achievement Motivation* (pp. 225-248). New York: Plenum.

Seeley, D.S. (1981). *Education through partnership: Mediating structures and education.* Cambridge, MA: Ballinger.

Seginor, R. (1983). Parents' educational expectations and children's academic achievements: A literature review. *Merrill-Palmer Quarterly, 29*(1), 1-23.

Sigel, I.E., Dreyer, A.S., & McGillicuddy-Delisi, A.V. (1984). Psychological perspectives of the family. In R.D. Parke (Ed.), *Review of Child Development Research,* (p. 7). Chicago, IL: University of Chicago Press.

Simich-Dudgeon, C. (1986). *Parent involvement and the education of limited English proficient students.* ERIC Digest, December. Washington, DC: ERIC Clearinghouse on Languages and Linguistics.

Simmons, R.G., Blyth, D.A., Van Cleave, E., & Bush, D. (1979). Entry into early adolescence. *American Sociological Review, 44,* 948-967.

Slaughter, D.T., & Epps, E.G. (1987). The home environment and academic achievement of Black American children and youth: An overview. *Journal of Negro Education, 86*(1), 3-20.

Smith, M.S., & O'Day, J. (1990). Systematic school reform: The politics of curriculum and testing.

Snider, W. (1990a, November 21). Parents as partners: Adding their voices to decisions on how schools are run. *Education Week, 10*(21), 27-33.

Snider, W. (1990b, November 21). Role of parents in school decisions long debated. *Education Week, 10*(21), 29.

Snider, W. (1990c, November 21). U.S. programs recognize parent contributions. *Education Week, 10*(21), 33.

Solomon, Z. (1991). California state policy on parent involvement: Initiating a process for State Leadership. *Phi Delta Kappan, 72,* 359-362.

Stevenson, D., & Baker, D. (1987). The family-school relation and the child's school performance. *Child Development, 58,* 1348-1357.

Stipek, D.J. (1984). The development of achievement motivation. In R. Ames & C. Ames (Eds.), *Research on Motivation in Education,* (p. 1). Orlando, FL: Academic Press.

Tangri, S., & Moles, O. (1987). Parents and the community: An educator's handbook. In V. Richardson-Koehler (Ed.), *Educator's Handbook* (pp.1-82). New York: Longman Press.

Taylor, B. & Levine, D. (1991). Effective schools projects and school-based management. *Phi Delta Kappan. 72,* 394-397.

U.S. Department of Education. (1986). *What works: Research about teaching and learning.* Washington, DC: U.S. Government Printing Office.

Useem, E.L. (1990, April). *Social class and ability group placement in mathematics in the transition to seventh grade: The role of parent involvement.* Paper presented at the annual meeting of the American Educational Research Association, Boston, MA.

Walberg, H.J. (1984). Improving the productivity of America's schools. *Educational Leadership, 41*(8), 19-27.

Warner, I. (1991). Parents in touch: Indianapolis public schools' investment in family involvement. *Phi Delta Kappan, 72,* 372-375.

Williams, D.L. (1984). *Parent involvement in education: What a survey reveals.* Austin, TX: Southwest Educational Development Laboratory. (ERIC Document Reproduction Service No. ED 253 327)

Williams, D.L., & Chavkin, N.F. (1990). Essential elements of strong parent involvement programs. *Educational Leadership, 47*(4), 18-20.

Williams, D.L., & Stallworth, J. (1983/4). *Parent Involvement in Education Project, Executive Summary of the Final Report.* Austin, TX: Southwest Educational Development Laboratory.

Zeldin, S. (1989). *Perspectives on parent education: Implications from research and an evaluation of new partnerships for student achievement.* Washington, DC: Policy Studies Associates.

Zeldin, S. (1990). Implementation of home-school-community partnership policies: Policy from the perspective of principals and teachers. *Equity and Choice, 6*(3), 56-67.

Part II

Literature Related to the Middle Grades

Chapter 1

Comprehensive Districtwide Reforms in Parent and Community Involvement Programs

Nancy Feyl Chavkin

It lies within our reach, before the end of the twentieth century, to change the futures of disadvantaged children. The children who today are at risk of growing into unskilled, uneducated adults, unable to help their own children to realize the American dream can, instead, become productive participants in a twenty-first-century America whose aspirations they will share. The cycle of disadvantage that has appeared so intractable can be broken (Schorr, 1988, p. 291).

In *Within Our Reach: Breaking the Cycle of Disadvantage*, Lisbeth Schorr provides compelling evidence that we have the requisite resources and skills to alter the future. This paper examines one part of Lisbeth Schorr's challenge to us—the role of school districts in reforming current parent and community involvement in education. The focus is on identifying both the resources and skills that school districts already have and those resources and skills that school districts can develop in order to increase educational success for all students.

This paper is divided into six parts. Part I presents the definition and guiding questions that introduce the topic of district-wide reform along with a discussion of the importance of key people who share a common vision for change. Part II reviews the research about parent and community involvement. Part III describes two key facilitating factors found in districts with promising parent and community involvement programs: policy and support for policy. Part IV considers the critical issues of allocating budgets and resources, assessing outcomes, and the collaboration process for parent and community involvement programs. Using case studies from middle schools, Part V reviews ways districts can enhance parent involvement. Part VI discusses both recommendations and further issues for school districts for improving parent and community involvement.

Part I: Introduction

The issue of comprehensive district-wide reform in parent and community involvement at the middle school level is a complex topic. This paper begins the discussion with a definition of comprehensive parent and community involvement. Then the paper focuses on important questions that guide the reform movement, key people in the reform process, and a clear statement of the vision needed for district-wide reform.

Definition. Comprehensive district-wide parent involvement programs are defined as programs that emphasize a variety of educational roles for parents in various schools throughout the community, particularly in schools with many students who are educationally at-risk. These parental roles might include volunteering in schools and classrooms, perhaps along with other members of the community, sitting on school governance and advisory boards, participating in parent/teacher organizations, and learning how to enrich the home learning environment. Collaboration with businesses and community service agencies, such as flextime for school conferences and referrals for parents' health and employment needs, are other possibilities. From such a set of options, parents can choose activities which best suit their circumstances. Such comprehensive programs might use innovative methods of communicating with parents, provide information to parents on various educational and child development issues, recruit and use volunteers in new ways, and in other ways make the programs attractive to different kinds of parents.

Guiding Questions. The following questions confronting district-wide reform are significant because the answers to these questions guide the nature of the reform.

1. What are key characteristics of model approaches to district-wide parent and community involvement? How do these new or reformed approaches differ from traditional practice or from prior practice?

2. What are supports and barriers to district-wide parent and community involvement programs?

3. To what extent do district-wide written parent involvement policies lead to changed behaviors and practices?

4. How do federal, state, and local policies, programs, budget priorities, and resource allocations affect district parent and community involvement programs?

5. How can federal, state, and local agencies be encouraged to collaborate in the development of a cooperative district-wide approach to family support and parent involvement?

6. What specific guidance from a systems perspective can facilitate understanding of how to reform/enhance district-wide programs of parent and community involvement?

7. What strategies and approaches have been developed to assess the impact of district-wide parent and community involvement programs?

8. What are the outcomes of the new or reformed district-wide parent and community involvement programs for parents, students, school administrators, teachers, other school staff, and community residents?

Finding the answers to these questions and others will be an ongoing process and will require the commitment of key people with a common vision of successful schooling.

Key People and Common Vision. Administrators and teachers are always quick to point out the many barriers to effective districtwide reform of parent and community involvement. Their lists usually begin with a plethora of grim statistics about poverty, underachievement, school dropouts, teenage parents, substance abuse, homelessness, and other societal problems. Research supports the correlation between these statistics and educational achievement (Levy & Copple, 1989). The plight of these families and the reality of these students' social systems is nothing new to district administrators and teachers who see these facts as major hindrances to parent and community involvement.

There is another perspective one can take on these crises occurring within our educational, health, welfare, and justice systems: these crises within our social systems help remind us daily of the failures of our current system of piecemeal efforts. All of our current systems function in isolation, and these multifaceted crises in our educational and social systems demand a convergence of reform now. Levy and Copple (1989, p. 1) call this "a propitious time for collaboration because education and human services face common challenges as they try to help the same people and respond to the same problems."

These crises have caused leaders from diverse fields to "join forces" in the reform movement. James Coleman (1991) calls for "the rebuilding of social capital" by schools when the social capital of the family and community is weak. The Council of Chief State School Officers (1989) says "the time is ripe" for "comprehensive family support, education and involvement efforts." The National Coalition for an Urban Children's Agenda (1991) is asking schools and communities to define "desirable outcomes for children" because its ten members are deeply concerned about the plight of urban children and families.

A recurrent theme in all these reports is that school districts can not solve the problems of today's students alone. Collaboration with parents and community is imperative. Many people automatically assume that the key people in the reform effort are either at the state department of education level or are school district personnel such as principals, superintendents, and school board members. We must recognize the importance of another group of constituents—parents and community members. They are key people in the reform process. Districts must develop a common vision that is shared by families, community members, and educators. This vision must be grounded in a social systems perspective that recognizes the importance of working together for the educational success of all students. Educational reform, and especially reform in the area of parent and community involvement, must include people both inside and outside the school. At the middle school level, these key people are school administrators, teachers, parents, community members, and the students themselves.

The conceptual framework of the whole student as part of a larger social system that extends beyond the school and the family to the community is being welcomed in districts across the nation. Educators are realizing that they can't do it alone. Districts cannot fix the problems of health, hunger, and unemployment, but they can collaborate and help students and families get services. Just changing the structure of schools and the academic curriculum is not enough; districts need to have a common vision that emphasizes reaching out to parents and the community and using the resources within the home and community to help students. Any vision that does not include reaching out to families and communities is a limited vision that is failing to look beyond the school building at the needs of the whole child and the community.

The importance of key people and a common vision can not be overstated. It does not matter exactly where the efforts for districtwide parent and community involvement begin. These efforts can be initiated by parents, by teachers, by superintendents, by principals, or by others. What is important is that key people promote and support parent and community involvement and that these key people develop a common vision with others in the school's social system. The common vision must include a broad view of the school that includes the community as an important part of its social system.

This paper continues to examine key issues surrounding the guiding questions, key people, and a common vision by reviewing the research and practice literature. Next, the paper describes two facilitating factors found in districts with promising parent and community involvement; these two factors are districtwide policy and support for policy. The paper discusses critical issues concerning budgets/resource allocations, assessment of outcomes, and the collaboration process. Case studies at the middle school level provide specific examples of how districts are reforming parent and community involvement. There are no easy answers or shortcuts to the development of districtwide parent and community involvement. Each district must harness the skills of key people and develop its own common vision for a successful school that reflects the specific community where the school is located.

Part II: Research Background

Research tells us that parents and community members are part of the rich resources and skills that each school district has. Walberg's (1984a) synthesis of 2,575 studies of academic learning reveals that parents influence key determinants of cognitive, affective, and behavioral learning. Henderson's *The Evidence Continues To Grow: Parent Involvement Improves Student Achievement* (1987) summarizes 49 research studies and documents the incontrovertible fact that parent involvement increases student achievement. The research has demonstrated that all children benefit from family involvement in education.

Furthermore, there are other important benefits of family participation in the schools. Chavkin (1993), Rich (1985), and Sattes (1985) found that parent involvement in education helped produce increases in student attendance, decreases in the drop-out rate, positive parent/child communication, improvement of student attitudes and behavior, and more parent/community support of the school. Swap (1987) discussed the benefits that both parents and teachers reap from collaboration. She reported that collaboration broadens both parents' and educators' perspectives and brings additional resources to both groups. Nardine (1990) discusses the reciprocal benefits for parents who are involved in their children's education. He cites specific examples of the mutually reinforcing effect that parents and children have on each other's educational outcomes and suggests that involving parents in the educational process is an asset.

These beneficial effects of parent involvement in education have been reported from early childhood through high school. Rhoda Becher's (1984) review of the literature on parent involvement in early childhood education supports the notion that parent education programs improve children's language skills, test performance, and behavior. Berla, Henderson, and Kerewsky (1989) advocate for more middle school involvement because this age period is such a critical time in adolescent development. Dornbusch and Ritter's study (1988) found parents of high school students a neglected resource.

Chavkin and Williams' study (1987) found that more than 70% of both superintendents and school board presidents believed it was the school district's responsibility to provide a policy and guidelines for involving parents in their children's education. Parents' responses were very similar to administrators' responses. Most parents wanted the school to take the lead in parent involvement and give them ideas about working with their children, particularly in the area of homework. In short, both parents and educators want school districts to provide policies and supports for parent involvement in education.

With both groups in favor of parent involvement, it would seem that schools would have more parent involvement than they do now. The reason for infrequent parent involvement is not clear. Sometimes it is the result of a stereotypical view of parents and the erroneous assumption that they do not care about their children's education (Chavkin, 1989). Unfortunately, parents are often typecast as indifferent to parent involvement when they do not participate in traditional parent/school activities.

According to James Comer (1986), parents' lack of participation in traditional parent/school activities should not be misinterpreted as a lack of interest in their children's education. He points out that many parents do not participate in traditional parent/school activities such as PTA meetings because they feel uncomfortable at the school. Comer's work with the New Haven schools reveals that parents often lack knowledge about school protocol, have had past negative experiences with schools, and feel unwelcome at a middle class institution. Because of racial, income, and educational differences, parents are reluctant to become involved in the schools.

Comer suggests that just inviting parents to school is not enough; parents need clear mechanisms for involvement and district programs must be restructured to attract parents who have been reluctant to involve themselves in the school. Comer (1988, p. 42) concludes: "Schools must win the support of parents and learn to respond flexibly and creatively to students' needs."

All students could benefit prodigiously from effective approaches to parent involvement in education. It is not appropriate to place the blame for illiteracy and dropouts solely on the home or solely on the school. As Davies (1993), Seeley (1989), and Chavkin (1990) suggest, the solution to these educational problems requires collaboration among a wide range of community entities with families and schools as the central partners in the process of education. Community organizations, businesses, health care institutions, and social service agencies are all important in the educational process, and a positive relationship between parents and schools is essential.

Clearly, districtwide reform of parent and community involvement is a crucial part of the change that needs to take place in the United States if we are going to break the cycle of disadvantage. Regardless of the communities they serve, all school districts can develop effective programs to involve parents in the education of their children. James Comer's (1988) work, which began with the Yale University Child Study Center and two inner-city schools in New Haven, Connecticut and now includes more than 50 schools around the country, shows that supportive bonds between home and school can increase academic achievement and improve attendance and discipline without any change in the socioeconomic makeup of the schools. Herb Walberg's (1984b) examination of 29 studies on family involvement in education found that participation in parent involvement in education programs is twice as predictive as socioeconomic status.

Research tells us that school districts with policies about parent involvement have more parent involvement. In the Chavkin and Williams' study (1987), researchers found that the existence of formal, written policies about parent involvement led to increased parent involvement activities. Policies about parent involvement in education and support for these policies are two key facilitating factors. Part III of this paper will examine policy and support for policy.

Part III: Policy and Support for Policy: Two Key Elements in Districtwide Reform of Parent Involvement

Williams and Chavkin (1989) used a key informant approach to identify and describe the essential elements of promising parent involvement programs in five southwestern states. These essential elements begin with two key components: written policies and administrative support for parent involvement. The other elements all fit under the general umbrella of ways school districts help support educators working with families. These additional elements include: training for staff and parents; a partnership approach in every aspect of programming; two-way communication; networking within and outside the district; and evaluation. In each case, the school board set the official district policy on parent and community involvement and then provided administrative support for policy implementation. Individual schools within the district developed their own strategies for implementation with support from the central office as necessary.

The word policy often means different things to different people. For the purposes of this paper policy means the formal, written policies of the school district. These are the policies on which the school board takes an official vote. This paper uses the phrase *school district policies* to mean rules and regulations that are written down, officially approved by the Board of Education, and followed by all in the district.

This paper uses the word *support* in the traditional sense of sustaining or upholding something. Support is considered during three different stages of policy—development, implementation, and maintenance. Support is what helps a policy come into formal existence (development), what helps a policy translate into practical actions (implementation), and what helps us maintain the policy (maintenance).

The Institute for Responsive Education's research (Davies, 1987) points out that because school districts have unique features which make them resistant to change, policies about parent involvement are necessary. The goals of schools as organizations are diffuse; the method of goal achievement is fragmented and responsibility is diffused among administrators, counselors, teachers, families, and students. In addition, the informal norms of schools are powerful, and the formal structure is complicated and not always well-coordinated. These organizational realities make the idea of parent involvement in education an idea that is both difficult to introduce and maintain without a formal, written policy. Davies (1987) makes a recommendation that a mandate or policy for parent involvement is essential. His work and the study by the Institute for Responsive Education clearly show that policy is a critical element if the natural organizational resistance to change is to be overcome.

The National Coalition for Parent Involvement in Education (NCPIE) is dedicated to the development of family/school partnerships. This group of organizations used their broad and diverse experiences in working with teachers, administrators, families, and community leaders to develop general policy suggestions. Based on the assumption that all parent involvement policies are developed with input from teachers, administrators, parents, students, persons from youth-serving groups, and the community, NCPIE suggests that all policies should contain the following concepts:

- Opportunities for all parents to become informed about how the parent involvement program will be designed and carried out.

- Participation of parents who lack literacy skills or who do not speak English.

- Regular information for parents about their child's participation and progress in specific educational programs and the objectives of those programs.

- Opportunities for parents to assist in the instructional process at school and at home.

- Professional development for teachers and staff to enhance their effectiveness with parents.

- Linkages with social service agencies and community groups to address key family and community issues.

- Involvement of parents of children at all ages and grade levels.

- Recognition of diverse family structures, circumstances and responsibilities, including differences that might impede parent participation. The person(s) responsible for a child may not be the child's biological parent(s) and policies and programs should include participation by all persons interested in the child's educational progress.

But policies alone are not enough. Davies (1987) says policies only provide the framework; policies need to be supported by mechanisms for monitoring, enforcing, and providing technical assistance. District support for parent and community involvement must occur during three critical stages. These stages are: (1) the development stage; (2) the implementation stage; and (3) the maintenance stage. Each of these stages is critical to ensuring the effectiveness of policy about parent and community involvement.

Based on information from actual programs, the National Coalition for Parent

Involvement in Education (NCPIE) and the National School Boards Association (1988) recommend several supports for policies for involving parents in school activities during the development phase. These begin with assessing parent needs and interests about ways of working with the schools and setting clear and measurable goals with parent and community input. The understanding of what a true partnership means is critical during this first stage. School districts need to see parents and community members as equal partners and seek their input. Districts need to take the leadership role and reach out into communities and actively seek the involvement of parents and community.

Once a policy is adopted, school districts need to successfully implement the policies through a strong support system. NCPIE's keys to success at the implementation stage include a variety of strategies. Some suggestions that have worked for districts include the following:

- Hire and train a parent liaison to directly contact parents and coordinate parent activities. The liaison should be bilingual where needed and sensitive to the needs of parents and the community, including the non-English speaking community.

- Develop public relations to inform parents, businesses, and the community about parent involvement policies and programs through newsletters, slide shows, videotapes, and local newspapers.

- Recognize the importance of a community's historic, ethnic, linguistic, or cultural resources in generating interest in parent participation. Even when there are problems, such as desegregation issues, a parent involvement program can serve as a forum for discussion and a conduit for change.

- Use creative forms of communication between educators and parents. This may include parent/teacher conferences which yield individual parent/child and teacher/child plans, and newsletters mailed to parents.

- Mobilize parents as volunteers in the school assisting teachers with instructional tasks, assisting in the lunchroom, and helping with administrative office functions. Parents might act as volunteer tutors, classroom aides, and invited speakers.

- Train educators to include techniques for surmounting barriers between parents and schools so that teachers, administrators, and parents interact as partners.

The maintenance stage follows the coming together of the partnership and the establishment of an official group; the maintenance stage focuses on working together with all partners. The work is not done after policies are developed and implemented. In fact, most partnerships report that very difficult tasks occur during the maintenance stage.

After implementing policies about parent and community involvement, it is essential to enhance the success of policies during the maintenance stage. NCPIE makes the following three recommendations. First, integrate information and assistance with other aspects of the total learning environment. Parents should have access to information about such services as health care and nutrition programs provided by schools or community agencies. Second, schedule programs and activities flexibly to reach diverse parent groups. Third, monitor and evaluate the effectiveness of parent involvement programs and activities on a regular basis.

It is important to be aware of the factors that may inhibit districtwide reform through policies and supports for policies. Critics of parent involvement policies/supports will state that the attitudes of the parents or the educators cannot be legislated. Others will argue that policies take too long to develop or the district already has too many policies that no one pays any attention to. Still other critics will point to the need for a national family resource policy, not an individual school district policy (see Heath & McLaughlin, 1987).

Policies will not help if they are not supported at every level (federal, state, and local) and at every stage (from development through implementation and maintenance). Flexibility is being encouraged at the federal level, and state departments of education are currently changing their role from "state as regulator" to "state as facilitator" in order to help districts reshape parent and community initiatives to fit their own community. It is essential that school districts provide opportunities for broad input from parents, teachers, and community members and develop and support their own policies about parent and community involvement. Each district's policy needs to be individualized and should reflect its own community.

Part IV: Critical Issues in Policy and Support of Policy

Any discussion of districtwide reform must include consideration of three critical issues: budget/resource allocations, assessment of outcomes, and the collaboration process. Because these concerns are critical to support for policy about parent and community involvement, this paper addresses the issues at the local district level and the state and federal levels.

Budget/Resource Allocations. All districtwide reform efforts cost some money and the perennial question is, "Where will the money come from?" As Seeley, Niemeyer, and Greenspan (1991) write in *Principals Speak*, the answer can be found in the word priorities. Our schools, even in times of high expenditures, have not spent very much money on parent and community involvement. The United States Department of Education (1991) reports that using constant 1990 dollars, our schools have increased per pupil expenditures more than $3600 per pupil (from $1389 to $4992)in the last thirty-five years, and almost none of it has been spent on parent and community involvement. Although looking at the past does not correct the budget problems, it does serve as a guide for what schools could be doing. The word priority comes into play. If we really believe parent and community involvement are linked to student success, we must stop giving lip service to partnerships and allocate modest sums for staff development, outreach, and coordination activities.

Of course, some of the goals of parent and community involvement can be accomplished without new district dollars; resource reallocation can help. Teachers and staff can be reassigned and existing staff development time can be used for training on parent and community involvement. Additional funding can also be sought from local businesses and community groups. Foundations can be another source of support.

State and federal funds are other possible sources of support. Seeley, Niemeyer, and Greenspan (1991) suggest that one promising place to look for funding is the use of federal Chapter 1 dollars because they have been increasing. They urge districts to review their priorities for the use of Chapter 1 funds and see whether continuing to spend dollars on remedial instruction is in the best interest of students. They suggest the dollars might be used more productively if they were invested in mobilizing home/school/community resources to help children. The recent U. S. Department of Education publication (1992) on flexibility in using Chapter 1 funds supports this idea, but Palanki and Burch (1992) report few programs are taking advantage of this opportunity.

In addition to Chapter 1 funds, there are other special funding sources to consider. These sources include special education funds, drug education funds, funds for at-risk youth, and dropout prevention funds. Many of these funding sources welcome plans that include parent and community involvement.

Davies, Burch, and Johnson (1992) suggest that there is little reliable data about either the actual costs or funding sources of family/community/school activities. Districts in the League of Schools Reaching Out Project reported that they were spending local district funds, but further investigation revealed that the local funds are actually federal dollars channelled through districts. Another important finding from the League of Schools Reaching Out Project was that the schools reporting comprehensive reaching out strategies also had a range of funding supports. These funding supports include dollars from federal, state, and district levels as well as private funds.

The role of local communities in funding for parent and community involvement can be a significant factor for many school districts. Not only are funds available from businesses and foundations, but social service and community agencies can pool resources, share space and staff, and exchange in-kind resources. There are a wide range of funding supports that can be used when the emphasis is placed on community. The options increase dramatically when districts broaden their vision to include the whole community and see students as part of a larger social system than home and school.

The National Coalition for an Urban Children's Agenda (1991) suggests that a major part of the budget/resources issue is that we are not effectively using the resources we have. Because of our past history of programmatic fragmentation, we are driven by a traditional view of funding that puts dollars for children in specific categories of programs. This categorical funding mentality divides program dollars vertically to address piecemeal concerns of drug use, teenage pregnancy, drop-out prevention, and remedial education. The result has been a duplicative and inadequate system. The Coalition suggests that more districts look at ways to decategorize money and address issues of the whole student and whole family. In some areas this change will require state and federal legislation.

Nardine and Morris (1991) studied the current status of state leadership, staffing patterns, funding, training, and technical assistance for parent involvement activities in all fifty states. They followed this study by another survey of state legislation, guidelines, and regulations dealing with parent involvement. The responsibilities for parent involvement were not comparable across states because states had separate divisions for federal programs like Chapter 1, migrant, and bilingual education. Often the staff only worked part-time on parent and community involvement. No state had the equivalent of one full-time person for parent involvement per $100 million dollars budgeted. Although some states have legislation suggesting parent involvement, most states have not made legislation about parent involvement or funding of parent involvement a high priority.

The issue of district funding for parent involvement cannot be addressed without mention of the inequities in school funding. The current school funding system favors wealthy districts because the bulk of school funding comes from local property taxes. Education dollars do not exist in places of greatest need such as our inner cities. Court cases challenging present funding practices are active across the nation, and many believe the time has come to develop a new finance system which means increased state funding and decreased emphasis on the property tax (NASBE, 1989b).

Assessment of Outcomes. If we want more budget/resource allocations for parent and community involvement, we must be clear about the outcomes of these activities. It is important to specify clear and measurable goals for district-wide parent and community involvement, and it is essential to go one step further and delineate how we will know when we have reached our goals. We must describe the outcomes we expect for parents, students, school administrators, teachers, school staff, and community residents. The National Coalition for an Urban Children's Agenda (1991) says we must specify the outcomes so we can track progress and judge whether districts are fulfilling their responsibilities.

We need to look beyond inputs (who was served, what services were provided) and move toward examining outcomes. The Coalition suggests several indicators that districts might consider: health and well-being; development; deviant behavior; and satisfaction. It is a difficult process to define outcomes for partnership programs because they combine the elements of education, social service, and community activities. It is not an easy task, but it is an important challenge.

After defining outcomes, it is necessary to measure them. Assessment is nothing new to educators; teachers use assessment daily. In this paper we have already talked about assessment as a key component of the policy development stage and the policy maintenance stage. Assessment is definitely a major component of supporting parent and community involvement policy. Palanki and Burch (1992) suggest seven ways districts can evaluate whether their policies about parent and community are effective. They suggest policies need to be evaluated by looking at flexibility, intensity, continuity, universality, participation, coordination, and comprehensiveness.

Assessment will need to undergo quite a bit of change from our usual understanding if it is truly going to measure outcomes. Most of the current assessments used by districts measure inputs rather than outputs. Assessments in current parent and community involvement programs typically count how many people attended instead of measuring the quality of their interactions with the school; quality is at least as important as quantity. Some districts are now incorporating assessment about parent and community involvement in the annual performance reviews of both teachers and administrators. Changes in attitudes and perceptions of both parents and teachers should occur and be measurable. A "vignette" approach and other qualitative measurement techniques may work best and also provide the most insight for districts. Districts need to continue to develop accountability systems that accurately assess outcomes for collaboration and coordination activities.

Heath and McLaughlin (1987) call for a national child resource policy. They argue against a narrow view of the outcomes of schooling as academic achievement and propose that there are other important nonacademic outcomes such as social competence, physical and mental health, formal cognition, and emotional status. In addition to arguing against a narrow conception of outcomes, they suggest that schools are relying on outdated assumptions about the role of families and schools. Demographic, cultural, and ethnic realities in American families have altered the idealized, nuclear family of yesterday. Heath and McLaughlin call for a broader view of both strategies and institutions to help children succeed and suggest that school districts need to shift to a collaborative mode and focus on identifying and coordinating the social networks of students.

Collaboration Process. Districts must work with all aspects of the community to ensure that students and their families have access to needed health and social services, employment, food, and housing so that they come to school ready to learn. Whether schools link students and their families to needed services or whether these services are provided at the school will require new roles and commitments (NASBE, 1989a, 1989b). Districts need to be sensitive to racial, ethnic, and economic differences, as well as language and literacy obstacles because insensitivity inhibits both communication and collaboration. Too often this lack of sensitivity prevents effective interaction with families and the community.

School districts will have to provide training for staff to learn to coordinate with staff in other systems. Districts will need to examine existing job descriptions and reward systems. There needs to be a wide range of activities, service directories, and resource materials available at the school. Districts have to look at the possibility of locating some community services or community personnel in school buildings. Districts will want to hire parent and community coordinators to link families with the school and community services. Sometimes this person will be a professional social worker trained in community organization and working with families; other times the person will be a long-time member of the community.

Whenever possible, districts need to work with nearby teacher-training institutions to assure preservice training in parent and community involvement and the collaboration process. Higher education institutions may also be able to provide district-wide in-service training that meets the needs of local teachers, community members, and parents.

In addition, district-wide partnerships with business and industry can be an important part of the collaboration process. Businesses can contribute in a wide variety of ways (e.g., employee mentorships with individual students, participation in the classroom, providing "real-world" challenges and fun, providing released time for employees and parents to attend to school matters during regular work hours, helping students explore possible career options).

It is difficult to get collaboration programs underway. There are many barriers because each system has a different governance structure. There are often conflicting regulations and time schedules. Professional practices such as intake forms, budget cycles, confidentiality rules, and reimbursement plans are often contradictory and cause disagreements (Cohen, 1989a, 1989b).

These differences are not insurmountable, but it does take school districts time to work these problems out with other agencies. Superintendents and principals are key people who can exert leadership in this collaboration process; they can be the guiding force that makes collaboration work. Collaboration programs can be successful when there is a strong district policy and support for the policy about parent and community involvement.

The need for cooperation among systems at the federal, state, and local levels is well-established. Districts need support from state and federal agencies so that collaboration programs can work. The fragmentation of local communities is mirrored at the state and federal level. Very often there are numerous federal and state agencies with policies and programs that overlap, but these programs do not coordinate with each other. Federal and state agencies need to be modelling the collaboration process for local districts. These federal and state efforts can establish direction and tone, as well as provide model policies and strategies that can readily be adapted at the local district level. Often leaders at state departments of education are well-positioned to serve as catalysts for statewide reform in parent and community involvement and can help local districts develop their own district-wide reform efforts.

Part V: Case Examples and Analysis

This part of the paper examines effective ways that districts can enhance parent and community involvement. The focus is on parent involvement in middle schools because the Carnegie Council on Adolescent Development's report *Turning Points: Preparing American Youth for the 21st Century* (1989) indicates that this is the typical time that involvement starts to decrease and seems more difficult than at the elementary level. Epstein (1986) reports that by the middle school years parent involvement has decreased significantly and in some cases is nonexistent.

Berla (1991) believes that there are several barriers to parent involvement at this age level, including the impersonal structure of the middle schools, the attitudes of students who are striving for independence from parents during early adolescence, and the attitudes of school staff that parent involvement is not as important as when the student was younger. The following examples from middle schools are descriptions of promising approaches to district-wide reform. This section presents the key characteristics of these effective programs and what the districts have learned about promising reforms at the middle school level.

San Diego City Schools

San Diego City Schools was the first district in California and the first large urban district in the nation to have a comprehensive policy about parent involvement approved by the school board. The district's Parent Involvement Task Force is a broad-based group of parents, community representatives, and district staff who developed this policy and serve as an advisory group to the district on ongoing district-wide parent involvement activities. The overall responsibility for implementation of the policy was assigned to the Community Relations and Integration Services Division which has contained a Parent Involvement Department since 1989. The Parent Involvement Department has a coordinator and two resource teachers who provide coordination to district-level efforts in parent involvement and provide technical assistance to schools as they develop parent involvement programs at school sites.

Three major support activities have helped implement and maintain the district's parent involvement policy. These are staff development, partnership development, and follow-up activities. In the area of staff development, the Parent Involvement Department provides technical assistance (materials, planning/evaluation assistance or resources) and training sessions on program planning, home/school communication, parent/teacher conferences, and home visits. The department also publishes a quarterly newsletter to build staff awareness about the importance of parent involvement and has a parent involvement handbook that is presented to all new administrators each year. Special workshops are given for new principals, for leadership candidates, bilingual teachers, and counselors.

In the area of partnership development, the Parent Involvement Department has a strong belief in comprehensive, systemically planned, and long-lasting programs. Contrary to popular perception that the level of parent involvement is determined by parent interest or apathy, San Diego's Parent Involvement Department believes the level of parent involvement is determined by whether or not appropriate strategies and structures are in place to facilitate the participation of parents. The department works to ensure that each school's programs respond to a variety of needs. For example, at the third annual countywide parent involvement conference, workshops were presented in English, Spanish, Lao, Cambodian, and Vietnamese. Staff provided assistance to conferences on the African-American Family and the Latino Family. Family Reading, Parents Growing Together, and other workshop programs are supported. Recently a bus has been purchased and will be staffed and used as a mobile Parent Resource Center for schools.

Another interesting component in the area of partnership development has been the Parent Involvement Incentive Grants. These grants were awarded to support the parent involvement policy by encouraging schools to develop promising practices and innovative programs that strengthen partnerships between home and school. Some of the grants were for innovative projects linking parents and specific curriculum areas, and others were for projects linking schools and community agencies. Some of the middle school grants included: working with community agencies to implement "Parenting your Teenager" workshops; linking with community agencies serving families from different cultures; hosting a conference for families of a middle school and its feeder schools; developing and testing a community mentoring model; organizing a community-wide parent conference; working with community agencies to promote involvement of the African-American community.

The San Diego City Schools have also been active in the area of follow-up and support for parent involvement. The Parent Involvement Task Force continues to meet regularly and play an active role as an advisory group for policy implementation issues. Members have participated in the School Accountability Report Card and have been leaders in urging the district to establish translation/interpretation services for schools to enhance home/school communication. The district tries to link parent involvement activities to community resources and staff are working to build relationships with community groups in order to maximize benefits to students. The district is also working to link district parent involvement efforts to state and national resources and information. The District has suggestions specifically tailored for the middle school level in five areas of parent involvement (communication, support, learning, teaching, and advisory/decision making). For example, in the area of home and school support strategies, one suggestion is to organize a beginning-of-the-year Saturday Family Day where parents and students can learn about study skills, adolescent development, college preparation, family communication, healthy living, and also have student clubs raise funds on fun activities. In addition to the suggestions for activities at the middle school level, the district guide also lists the expected outcomes for teachers, students, and parents.

More information about parent and community involvement in San Diego can be found in the following publications of the Community Relations and Integration Services Division: *Partners for Student Success: A Handbook for Principals and Staff* (Chrispeels, Fernandez, & Preston, 1991) and *Report on Efforts to Build Home-School Partnerships* and *Announcement of Parent Involvement Incentive Awards* (San Diego, 1991). Chrispeels (1991) discusses the California State Board of Education's policy, efforts of the San Diego County Office of Education (the intermediate unit of the educational structure), and activities in the San Diego City Schools.

Seattle Middle Schools

For two years the National Association of State Boards of Education (NASBE) with support from the Edna McConnell Clark Foundation worked in a partnership effort with ten middle schools in the Seattle Public School District. This collaborative effort was a complex undertaking that was designed to initiate systemic change in a school district and in broader community institutions in a short time.

The project had three phases of planning, starting up, and implementing activities. During the planning phase, the objectives were: creating a vision of what middle school education could look like in Seattle; initiating a broad-based planning process that would ensure support for reform at the district, community, and state levels; developing an action plan for systemic change; and enhancing staff development opportunities. The second phase consisted of creating a blueprint for action about how change would take place. The third phase involved piloting the recommendations in two Seattle middle schools.

The creation of a broadly based group was a significant part of the reform effort.

Participants on the Seattle Middle Schools Commission included representatives from the business community, the department of social and health services, parents, the state board and department of education, the middle school principals' association, district staff, community-based organizations, and the Seattle Board of Education. The reason for this diverse group was the conviction that past reform efforts have not succeeded because the education community had not sufficiently engaged others in proposed reforms.

Another significant part of the project was the agreement from the very beginning that the budget line would include released time for teachers so they would be able to play a key role in guiding the project. During the second phase this budget commitment was extended to obtain a minimum of $100,000 of district funds per year for the next four years to support middle school reorganization.

The district did not try to do everything themselves; networking was a key component of the reform effort. The project brought in resource people and materials to inform discussions and planning. Staff also linked the project with the State Board of Education, Governor's office, legislature, and State Department of Public Instruction.

Four key recommendations concerning school structure, organization, climate, and outside support evolved: (1) all middle schools should be divided into smaller, more easily managed units called "houses"; (2) teachers should be organized into interdisciplinary teams; (3) schools should sustain the present Dropout Prevention Retrieval Program; and (4) the district should provide each middle school with a parent/outside service coordinator.

The major activities that helped foster districtwide parent and community involvement began with the school board's official adoption of the Commission's recommendations. Then leadership teams were developed in each school with two schools being chosen to pilot the reforms.

The Commission created staff development programs for the leadership teams at all the schools. These staff development programs included preparations for working with adolescents and their families at the middle grades. A retreat was planned for problem-solving, hearing from experts, and interacting with the superintendent.

Parent/outside service coordinators were hired to provide effective support for at-risk middle school students. These coordinators provided support for all students but placed a special emphasis on potential dropouts and their families. The coordinators provided services such as home visits, tutoring, helping students deal with parents' substance abuse problems, and conducting parenting classes. The coordinators worked flexible hours including nights and weekends and were instrumental in providing personal attention to students and families.

Other key activities included piloting the plans for "houses" and interdisciplinary teams at two middle schools and sustaining leadership within the district for middle school restructuring by keeping it visible among teachers, principals, the business community, and the superintendent.

There were three activities directly related to evaluating the results of the project. First, an Oversight Committee was created to hear regular reports concerning project activities and to provide guidance. Second, semi-structured interviews were conducted by NASBE staff during regularly scheduled site visits. Third, each school collected information on itself. These school portraits included: demographic information on students and staff; suspension, attendance, expulsion and retention data; achievement test data; student grouping practices; and school climate.

More information about the Seattle Middle School Project can be found in a publication entitled *The Steps to Restructuring: Changing Seattle's Middle-Schools* (1989) by Janice Earle.

Alachua County Middle-School Family Service Center

In August 1990 the Family Service Center, a full-service school, opened at Lincoln Middle School in Alachua County, Florida. The school is located next to a subsidized housing project and a majority of the racially mixed students qualify for free or reduced price meals.

The Center's goal is to address the major problems facing at-risk students and families by using the school site to bring together health, education, and social services. With the ultimate goal of increasing student achievement, the Center works to improve other factors of student and family well-being that influence a student's ability to be successful at school.

The director of the Center is hired by the school board and views herself as an advocate for empowering disadvantaged parents. Home/school communication is a major component of her job. To assess the services a family needs, a family liaison specialist conducts a needs assessment on-site where eligibility for services is established. A plan is developed and progress is monitored.

Services to families are provided both on-site at the school and off-site. Extensive interagency cooperation is critical to the success of the project. Using a holistic approach, the project provides both education and social services to students and their families.

The key people in the project include the principal of Lincoln Middle School, two family liaison specialists, a nurse practitioner, a social worker/guidance counselor, after-school teachers, and clerical assistants. Other agencies provide the services of their staff on an in-kind basis. The school district is working in partnership with the Department of Health and Rehabilitative Services, the University of Florida's College of Medicine, Santa Fe Community College, community social service agencies, city government, and county government.

Funding for this project comes from numerous sources. The city has contributed technical services and the property for site location. The State Department of

Education, Head Start, Florida First Start, and Even Start have all contributed dollars.

The evaluation of the project is being done by a collaborative team from the Department of Health and Rehabilitative Services, and the School Board of Alachua County. The team is looking for the achievement of the following objectives: increased student learning, increased student grade point average, gain in family involvement in school activities, reduced health problems related to behavioral disorders and substance abuse, increased efficiency and effectiveness for personnel and resources, reduced incidence of teenage suicide, reduced criminal activity, and assisting disadvantaged families with achieving economic and social independence. The evaluation component includes a control group of 80-100 middle school students with similar educational and economic backgrounds not served by the Center.

More information about parent and community involvement in Alachua County can be obtained from a 1991 publication of the Council of Chief State School Officers entitled *Families in School: State Strategies and Policies to Improve Family Involvement in Education.*

Other Promising Districtwide Practices

Many districts across the nation are initiating parent and community involvement programs that contain promising practices; not all are labeled middle school programs. Many of these practices are being adapted at the middle grades.

In McAllen, Texas, the district's parent involvement programs were originally administered under the auspice of federal programs such as Chapter 1, bilingual education, or migrant funding. By making parent involvement a districtwide effort instead of a special program effort, the district's parent and community efforts have grown tremendously. Because the district integrated its parent involvement efforts into the regular school program, all support personnel for parent involvement are supervised by a centrally located administrator. Each school has its own home/school partnership program that is supported at the district level. Many of the services provided to parents are paid for by combining funding sources so that all parents may participate; the emphasis is on parent and community involvement for all families.

Some of the promising practices in McAllen include allowing teachers at a junior high two planning periods a day during which they may confer with parents or conduct home visits while an administrator teaches their classes. There is a weekly radio program in Spanish called *Discusiones Escolares* that encourages parents to become more involved in their child's education; parents can check out audiotapes of the radio show or videotapes of other parent meetings.

In Illinois, the State Board of Education established a major objective of improving the education of at-risk children and youth through collaborative partnerships. The Urban Education Partnership Grants program, although school-based in its present form, has accomplished major changes with relatively low costs. The program uses money from Chapter 2 of the Education Consolidation and Improvement Act of 1981 and requires that each grant have the participation of the principal, the school staff, the parents, and a variety of partners from the community.

In a suburban junior high school with a racially diverse student body that had declining test scores and only about 40% of the student body turning in homework, the Urban Partnership Grant had three components: a homework lab that was available to students two days a week; improvement contracts for individual students; and two kinds of videotapes. There were instructional videotapes on critical lessons in mathematics, English, social studies, and writing research papers and parent education videotapes on how to help motivate students to learn.

The positive experience of this program has led districts to consider replicating the state's grant program. Local Illinois districts themselves are now offering multi/year grants so that schools are able to establish and stabilize their programs. The districts are examining the importance of multiple outcomes such as attendance, discipline, and level of parent involvement in addition to achievement.

In Indianapolis, Indiana, the emphasis has been on developing a multifaceted, districtwide parent involvement program that facilitates two-way communication enabling parents to stay in touch with the school and become partners with the schools in the education of their children. Called *Parents in Touch*, the program focuses on conferences, folders, Student/Teacher/Parent (STP) Contracts, and a weekly calendar. For the conferences, the district has arranged adjusted hours with the Indianapolis Education Association so that working parents can be accommodated and each school has a coordinator to schedule conferences. In addition to sharing report card information, assessing progress, and setting goals for students' achievement, the conferences are an opportunity to distribute parenting materials developed by *Parents in Touch*.

Teachers give middle school parents folders at the first conference that contain school policies on homework and attendance, on grading procedures, and on dates for distributing report cards. The STP contracts are tailored to the needs of middle schoolers and include information to help parents improve their interactions with their young adolescents. The contracts are prepared in triplicate so that the parent, teacher, and student each have a signed copy of the agreement. All of the middle schools provide weekly calendars to students so that they can list their daily assignments in each class and enable parents to monitor their children's homework.

In New Jersey, the Linking Schools and Community Services Project has mobilized resources to address educational and social issues in two middle school programs. With strong districtwide support from their respective districts, Camden Middle School was chosen as the urban site and Woodruff School was the rural site for the pilot project. The emphasis of the program was on establishing cooperative relationships between schools and community agencies to address the multiplicity of social problems that children bring with them to the classroom. This project highly recommends that both school districts and agencies keep detailed logs of the collaboration process so that the networking process is an active, reciprocal process that focuses on the recurring themes of needs identification, resources identification, organizational issues, and project linkages. Each middle school developed a different collaboration project, but the general process of focusing on recurring themes was the same.

More information about parent and community involvement in McAllen, Texas, can be found in D'Angelo & Adler (1991) and D'Angelo (1991). Chapman (1991) describes the Illinois experience, and Warner (1991) writes about the Indianapolis program. Robinson and Mastny (1989) describe the Linking Schools and Community Services Project in further detail. The Council of Great City Schools (1987), Davies (1991), Epstein and Salinas (1992), Filby, Lee, and Lambert (1990), Goodson, Swartz, Millsap, Spielman, Moss, and D'Angelo (1991), Liontos (1992), and the Quality Education Project for Minorities (1990) also provide rich case examples of districtwide efforts to increase parent and community involvement.

Part VI: Recommendations for Districtwide Reform

The review of research and practice in this paper unquestionably points to essential elements of districtwide reform of parent and community involvement. All districts must have key people with a common vision who have a policy and support for policy about parent and community involvement in education. Clearly, policy alone is not enough; support for policy is critical for the development, implementation, and maintenance of districtwide parent and community involvement. Support for policy comes when a district has key people with a common vision of a successful school.

The school districts with effective reform programs at the middle school level all had strong district-wide support for their programs. Many of the programs were developed and implemented at the school building level, but there was always a strong element of districtwide support for the program. Sometimes the support was the written policy; other times the support went beyond the written policy and came in the form of home/school coordinators, technical assistance, staff development workshops, mini-grants, newsletters, or videotapes. The support was tailored to local needs and interests, but every successful middle school program was supported at the district level. The programs described in this paper have used existing resource materials and developed new ones to help facilitate district-wide parent and community involvement. For example, in response to the National School Board Association's (1988) recommendation that school districts conduct assessments on their community, families, and current policies before developing or revising policy about parent and community involvement in education, districts have used a variety of resources, including those developed by Cale (1990), Chrispeels (1988), and Henderson, Marburger, and Ooms (1986). In response to the call for more teacher training (Chavkin & Williams, 1988; Chrispeels, 1991), districts are using materials prepared by the professional associations.

In addition, the United States Department of Education (Moles, 1993) is piloting a workshop series for educators on strengthening students' home learning; Chavkin's workshop discusses school district policies about home learning. This policy workshop offers an opportunity to examine specific school district policies about parent and community involvement. It also presents four case studies of ways school districts are supporting parent and community involvement. The workshop concludes with a district checklist and "Next Steps" plan of action.

As Epstein (1991) suggests, we have much to learn from current district efforts to connect schools, families, and communities to promote the success of children in school. Indeed, there are real possibilities. In *Promising Programs in the Middle Grades*, Epstein and Salinas (1992) cite numerous examples of promising programs that keep the families of middle grades students informed as well as involved in their children's learning. Leaders in federal and state government as well as national organizations are encouraging these kinds of home/school/community partnerships. Although there are many barriers, there are important steps that districts can take to catalyze, support, and reinforce parent and community involvement.

Ooms (1992) says that it may take both encouragement and mandates to establish strong districtwide programs. One thing for certain, however, is that policy can set the direction by clarifying the definition of parent and community involvement and setting priorities and guidelines for the various groups from home, school, and community. Districts will need to invest some resources; school boards need to consider new dollars, personnel, and the reallocation of existing dollars and staff. Reaching out to homes and communities is not the norm in most schools, and this paradigm shift, as Lueder (1992) and Seeley (1989) call it, requires that reform of parent and community involvement be a districtwide effort during the development, implementation, and maintenance of policy.

Oakes and Lipton (1990) call for unconventional policy initiatives that mobilize the commitment of families, schools, and communities to work together to improve education. They argue that new districtwide policies can marshal federal, state, and local resources to help school reform. They caution, however, that the reforms will not survive unless families, communities, educators, and policymakers work together over the long term to change beliefs and practices.

Barriers to comprehensive districtwide reform of parent and community involvement still exist, and it is critical that districts recognize these barriers and take steps to alleviate them. Ineffective communication between and among all stakeholders (administrators, teachers, and parents) is compounded at the district level by the number of middle schools and feeder schools, the diversity of the neighborhoods, and the developmental changes of early adolescents. Another barrier is the inadequate training of administrators, teachers, families, and community members to work in the collaborative mode and to understand both the rationale and the "how to" of school/home collaboration. In addition to communication and training concerns, barriers include a lack of leadership among key administrators, unclear and limited vision of comprehensive parent and community involvement, and low budgetary priorities for parent and community involvement.

Addressing these barriers will take renewed effort and commitment; these barriers are "tough" issues that need to be raised. Districts need to have a reform mentality that helps them move beyond barriers to achieve the kind of parent and community involvement that is necessary for successful schooling. To meet Lisbeth Schorr's challenge is going to take major district-wide changes in key people, vision, policy, and support for policy. Oakes and Lipton (1990) suggest that three fundamental premises must underlie these district-wide changes. First, all schools need help. Second, some schools need more help than others. Third, good schools help all children. Clearly, change is within our reach. Districts can and must examine the ways they involve parents and community in education.

References

Becher, R. (1984). *Parent involvement: A review of research and principles of successful practices.* Washington, DC: National Institute of Education.

Berla, N. (1991). Parent involvement at the middle-school level. *Eric Review, 1*(3), 16-17.

Berla, N., Henderson, A. T., & Kerewsky, W. (1989). *The middle-school years: A parents' handbook.* Columbia, MD: National Committee for Citizens in Education.

Cale, L. (1990). *Planning for parent involvement: A handbook for administrators, teachers, and parents.* Phoenix, AZ: author.

Carnegie Council on Adolescent Development. (1989). *Turning points: Preparing American youth for the 21st Century.* New York: Carnegie Corporation.

Chapman, W. (1991). The Illinois experience. *Phi Delta Kappan, 72,* 355-358.

Chavkin, N. F. (1989). Debunking the myth about minority parents and the school. *Educational Horizons, 67,* 119-123.

Chavkin, N. F., Ed. (1993). *Families and schools in a pluralistic society.* Albany, NY: State University of New York Press.

Chavkin, N. F. (1990). Joining forces: Education for a changing population. *Educational Horizons, 68,* 190-196.

Chavkin, N. F., & Williams, D. L., Jr. (1988). Critical issues in teacher training. *Educational Horizons, 66,* 87-88.

Chavkin, N. F., & Williams, D. L., Jr. (1987). Enhancing parent involvement: Guidelines for access to an important resource for school administrators. *Education and Urban Society, 19,* 164-184.

Chrispeels, J. (1991). District leadership in parent involvement: Policies and actions in San Diego. *Phi Delta Kappan, 72,* 367-371.

Chrispeels, J., Fernandez, B., & Preston, J. (1991). *Home and school partners in student success: A handbook for principals and staff.* San Diego, CA: San Diego City Schools.

Chrispeels, J. (1988). *Home-school partnership planner.* San Diego, CA: San Diego County Office of

Education.

Cohen, D. (1989a, March 15). Collaboration that works. *Education Week, 8,* 13.

Cohen, D. (1989b, March 15). Joining forces: An alliance of sectors envisioned to aid the most troubled young. *Education Week, 8,* 7-11.

Coleman, J. S. (1991). *Policy perspectives.* Washington, DC: United States Government Printing Office.

Comer, J. (1988). Educating poor minority children. *Scientific American, 259*(5), 42-48.

Comer, J. P. (1986). Parent participation in the schools. *Phi Delta Kappan, 67,* 442-446.

Council of Chief State School Officers. (1989). *Family support, education and involvement: A guide for state action.* Washington, DC: Author.

Council of Chief State School Officers. (1991). *Families in school: State strategies and policies to improve family involvement in education.* Washington, DC: Author.

The Council of Great City Schools. (1987). *Results in the making.* Washington, DC: Author.

D'Angelo, D. M. (1991). Meeting the challenge in McAllen, Texas. *Phi Delta Kappan, 72,* 352-353.

D'Angelo, D. M., & Adler, C. R. (1991). Chapter 1: A catalyst for improving parent involvement. *Phi Delta Kappan, 72,* 350-354.

Davies, D. (1993). Benefits and barriers to parent involvement: From Portugal to Boston to Liverpool. In N.F. Chavkin (Ed.), *Families and schools in a pluralistic society* (pp. 205-216). Albany, NY: State University of New York Press.

Davies, D. (1987). Parent involvement in the public schools: Opportunities for administrators. *Education and Urban Society, 19,* 147-163.

Davies, D. (1991). Schools reaching out: Family, school, and community partnerships for student success. *Phi Delta Kappan, 72,* 376-382.

Davies, D., Burch, P., & Johnson, V. (1992). *A portrait of schools reaching out: Report of a survey on practices and policies of family-community-school collaboration.* (Report No. 1). Baltimore, MD: The Johns Hopkins University Center on Families, Communities, Schools & Children's Learning,

Dornbusch, S. M., & Ritter, P. L. (1988). Parents of high school students: A neglected resource. *Educational Horizons, 66,* 75-77.

Earle, J. (1989). *The steps to restructuring: Changing Seattle's middle school.* Alexandria, VA: National Association of State Boards of Education.

Epstein, J. L. (1986). Parents' reactions to teach practices of parent involvement. *Elementary School Journal, 86,* 277-294.

Epstein, J. L. (1991). Paths to partnership: What we can learn from federal, state, district, and school initiatives. *Phi Delta Kappan, 72,* 344-349.

Epstein, J., & Salinas, K. C. (1992). *Promising programs in the middle grades.* Reston, VA: National Association of Secondary School Principals.

Filby, N. N., Lee, G. V., & Lambert, V. (1990). *Middle grades reform: A casebook for school leaders.* San Francisco, CA: Far West Laboratory for Educational Research and Development.

Goodson, B.D., Swartz, J. P., Millsap, M. A., Spielman, S.C., Moss, M., & D'Angelo, D. (1991). *Working with families: Promising programs to help parents support young children's learning.* Final report for the U. S. Department of Education, Office of Planing, Budget and Evaluation. Washington, DC: Government Printing Office.

Heath, S. B., & McLaughlin, M. W. (1987). A child resource policy: Moving beyond dependence on school and family. *Phi Delta Kappan, 68,* 576-580.

Henderson, A. (1987). *The evidence continues to grow: Parent involvement improves student achievement.* Columbia, MD: National Committee for Citizens in Education.

Henderson, A., Marburger, C., & Ooms, T. (1986). *Beyond the bake sale: An educator's guide to working with parents.* Columbia, MD: National Committee for Citizens in Education.

Levy, J. E., & Copple, C. (1989). *Joining forces: A report from the first year.* Alexandria, VA: National Association of State Boards of Education.

Liontos, L. B. (1992). *At-risk families & schools: Becoming partners.* Eugene, OR: ERIC Clearinghouse on Educational Management.

Lueder, D. (1992, April). With open arms: Reaching out to re-engage parents in the education of their children. Paper presented at the Fourth Annual International Roundtable on Families, Communities, Schools and Children's Learning, San Francisco, CA.

Moles, O. (1993). *Schools and families together—Helping children learn more at home: Workshops for urban educators.* Washington, DC: U. S. Department of Education.

Nardine, F. E. (1990). The changing role of low-income minority parents in their children's schooling. *New directions for adult and continuing education, 48*(Winter), 67-80.

Nardine, F. E. & Morris, R. D. (1991). Parent involvement in the states: How firm is the commitment? *Phi Delta Kappan, 72,* 363-366.

National Association of State Boards of Education. (1989a). *Partners in educational improvement: Schools, parents, and the community.* Alexandria, VA: Author.

National Association of State Boards of Education. (1989b). *Today's children, tomorrow's survival: A call to restructure schools.* Alexandria, VA: Author.

National Coalition for an Urban Children's Agenda. (1991). *Implementing the children's agenda: Critical elements of system-wide reform.* Alexandria, VA: National Association of State Boards of Education.

National Coalition for Parent Involvement in Education. (n.d.). *Parent involvement.* Washington, DC: Author.

National School Board Association. (1988). *First teachers: Parent involvement in the public schools.* Alexandria, VA: Author.

Oakes, J. & Lipton, M. (1990). *Making the best of schools: A handbook for parents, teachers, and policymakers.* New Haven, CT: Yale University.

Ooms, T. (1992). *The family-school partnership: A critical component of school reform.* Briefing paper for Family Centered Social Policy: The Emerging Agenda, conducted by the Family Impact Seminar, February 21.

Palanki, A. & Burch, P. (with D. Davies). (1992). *Mapping the policy landscape: What federal and state governments are doing to promote family-school-community partnerships.* (Report No. 7). Baltimore, MD: The Johns Hopkins University.

Quality Education for Minorities Project. (1990). *Education that works: An action plan for the education of minorities.* Cambridge, MA: Massachusetts Institute of Technology.

Rich, D. (1985). *The forgotten factor in school success: The family.* Washington, DC: The Home and School Institute.

Robinson, E. R., & Mastny, A. Y. (1989). *Linking schools & community services.* New Brunswick, NJ: Rutgers, The University of New Jersey, Center for Community Education, School of Social Work.

San Diego City Schools. (1991). *Report on efforts to build home-school partnerships and announcement of parent involvement incentive grant awards for 1991-92.* San Diego, CA: Author.

Sattes, B. D. (1985). *Parent involvement: A review of the literature.* Charleston, WV: Appalachia Educational Laboratory.

Schorr, L. B. (1988). *Within our reach: Breaking the cycle of disadvantage.* New York: Doubleday.

Seeley, D. S. (1989). A new paradigm for parent involvement. *Educational Leadership, 47*(2), 46-48.

Seeley, D. S., Niemeyer, J. H., & Greenspan, R. (1991). *Principals speak.* Report No.2. Staten Island, NY: Principals Speak Project/City University of New York.

Swap, S. M. (1987). *Enhancing parent involvement in schools.* New York: Teachers College.

United States Department of Education. (1992). *Chapter 1 flexibility: A guide to opportunities in local projects*. Washington, DC: U. S. Department of Education.

United States Department of Education. (1991). *Youth indicators 1991. Trends in the well-being of American youth*. Washington, DC: U. S. Department of Education.

Walberg, H. J. (1984a). Families as partners in educational productivity. *Phi Delta Kappan, 65*, 397-400.

Walberg, H. J. (1984b). Improving the productivity of America's schools. *Educational Leadership, 41*(8), 19-27.

Warner, I. (1991). Parents in touch: District leadership for parent involvement. *Phi Delta Kappan, 72*, 372-375.

Williams, D. L., Jr., & Chavkin, N. F. (1989). Essential elements of strong parent involvement programs. *Educational Leadership, 47*(2), 18-20.

Chapter 2

School Restructuring to Facilitate Parent and Community
Involvement in the Middle Grades

Janet Chrispeels

Introduction

The middle grades student represents a bundle of human energy undergoing rapid physical, psychological, intellectual, and social development that is akin to the first few years of a child's life. The titles of two recent reports about the middle grades, *Caught in the Middle* (1987) published by the California State Department of Education and *Turning Points: Preparing American Youth for the 21st Century* (1989), a report prepared by the Carnegie Council on Adolescent Development, capture well these difficult years of growth and transition from childhood to adolescence. Pre-adolescents and young adolescents are indeed often caught in the middle—too old for childhood activities and too young for the adolescent world into which they are being pushed. These critical years represent key turning points in their lives. As the *Caught in the Middle* report states:

> For many students the middle grades represent the last chance to develop a
> sense of academic purpose and personal commitment to education goals.
> Those who fail at the middle grade level often drop out of school and may
> never again have the opportunity to develop to their fullest potential. (p. v)

The middle grades typically refer to students in grades five or six through eight. Students in this age-span find themselves housed in a variety of school settings and grade configurations such as K-8, 4-6, 5-8, 6-8, 7-8, 7-9, 7-12, and 4-12, to name a few (Epstein & Mac Iver, 1990). The great diversity in the way middle grades students are clustered complicates the job of schools in designing programs and approaches that will best meet these students' educational, social, emotional, and physical needs. As a result, a third level of schooling, which falls between elementary and high school has emerged to serve many middle grades students (George, Stevenson, Thomason, & Beane, 1992). The majority of middle grades students now attend separate middle or junior high schools typically serving grades 6-8, 7-8 and 7-9. For purposes of this paper, references to middle grades and middle schools will encompass and focus primarily on these grade configurations. The ideas and examples given, however, can be adapted by schools serving any middle grades students.

Middle schools and a middle school philosophy have emerged over the last 25 years as a means of responding to the needs of young adolescents during these exciting and turbulent years of growth and development. Studies that have helped to define the type of education needed by young adolescents include the two studies mentioned earlier, *Caught in the Middle* and *Turning Points*, as well as the work of Lipsitz (1984), *Successful Schools for Young Adolescents*; the National Association of Secondary School Principals' *An Agenda for Excellence at the Middle Level* (1985); and the recent Association for Supervision and Curriculum Development study, *The Middle School—And Beyond* (George et al., 1992). These studies are very important for setting the context for schools to restructure and facilitate parent and community involvement in the middle grades. The reports urge that families be more involved in the education of their young adolescent children and that schools need to be connected with their community. The critical issue is how to translate the recommendations from rhetoric into action. How do schools serving middle grades students need to change or restructure to reengage parents and community in support of student learning and school success?

This paper addresses five major issues regarding how to change or restructure middle schools and middle grades education to involve parents and community in students' learning. First, a conceptual framework is presented for thinking about the ways parents, community, and school staff can work together in partnership. Second, several examples are given of how middle schools are changing and restructuring parent involvement programs to reach out to parents and community. Third, emerging structures and instructional practices in middle school reform are discussed and ideas presented on how these restructuring efforts could be used to connect more fully students, their families, and communities with schools. Fourth, the paper discusses potential staff development needs that must be addressed if teachers and school staff are to more actively involve and work with parents and community. Finally, the paper outlines further areas for research about family/school connections in the middle grades.

Home/School/Community Partnerships: A Conceptual Framework

The reports about middle schools recommend greater parent and community involvement; however, how to accomplish this goal is not spelled out with much specificity. The *Caught in the Middle* report points out that the successful transformation of a junior high to a middle school usually resulted in greater overall parent involvement in the restructured school (George & Oldaker, 1985). One of the reasons for this increased involvement may be that teachers and principals, who are working to convert a junior high to a middle school, often display an enthusiasm and commitment to change. The conversion process requires examining old relationships and practices, which allows the school to reevaluate relationships with parents as well. Another reason for the increased involvement may be that parents must be involved to sanction the conversion. The report also urges that schools serving middle grades students recognize parent concerns about their children's emergence into adolescence. If these developmental concerns are recognized and dealt with openly, the report states, the distance between classroom and home will be diminished. The changing demographics, deterioration of inner city communities, the diverse combinations of individuals that represent the modern family, however, require more than exhortations to increase parent involvement. It will take hard work, resources, and school changes to translate the policy rhetoric into school practices. Restructuring is required both within schools and in the ways schools, families, and communities work together to support student success in school, at home, and in the community.

From the research on parent involvement, it is clear that families and schools need to be connected in a variety of ways. There are critical roles that each play. The following typology of home/school/community partnership roles, built on the work

Figure 1   **Home—School—Community**
◄— Parnership Roles Continuum —►

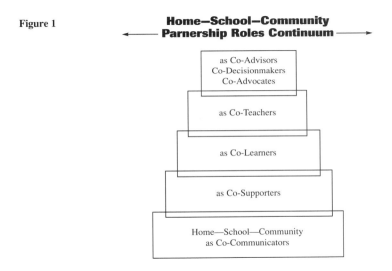

of Lyons, Robbins and Smith (1983), Epstein (1987a), and Chrispeels (1987, 1992), is offered as one way of thinking about the multiple ways that schools, communities, and families need to be linked. The typology forms a scaffolding on which to build a home/school/community partnership. The typology encompasses five mutual and interactive roles, which is the reason the concept and label of co-communicator, co-supporters, co-learners, co-teachers, and co-advocates, advisors and decision-makers are used. First, the "co-" implies both school and family perform these roles. Sometimes these roles will be performed independently (e.g., both need to learn important information relative to their role, or both are involved in teaching, one primarily at school the other at home). Second, the "co-" implies that schools and families need to interact and work together to support best student learning and school success. The roles, depicted in Figure 1, are arranged in a pyramid and overlapping fashion to suggest that the roles are not mutually exclusive and build on each other.

Communication serves as the foundational role and is pivotal to and impacts the successful implementation of the other roles. Each role is likely to involve fewer teachers, school staff, parents and community members than the previous role. To some extent the level of participation is also an indication of the increasing complexity of skills and level of engagement required to fulfill the role.

Home and School as Co-Communicators. The co-communicators role is the most critical to all other partnership endeavors. Without adequate communication between families and school personnel, other partnership efforts are likely to falter. Furthermore, as the "co-" implies, the communication must be two-way. Both school and parents have information that is vital to children's success; however, the school, because of its power and authority, is in a stronger position to initiate, promote, and sustain home/school communications. The school can invite and encourage active communication or it can create barriers that make it difficult for parents to communicate. Epstein and Becker (1982) found a steady decrease in the communication between home and school and the degree of involvement of parents as students moved into the middle grades. There are several reasons for this decline of home/school engagement and interaction. First, as students mature, they may be less reliable couriers as they make decisions themselves as to which information they will or will not share with their family. Second, given the increasing maturity and intellectual development of students, teachers may feel their primary focus of communication should be with the child, not the parent. Third, parents are likely to have less direct contact with the school as the children are able to get to and from school on their own. Fourth, teachers in the upper elementary grades and in middle schools are usually much more reluctant to have parent volunteers in the classroom, breaking a channel of communication with parents and the community. Fifth, as students move into middle schools and junior high schools, the school itself becomes a barrier to communication. The school is often larger and more impersonal in nature. Students frequently move from class to class working with several different teachers, making it more difficult for parents to stay in touch or to know whom to contact. Also, not all middle and junior high schools hold regularly scheduled parent/teacher conferences. In some schools, teachers are available for conferences when students and parents receive the first report card. Unless these conferences are well-structured, it is not always easy for parents to know with which teachers to meet. In the case descriptions that follow, examples will be given of how some middle schools are trying to close the communication gap with parent centers, through the telephone, through special meetings in neighborhoods, and through hiring community liaison workers or teachers who have special responsibilities for community outreach.

Home and School as Co-Supporters. Like communication, home and school as co-supporters need to involve almost everyone at sometime during the school year in expressions of support. There are several dimensions to the concept of support. Traditionally, parent support for the school consisted of two critical aspects. The first aspect of support comes from parents fulfilling their basic parenting obligations by providing safety, shelter, food, clothing, nurturing, guidance, and love (Epstein, 1987a). The second dimension is parental support for the school in terms of volunteering to assist the school in clerical or chaperoning tasks, serving as room representatives, raising funds, participating in social activities, attending school events such as back-to-school nights, open houses, awards ceremonies, or student performances.

It is only in the last few years that schools are beginning to understand their role as co-supporters. The ever-increasing levels of poverty, the changes in families, especially the need for mothers to work, and the rise in the use and abuse of harmful substances such as drugs and alcohol, are changing the notion of support. To address these critical needs, schools now find themselves having to offer more support for families. Schools are being called upon to provide not only a safe and positive learning environment during the school day, but also to offer a safe environment before and after school hours. Schools cannot provide all the resources families need for their children to be successful in school; therefore, the school support role requires schools to collaborate with other social service, community, and government agencies in ways that have not previously occurred. The school support role for young adolescents requires both considerable thought and restructuring of traditional school roles and responsibilities. The case studies will illustrate innovative ways that the schools are providing support for families.

Home and School as Co-Learners. Through communications such as newsletters, open houses, progress reports and report cards, and parent workshops, schools have traditionally tried to help parents learn about school programs and how their children are achieving. The learning opportunities are usually unidirectional, with a focus on parents learning about the school. If parents and teachers, especially parents and teachers from diverse cultures, are to interact in new ways, the role of home and school as co-learners takes on new meaning.

The sporadic and infrequent communication typical of most schools serving middle grades students does not allow adequate opportunities for mutual learning to take place. As children move into the middle grades, there is much that both teachers and parents have to learn. Many parents feel ill-equipped, especially in their communication skills, as their children become teenagers. The problems of communication and parenting are further complicated for many inner-city parents who may have to deal with a culture in which they themselves were not raised. The problems of interface between home and school for immigrant families (and families in poverty who have never experienced success in school) is captured by Howard Gardner in his book *To Open Minds* (1989).

My diligence at the piano was possible only because of the example of regularity and fidelity my parents displayed on every front. Yet at the same time, they felt inadequate to instruct me and Marion about the operation of school and other communal institutions, about how to interact with peers, about hobbies to pursue or scholastic choices to make. Nor could they model the behavior appropriate to an American parent: we had to take these from the pages of Life magazine, from the situation comedies of television, from the examples of our own teachers or our more Americanized friends and their families. Indeed, as the image of "reverse rearing" suggests, our parents looked to their children for clues about how to negotiate their way in this new land, for which they had no preparation. (p. 25)

If the school leaves it to the student to do the teaching of the parent about school life, the lessons may not always be ones that will serve well the family, student, or school. The school needs to assume a more systematic approach to helping parents learn about the school, its programs and opportunities for their children, as well as about adolescent development and parenting practices that will foster a smooth transition during the middle school years.

In addition, many teachers of middle grades students find themselves equally ill-equipped to work with middle grades students. Some were trained as secondary teachers with a strong focus on subject matter, not on adolescent development. Teachers working in multicultural settings also need to learn about the cultures of the students they are teaching and how to best work with families from such diverse backgrounds. Parents and students can help teachers acquire knowledge about their culture and can also be valuable resources for teachers on the student's interests and learning styles. Seeking out this information can help teachers to engage students and their families in more active learning processes both at school and at home. Greater knowledge about the students' culture and interests will help teachers recognize and validate parenting practices and family values from diverse cultures. Such recognition should help families from diverse backgrounds feel more comfortable in contacting the school and working with teachers. Only through more systematic learning opportunities for both teachers (which will be discussed more fully in the section on staff development) and parents, will schools help to reengage the family in support of student learning.

Home and School as Co-Teachers. Many of the reform reports, such as *A Nation at Risk* (1983), stress that parents are children's first teachers. The critical role that parents play in early language development and intellectual stimulation of children that prepares them to enter school ready to learn is well understood. The lack of active parent teaching in the early years creates learning deficits that schools struggle to overcome. Less well understood is the teaching role that parents play as students enter the middle grades. Parents frequently feel less competent as teachers as their children move into middle and junior high schools. The sense of competence is greatly decreased if the child has not experienced much school success. Homework may become a battle ground if parents are unsure how to help and students do not understand the assignment. Once students enter the middle grades, parents are much less likely to continue reading to their children, even if they actively enjoyed books together in the primary grades (Smith, 1993). In addition, peers and other adults, such as club leaders, coaches, or youth leaders at churches, also become important teachers; however, the teaching role of parents needs to be encouraged and supported.

Teachers play a critical role in either welcoming and reinforcing or in discouraging parents' teaching role at the middle grades level. Creating opportunities for parents and community members to share information and their talents in the classroom, sanctions and models a more active teaching role for parents at home. Yet, few middle schools actively involve parents as classroom volunteers. The design of homework and home learning activities also can encourage or discourage the active participation of parents in their home teaching role. As some of the examples given below indicate, schools that support teachers to involve parents in the teaching process both at home and at school, also impact the nature and quality of the teaching at school.

Not all parents will be able to fulfill this role in ways that the school envisions, especially in the area of homework support. Therefore, this role requires special care and consideration so that students are not penalized by a parent's reluctance or feelings of inadequacy to be actively engaged. Community volunteers, college or peer tutors, adult mentors, and concerned teachers will all be needed as teachers to provide extended learning opportunities for some students.

Home and School as Co-Advisors, Advocates, and Decision-makers. This role caps the pyramid. It is at the top or end of the continuum because it is a role in which not all parents or school staff may be involved, especially in the formal aspects of advising and decision-making. This role has three dimensions. The first is the governance role implied in the notions of home and school as co-advisors and decision-makers. This role is fulfilled by teachers, school administrators, parents, and often students, when schools establish governance committees, school councils, Chapter 1 or Bilingual Advisory committees, ad hoc task forces, such as a discipline committee, or for a parent/teacher organization. While advisory committees have been a feature of schools since the passage of Title I legislation, both parents and teachers often feel ill-equipped to assume these leadership roles. As schools move to more extensive decision-making roles at the school site through site-based management proposals, more training and support are required for this role to be fulfilled successfully. Being in a formal governance role requires skills in group dynamics and organization. It also requires a vision that is broader than the immediate concerns for one's own child or classroom and a commitment to serving the whole school. Few teachers or parents are willing to take on these additional duties and responsibilities.

The second dimension of this role is the more informal way in which parents and teachers are co-advisors and co-decision-makers. When parents and teachers meet to conference about a student, teachers frequently give advice to parents. (Teachers, sometimes, find it more difficult to accept advice from parents about teaching.) At the close of a conference, the teacher and family may mutually decide on a course of action, thus fulfilling the role of co-decision-makers. In secondary schools, counselors and advisory teachers may also play critical roles in giving advice and deciding a course of action for both students and parents. The day-to-day role modeling, advising and decision-making that occur both at school and at home shape and influence the course of student learning and their school success.

The third dimension of this role is that of co-advocates. An advocate, according to Webster's dictionary, is one who speaks on behalf of another. Upper-middle-class parents have often played this role for their children, intervening at the school to ensure correct placement in a class, insisting on testing for giftedness or other special programs, and registering concerns about an assignment, grade, or teaching practice. In contrast, parents who do not speak English, who themselves did not experience success in school, who are distanced from the school by poverty, or who are immigrants to this country, are less likely to be able to be advocates for their children in the same way. While teachers are not always happy when parents become advocates for their children, the advocacy does establish a point of contact and potential for dialogue. The lack of contact between parents and teachers is often construed by teachers as parental apathy or disinterest in their child's school success. When teachers form these negative views about parental interest, they may also be forming negative and detrimental views about the child's potential for success in school (Johnson, Brookover, & Farrell, 1989). Occasionally teachers have played an advocacy role for some of their students, helping them to get needed services such as health care or tutoring. In crisis cases counselors may step in as the child's advocate. Teachers as advocates is one role that may need much more attention and development during the vulnerable middle grades years.

Home/School/Community Partnership Models

This section of the chapter uses the conceptual model presented above to examine some of the ways that schools have restructured or changed their practices to enhance home/school/community partnerships. Many of the practices described will fall into more than one role. For example, as parents learn about the school through improved communications, they will be in a better position to fulfill their teaching role and will be stronger advocates for their children. It is valuable, however, to highlight specific changes and actions that primarily typify one of the roles. Many of the examples presented below are drawn from three middle schools in San Diego County that are working to develop partnership programs—Muirlands and Mann Middle Schools, both in San Diego Unified School District, and Montgomery Junior High in Sweetwater Union High School District. Other examples are included from a review of the literature on middle school parent involvement programs. The examples given are meant to be suggestive of innovative ways schools are changing to meet the needs of parents. They do not reflect all that schools are doing to build partnerships, nor do they adequately capture the full developmental process these schools have undergone to accomplish their current levels of partnership. Data from these schools were collected in the 1991-1992 school year.

School Practices that Enhance Home/School/Community as Co-Communicators. Muirlands Middle School, located in La Jolla, California, has had to rethink how it reaches out to parents. The school brings together two distinct student populations: the affluent resident population and a largely Hispanic student population bused to the school from a less affluent southeast San Diego neighborhood. The bused students are participating in the Voluntary Ethnic Enrollment Program (VEEP), part of San Diego's integration plan.

Mann Middle School is located in east San Diego and serves a diverse student population consisting of Hispanic, African-American, Laotian, Vietnamese, Cambodian, Hmoung, and white students. Mann Middle is faced with the problem of how to reach out to its very diverse community, especially when most of the school staff does not speak the languages of its students. Through a grant from the Edna McConnell Clark Foundation both Muirlands and Mann have been working to close the language and cultural gaps between school staff and their diverse parent and student communities.

As Pumell and Gotts (1983) have shown, school newsletters at the secondary level represent an important communication link between home and school. Muirlands has always had a monthly PTA newsletter, however, the newsletter was not printed in Spanish. Initially the principal's message, key dates, and one or two articles were translated; however, during a joint leadership development workshop for the PTA boards of Muirlands and Mann, representatives of each school's Hispanic parents strongly expressed the need for translating the entire newsletter into Spanish. As a result of this meeting, Mann publishes the entire newsletter in English and Spanish. It has not resolved how to publish the newsletter in all four of the Asian languages. Muirlands is publishing increasing proportions in Spanish as resources permit. Montgomery Junior High has also found that publishing its newsletter in Spanish is essential for communicating with its large Spanish-speaking parent population.

Booker T. Washington Middle School in Baltimore, Maryland (Epstein & Herrick, 1991b) also turned to a school newsletter as a means of enhancing home/school communication. In addition to the regular principal's newsletter, a second newsletter was initiated "to make parents feel welcome to the school and to sum-marize key information about school programs and workshops held at the school for parents who did not attend" (p. 1). To find out how successful the newsletter was, the Parents and Teachers Project Team conducted a random telephone survey of parents. The survey reconfirmed the importance of newsletters as communication vehicles at the secondary level and gave the team valuable information about how parents per-ceived the newsletters and ideas for improving the newsletter. In addition, the par-ents interviewed felt valued because their ideas were being solicited. This example shows that it is not only important to distribute a school newsletter to parents in their native language, but also to periodically check parent opinions about the utility and value of the newsletter, thus facilitating two-way communication.

Since all three San Diego County schools serve diverse ethnic populations, the schools have had to develop new means of communicating with parents. As part of its grant activities, Muirlands launched a new outreach effort in the fall of 1991. Ten parents from the VEEP community were asked to serve as community leaders. They in turn were each asked to select another parent whom they would mentor. Each par-ent leader agreed to attend bimonthly regional leadership meetings as well as the bimonthly VEEP meetings. They also agreed to call a list of 15 parents once a month to inform them about school events and solicit questions and concerns that could be brought to the monthly meetings. At the regional and VEEP meetings, each parent leader reported on his or her calls. This communication network represents an impor-tant beginning step in encouraging two-way communication. Attendance and inter-est at the monthly meetings remained high throughout the year, although not all par-ents feel their points of view were listened to by the staff.

An important outcome of this unique outreach has been more contact between home and school. As Spanish-speaking and VEEP parents have developed greater confidence, they have made more direct contact themselves with the school. During 1991, calls from VEEP parents increased 300 percent over the previous year. However, many of the VEEP parents felt that the majority of the contacts they received from teachers were negative in nature and focused mostly on homework, attendance, or discipline problems. A few teachers attended the bimonthly regional leadership or VEEP meetings, opening up the possibility for more parent/teacher dia-logue. A Spanish-speaking community liaison and vice principal facilitated commu-nication between parents and the school. Both were instrumental in developing the skills of the parent leaders.

While Montgomery Junior High did not have the support to establish such a sys-tematic parent leadership development program as Muirlands and Mann, the home/school partnership coordinator identified key parent representatives of the dif-ferent ethnic groups served by the school. She developed their leadership skills by regularly involving them in school and parent activities. These parent leaders assist-ed with telephone contact, recruited volunteers, organized parent meetings, and assumed many other responsibilities. As a result of the outreach by these parent leaders, an active, multiethnic volunteer core for the school was established.

Mann Middle School also recognized it was essential to have representatives from the different ethnic groups to assist with outreach to parents. Given the diversity of its parent population, it was difficult to find effective leaders for each group. In the rush to identify representatives who can meet the translation needs of the school, the African-American parents frequently felt neglected. Efforts are now under way to ensure that they feel included too. The teachers at Mann also made a concerted effort themselves to reach out to parents through the telephone, a practice not found in the other two middle schools. The PTA at Mann supported the effort through funding additional telephones for the school. The school adopted a policy that for every call a teacher made to address a concern or problem, two positive phone calls must be made. The adoption of this policy was an evolutionary process. The telephone contacts with parents started with a few teachers. As other teachers saw the benefits, more began to participate until it became an accepted school practice. In 1992, the school planned to have a telephone in every classroom, or at least one for every interdisciplinary team.

One of the interdisciplinary teams at Mann Middle took on the special challenge of working with a group of 90 students who were at extreme risk of school failure. The team decided to increase the face-to-face contact with parents by devoting three Saturdays during 1991-1992 to conferencing with parents. The conferences were held on the teachers' own time without compensation from the school. The project-oriented curriculum, designed by the team, coupled with extraordinary efforts to reach out to parents resulted in considerable achievement gains for these students. The teachers received the intrinsic rewards of seeing the increasing achievements of their students; however, this level of parent contact is not likely to be maintained or replicated without more school support, such as released time or compensation.

Practices that Facilitate Home/School/Community as Co-Supporters. As a result of their increased communication, all three of these schools experienced increased interaction with parents. Muirlands has always enjoyed strong parental support from its resident white population. The development of the VEEP parent leadership team has now enabled Hispanic parents to find ways to demonstrate their support for the school. In a recent Cinco de Mayo celebration, VEEP parents organized a series of hands-on activities for students to introduce them to aspects of Hispanic-Mexican culture. This volunteer activity in many respects moved beyond traditional expressions of support into the families-as-teachers level of involvement. In addition, the activity showed that limited-English-speaking parents have important skills and knowledge to contribute to children's education.

Montgomery Junior High developed a very strong parent volunteer corps that performed thousands of hours of volunteer service for the school working in the library, copying materials for teachers, and performing other clerical tasks. Both teachers and parents, however, were reluctant to involve volunteers in the classroom in any teaching or tutoring capacities.

The needs of the parent communities served by Muirlands, Mann, and Montgomery pushed these school to find new ways to support parents. All three formed extensive partnerships with community agencies to provide workshops and support for parents. Muirlands and Mann benefited from an additional Edna McConnell Clark grant that was awarded to a coalition of seven community groups, with the June Burnett Institute for Children, Youth, and Families serving as grant coordinator. This coalition, called the Home-School Partnership Project, organized parenting classes for each of the ethnic groups, provided leadership training, and offered resources and support to each school's partnership building effort. For example, the Urban League conducted parenting classes for African-American families, the Parent Institute for Hispanic families, and the Union of Pan Asian Communities for Southeast Asian and Filipino families. At Muirlands, 65 parents completed the six-week Parent Institute class that taught parenting skills and helped parents learn how to be an advocate for their child. Even larger numbers of parents completed the classes at Mann. The Chicano Federation was involved in leadership development and advocacy for Hispanic parents. The San Diego City PTA Council's Project HOPE (Harness Our Parent Energy) worked with the predominantly white PTA boards to help them become more integrated and representative of the ethnic diversity found in the schools. In addition, Project HOPE encouraged the boards to undertake activities that involved and met the needs of all parents.

The Home-School Partnership Project resulted in several benefits. First, the partners enabled Muirlands and Mann to better meet the needs of their diverse parent populations in ways that the schools would be unable to do alone. Second, the project modeled collaboration for the school, demonstrating how representatives from diverse ethnic, linguistic, and cultural groups need to work together for the benefit of children. Third, the partners themselves grew and benefited from increased understanding from working with each other.

In addition to receiving support from the Home-School Partnership Project, Mann Middle School also benefited from being a part of the Crawford Community Cluster, a nine school coalition to coordinate community agency support to meet parent needs. The director of this coalition, who was based at the nearby high school, was paid in part by the school district and by funds received from each participating school. The coalition brought together an enormous array of service clubs, churches, community agencies, counseling services, food distribution programs, health services, police, and welfare agencies to help families. Teachers at the schools became involved through donating household items, food, and clothing to the resource bank to meet the needs of families in crisis. These coordinated models—the Crawford Community Coalition and the Home-School Partnership Project—represent important first steps in helping families be able to meet their basic parenting obligations, and thus increase the likelihood of their children's success in school.

Montgomery Junior High also found a way to form a support network for parents by collaborating with local community agencies. Five agencies (South Bay Community Center, South Bay Drug Rehabilitation Center, Union of Pan Asian Communities, Amancer, and Barrio Station) each adopted the school for a day. The school provided a room for agency staff to meet with small groups of students who were assigned to them or fell within their jurisdiction. These counselors or social workers held conferences with parents and students, conducted parenting classes in the afternoon or evening, and met with parents in their homes when necessary. This collaborative effort allowed the school to provide support for families beyond what the school counselors had time to do.

The school also formed links with the police and probation departments. Vista Hill and Southwood, two hospitals specializing in substance abuse rehabilitation, worked closely with school staff to provide free assessments for students and family members referred to them by the school. Montgomery's latest community partnership effort involved the San Diego Share Program, a food distribution center. For a small monthly fee, families received subsidized food. In exchange, participating families donated several hours of community service, which in this case meant more volunteers for Montgomery since the school served as a distribution center for the program. Such extensive support for families brought ever-increasing positive support for the school from parents.

Programs that Encourage Home and School as Co-Learners. The collaboration with community agencies described above was key in providing learning opportunities for parents at all three middle schools. The primary focus of these workshops was parenting and leadership development. In addition all three schools held back-to-school nights which were very well attended. Mann Middle had over 700 parents attend in 1991. Montgomery organized a parent/student orientation for incoming seventh graders, and each spring organizes a Shadow Your Student Day to give parents an opportunity to experience a day at school. A Baltimore middle school implemented a similar sixth-grade parent/student orientation where parents followed their student's schedule for a day and learned about expectations and the school's programs (Epstein & Herrick, 1991b). All three groups—parents, teachers, and students—felt the program was worthwhile. Parents who had previously had children attend the school, reported that this daylong experience gave them new and valuable insights into the school program.

Muirlands began the 1991-1992 school year by organizing a learning opportunity for its 10 designated VEEP parent leaders and their mentees. At the beginning-of-the-year staff development day, the twenty parents were introduced to the faculty. Teachers from the science and social studies departments presented demonstration lessons, helped parents learn how students should read and take notes from their text-books, and described the interdisciplinary approach used in teaching history and language arts. Parents were given tips on how to help their children make note cards and study vocabulary words; however, more specific strategies needed to be shared with the parents about what they could do at home to help. The missing dimension of the day was an opportunity for parents to share important cultural information with teachers. In other words, the teachers did not see themselves as learners or the parents as having vital information to share with them.

Two areas of home and school as co-learners were weak in these three schools. First, the schools made working with families a minimal focus of staff development. If schools are to build a more active partnership with families which fulfill a broad range of partnership roles, teachers need new knowledge and skills, just as parents do. Some of the knowledge, skills, and strategies needed by school staff will be discussed below.

A second neglected area was workshops for parents that would enable them to play a more active teaching role at home. For example, the Muirlands workshop presented to the parent leaders at the beginning of the year to introduce them to the science and math curriculum needed to be available to all parents and offered several times during the year. Montgomery Junior High and Mann Middle held a few Family Math, Family Computer, and Family Cooking workshops, but in general the schools had not offered parent and student workshops that focused on academic subjects that would enable parents to more effectively assist their children. Many elementary schools in San Diego County offer Family Math workshops (a K-8 program), and the workshops usually include or are even specifically targeted to fourth, fifth, and sixth grade students. Schools serving middle grades students, however, have been slow to venture into joint parent/student learning programs such as Family Math.

Parents Sharing Books (Smith, 1993), a project of Indiana University and supported by funding from the Lilly Endowment, is one potential home learning program that involves parents of middle grades students in reading at home. The purpose of the program is to promote family literacy and parent/student interaction around books at a critical time when young adolescents' interest in reading begins to diminish. During the first phase of the project, thirty-seven Indiana middle/junior high schools sent teacher/parent teams to be trained to implement the program. These teams then trained parents at their schools in techniques and strategies for effectively sharing and discussing books with their middle school children at home. The initial evaluation responses from parents were very enthusiastic. Some of the benefits for parents and students were increased time together, improved communication and discussion, and higher self-esteem and confidence (Smith, 1993).

Several major problems confronted Parents Sharing Books. First, the program's success depended upon the commitment of the teacher/parent leadership team. Strong principal support proved essential to effective implementation. For example, adequate time and support for the leadership team to organize, conduct and follow-up after the workshops frequently depended upon administrative support. Second, recruiting parent participants was a challenge for a number of the schools. Middle schools may be unfamiliar with recruitment strategies or the time it takes to involve parents. Third, time for parents to participate in the training or workshops and time for doing the activities with their children after the workshops was a bigger barrier than had been anticipated (Smith, 1993). One solution used by one of the Parent Sharing Books schools was to involve grandparents and other family members. Another school involved both parents and students in the workshop sessions which provided a built-in motivator for parents and students to do the reading activities at home after the session. Such joint parent/student learning programs can be an effective way to increase parent involvement in learning/teaching activities at home.

Programs that Encourage Home and School as Co-Teachers. None of these three schools substantially changed or restructured practices in ways that encouraged parents as co-teachers. Homework is a part of school life in all three schools. Assignment calendars are in use to help parents know what homework is assigned, but none had undertaken a systematic review of homework practices and problems. Nor had any of the schools developed home learning materials similar to the Teachers Involving Parents in Schoolwork (TIPS) (Epstein, 1987b) project developed under the auspices of The Johns Hopkins University by Baltimore middle grade teachers.

A recent study by Raul Pizarro (1992) in Chile indicated that when middle grades parents are given systematic training in how to help their children, important achievement gains can be reached. In his study, assistance was given in the area of mathematics and Spanish through twelve workshop sessions with parents. The achievement gains were more significant in mathematics than in Spanish, but students benefited from parental assistance in both subjects. This intervention was much more systematic and substantial than is offered in most parent workshops, and indicates that if the level of home support is to be dramatically affected, much more thorough and ongoing support will be needed.

The summer home learning packets developed by the Center for Effective Schooling for Disadvantaged Students at Johns Hopkins (Epstein & Herrick, 1991a) represent another way in which the teaching role of parents can be reinforced. Packets of activities in English and math were prepared for all seventh and eighth graders. The packets were prepared by teachers over the summer and mailed in July and August. Not all families reported receiving the packets or receiving them in a timely manner, but many of those who did receive them, responded to them favorably. Some students and parents found the directions unclear or needed more assistance, perhaps such as was provided in the Chilean project described above. Post-tests of student achievement showed that low-achieving students (as indicated by tests taken the previous spring) who had high use of the materials showed gains. Students who were fair students and high users of the materials maintained their scores, whereas a higher percentage of fair students who were low users showed declines from the spring to fall tests. This preliminary study indicated that students and parents are willing to do learning activities over the summer, but some families will need more guidance and support if more substantial learning gains are to be achieved and more families are to be involved.

Just as the three San Diego middle schools had not investigated or invested in more systematic home learning programs, neither had they involved parents in the classroom in teaching roles. There is some indication that parents can play a more active role in this area as well. As part of its TIPS project, parents were trained to share great art works with middle grade students (Epstein & Dauber, 1989). An Australian project also turned to art as a vehicle to involve parents as teachers in school (McGlip, 1992). Parents carried out lessons in the classroom in conjunction with the classroom teacher, in after-school sessions, or even in their own homes for small groups of students and parents in the evening. These two projects indicate that parents can play useful teaching roles in the classroom to support teachers' instructional programs. However, more research needs to be done to explore in what other subject areas parents or community members could assist teachers and what impact such programs will have on home/school/community relations and students' learning.

Developing, Home and School as Co-Advisors, Advocates, and Decisionmakers. There are Parent/Teacher Associations (PTA) at all three schools. Muirlands has always had a strong and active PTA, with the Board of Directors composed primarily of white parents in the resident community. During 1991-92, the Muirlands PTA board has made an effort to bridge the language, cultural, and distance barriers by occasionally attending meetings in the VEEP community. However, there was still not a sense of equality; Hispanic parent volunteers perceived themselves to be treated as second class citizens and no VEEP parents were recruited for the PTA board. In 1993-1994, five parents from the VEEP community served on the PTA Board and many more were involved through subcommittees. By providing transportation, VEEP parents have become more actively involved on campus. However, the school staff and community realizes there is a need to hold meetings in the VEEP community as well if all families are to be involved. Maintaining a PTA at Mann Middle and Montgomery has been more problematic. When Montgomery initiated its efforts to reach out to its diverse parent community, the PTA was found to be a barrier because the PTA board was perceived to represent only one faction of the community. The teacher coordinating the parent/community outreach program found it easier to organize informal groupings of parents. These parents became volunteers, undertook many projects, and assisted the coordinator in contacting other parents. A new PTA board was elected in 1991-92, which brought together a diverse group of parents more reflective of the community. This reconstituted group now may be able to play a more active role at the school. Parents at all three schools participated in school-site decision-making through School Site Councils (mandated if the school receives state School Improvement Funds) or School Governance Committees established as part of the school restructuring. In addition, parents served on other advisory or ad hoc committees. These committees served important roles in planning school improvement and change. Montgomery took the added step to have parents serve on all major school committees such as the dress code committee, the Student Attendance Review Board, and other ad hoc committees established to address a particular problem. The home/school partnership coordinator felt that giving parents more say in decisions that affect their children resulted in greater parent support in implementing the decisions.

The VEEP parent network at Muirlands empowered parents in ways that were unanticipated by the staff. Using the telephone network created by the school and its regional VEEP liaisons, a group of VEEP parents called other parents and invited them to meet to discuss their concerns. After several meetings, a document was prepared listing a number of issues about the treatment of their students, the perceived lack of opportunities for VEEP students to participate in extracurricular clubs and activities, the number of discipline referrals and suspensions given to VEEP students, and the placement of VEEP students in Special Education classes or in less rigorous and advanced classes than the resident students. The hardest lesson for the school staff has been accepting the collective action and demands of the parents. Traditionally the school staff dealt with parent concerns one-on-one, which usually allowed the school staff to remain in control. The collective advocacy of the parents and the strident manner in which the issues were raised shifted the balance of power and authority. The school turned to a mediation center to assist the school staff and parents in finding solutions to the concerns and problems presented by the parents. The actions of the VEEP parents caused the staff to do some soul searching about what it means when parents are truly involved, especially collectively, and the school is no longer the only one defining the terms of parent involvement. Fortunately, the parental concerns were resolved in ways that preserved the dignity of both staff and parents and led to solutions that were beneficial to students. Since this crisis, Muirlands has continued to move toward its goal—one school community: Home-School collaboration.

Restructuring the Middle Grades: Implications for Home-School Partnerships

In many respects, schools serving middle grades students have led the way in educational reform. The California High School Task Force Report, *Second to None* (1992), presents some recommendations that will be familiar to those involved in middle school reform, such as smaller, more personal learning units, re-engaging with families and communities, and interdisciplinary approaches to a core curriculum through grade ten. Although changes in the middle grades, especially the conversion of junior high schools to middle schools continues apace, additional reforms such as the ones listed below are being explored.

1. Continued development of more integrated, meaning-centered curricula.

2. Use of portfolio and performance-based assessments that will more accurately reflect depth of knowledge and understanding, and the diversity and multiplicity of intelligences.

3. Establishment of community-based learning and services.

4. Initiation of interdisciplinary teams and advisory periods.

5. Establishment of site-based management.

Each of these approaches for reforming and restructuring middle grades education offers opportunities for strengthening home/school partnerships. This section proposes a few strategies schools could pursue which currently are not widely found in schools serving middle grades students. In general the strategies call for more active engagement of teachers with families.

Development of integrated meaning-centered curricula. New insights into the process of learning and teaching and instruction are leading to calls for a curricula that begins with and builds on what students already know (Marshall, 1992). The recent research asserts that learning must take place in a meaningful, integrated context, not as decontextualized discrete facts. Knowledge is collaboratively constructed in a group and class context, not given as a fixed body of information to be acquired and assimilated by a passive student. Important learning can occur in collaborative groups with multiple opportunities for processing information in a variety of contexts and environments (Marshall, 1992).

The implications for home/school/community partnerships from these findings are considerable. First, if teachers begin with what students already know, the family is immediately brought into the learning environment. Much of what students know will derive from family and community experiences as well as previous school experiences. By valuing what students already know, teachers reinforce the family as a learning environment, regardless of educational or economic level of the family.

The following incident provides a concrete example of how the family can be integrated into a meaning-centered curriculum. In an integrated language arts/social studies class, the students were reading *Return from Manzanar*. In collaborative groups, the students analyzed various family values, customs, traditions, and practices that influenced the protagonists in the story. Then the teacher had the students individually write a short paper on their own family values, customs, and traditions. This activity provided an excellent way of linking the curriculum to students' lives. However, the teacher missed an opportunity to involve the family and community in the learning process. In their collaborative groups, the students could have developed a series of questions to ask their parents or other family members about family values, customs, and traditions. After conducting their interviews, the students could have written their papers, then compared their interview results with others in the class. A class summary illustrating similarities and differences in family customs and traditions would have provided fascinating learning experience in this ethnically diverse classroom. Based on the interview results, some parents could have been invited to share particular customs or traditions. Just as teachers are learning new instructional strategies to create a more meaning-centered curriculum, so too do they need to learn ways of linking that curriculum to family and community. The new middle grades TIPS (Teachers Involve Parents and Students) project at Johns Hopkins University represents one excellent way that middle grades teachers have collaborated to develop home learning materials that involve parents and students in joint learning activities. This model needs to be replicated by teachers in a variety of settings.

Portfolio and performance-based assessment. As with a more meaning-centered curricula, portfolio and performance-based assessments offer schools new opportunities for family and community partnerships. Portfolios generally involve students in selecting some of their best work for inclusion in the portfolio. Family members could be involved in the process in two ways. First, after selecting their work, students could take the portfolio home to explain their selection criteria and process to their families. In this way, family members would have an opportunity to see the growth and progress of their child and to share in their successes as opposed to just seeing a much less meaningful grade of A, B, or C on a report card or progress report. Second, family members could be involved in reviewing all of the student's work and helping to make the selection of work for inclusion in the portfolio. Again parents would have an excellent opportunity to see the growth, development, and progress of their child. In addition, parental insights can be included in the evaluative process.

Rather than a collection of the best work, a process folio contains all of the steps taken to complete a paper or project. It resembles a portfolio or notebook of an artist, designer, writer, scientist, or engineer that contains all of the rough drafts or sketches, designs or experiments that led to the final product. Such a folio, shared with parents, would help the family to see learning as a process. If schools are to move from a focus on factual learning to a greater emphasis on depth of understanding, such process folios will be essential in educating the family and community, which has come to expect much simpler measures of student achievement. Process folios will give parents and community a window on children's learning processes that has never been possible with traditional report cards or displays of students' best work.

Performance-based assessment and project work also give families and community members an opportunity to see what students have mastered in academic areas. Such performances and displays have previously been reserved for knowledge and skills mastered in the extra/curricular arenas such as theatre, concerts, arts, or sports. A teacher in a Colorado school demonstrated how performance assessment could be applied to an academic area when she organized a geometry fair and invited parents and community to view their children's mastery of geometry concepts displayed in an enormous array of projects. Some students who previously had not done well in the paper-and-pencil tests of geometry facts, proved to be master builders and able to apply their knowledge.

Another way in which community can be involved as schools restructure to use performance-based assessments is to have a parent/community advisory panel for each academic area. The panel would work with the teachers to design appropriate performance-assessment measures that relate school skills to the world of work. Such involvement with local businesses would greatly strengthen school/community/business collaboration around an important task—assessing students' knowledge. Teachers would learn firsthand the kinds of skills and knowledge needed by future workers, and businesses would gain a more accurate picture of what students are learning. Such collaborative assessment efforts would create opportunities for dialogue and problem solving and could help to identify community learning resources for students.

Interdisciplinary teams and advisory periods. To ease the transition from elementary self-contained classrooms, schools serving middle grades students have turned to interdisciplinary teams and advisory classes. Both of these restructuring strategies offer unique opportunities to connect with families, but in many cases they are not being used. For example, the advisory teacher is usually assigned a smaller class than may be typical for a regular academic class, and the advisor has only one class of advisees. Thus, the advisory teacher is in a unique position to be not only these students' advisor but also to be the primary person to establish contact with the home. This would mitigate against the common complaint of teachers in secondary schools that they cannot stay in close touch with parents because they have too many students. Since an advisor may have only 15 to 20 students, the advisor could conduct twice a year parent/teacher/student conferences as is done in elementary schools. The parents would have a point of contact that is less intimidating than trying to contact all of their child's teachers. The student would know he or she has an advocate to turn to for help.

The interdisciplinary team offers another vehicle for staying in closer touch with families. Research indicates that many parents want to help their children, but often feel unable to assist. To provide more information to parents, interdisciplinary teams could organize quarterly curriculum nights to review the next nine weeks' curriculum and offer tips on how parents could help their child at home. In addition, once the learning themes are identified, parents could be surveyed to find out if they had skills or information to share with the teacher and class. Such an approach would be more valuable for parents than the typical 15-minute rotation through the class schedule at back-to-school night. If students are involved in these curriculum nights to share their work, parents are more likely to attend.

Site-based management. Another major restructuring theme is increased decision-making at the school site by teachers and, in many site-based management plans, by parents and students as well at the middle grades level. Site-based teams offer opportunities for decision-making and advocacy beyond the traditional Parent/Teacher Association or parent club support roles. New roles and responsibilities have to be learned if effective site-based management teams are to be created. Often too little attention is paid to the training needs of the new team. If a school staff has had little previous experience in working together, teachers may feel reluctant and uncomfortable involving parents, students, and community members in new decision-making structures. Since parent and staff representation on the site-based management team is usually quite limited, it is important to set up a subcommittee structure that allows for participation of greater numbers of parents and teachers. These subcommittees can be ad hoc in nature, such as a dress code committee, or can be ongoing such as the departmental advisory panels suggested above in the section on portfolios and performance-based assessments.

Schools serving diverse ethnic populations need to be careful that all groups feel comfortable and welcome to participate. Leadership development may be necessary as was done by Muirlands and Mann Middle Schools. With careful planning and opportunities for training, service on a school site-based management team could become a valuable tool for developing the community leadership that is needed in many inner city neighborhoods.

Staff Development

Establishing new working relations with parents will not be an easy task. This is especially true because teacher pre-service and in-service training traditionally provide few opportunities for teachers to develop needed skills (Chavkin & Williams, 1988). Chavkin and Williams stress that teachers need knowledge about research on parent involvement and successful parent involvement models. In addition, teachers need specific skills that will enable them to work with families. To better develop the knowledge and skills, some changes must be made in pre-service teacher education programs. The states of Washington and California recently passed legislation and a legislative resolution, respectively, which call for parent involvement to be made a component of teacher education. The Council of Chief State School Officers (CCSSO) (Liontos, 1992) also recommends that family involvement information be a mandatory part of teacher training course work, not an optional interest area.

A recent survey of University of California pre-service teacher education programs showed that schools of education are gradually increasing the amount of time and attention paid to this issue (Ammon, 1992). In some courses, student teachers were learning how to identify community resources and gaining an understanding and appreciation of different school neighborhoods (Ammon, D'Emido-Caston, Evans-Schilling, Peretti, and Winkelman, 1992b). In other courses, student teachers developed curriculum materials which reflected the diverse backgrounds of students and served to link home and school through home learning activities (Ammon, Delgado-Gaitan, Evans-Schilling, & Leven,1992a). The University of Houston-Clear Lake in Texas, has also added a course to their pre-service program which helps teachers to identify barriers to family involvement and provides practice in overcoming those barriers (Liontos, 1992). These represent small, but very important, changes in pre-service education and should help new teachers to more easily form productive working relations with families.

To strengthen home/school relations in most middle schools, however, will require school and/or district-based staff development. School districts are beginning to recognize the need for staff development to ensure successful implementation of newly adopted parent involvement initiatives. For example, the Parent Involvement Policy Adopted by the San Diego City Schools stresses that building the capacities of teachers, administrators, and other staff members to work effectively with families is prerequisite for family/school partnerships (Chrispeels, 1991). The staff development, however, cannot be a one-shot workshop. Studies have shown that schools, which have implemented successful school improvement programs, engaged in systematic and ongoing staff development (Chrispeels, 1992). Similarly, unless the staff development addressing home/school partnership issues is of sufficient depth and duration, it is unlikely that significant changes will occur. The type of staff development will vary from school to school depending upon the current level of interaction with families and the community, and the needs and experiences of the school staff. The conceptual framework presented above can be used by schools to begin an assessment of areas of strength and areas needing improvement.

One area that may need attention is working with families from diverse backgrounds. Many schools have experienced rapidly changing demographics. Family structures and the number of families living at poverty levels have increased considerably in the last few years. These changes mean that teachers need new knowledge about the families and communities with whom they work. Unfortunately, as Liontos (1992) points out, there are few materials available to guide teachers in working with families, especially at-risk families. In addition, the current structure of the school day and year does not offer teachers much time for home visits or opportunities to become acquainted with families. Such first-hand contact is one of the best ways for gaining an understanding and appreciation of families. An occasional multicultural fair, while helping to build a sense of community, is no substitute for systematic staff development about the ethnic background, language, and culture of the students and their families. Davies found that an action research project of teachers in Portugal which brought the teachers out of the school and into the community to study, observe, and better understand the culture of working-class children greatly facilitated teacher learning and generated new appreciation for the lives and language of the children (Liontos, 1992).

The staff development needs to be at least two-fold: general information about the culture and community of students which expands knowledge and diminishes stereotyping; and information on how teachers can integrate family knowledge, culture, and traditions into the everyday life of the classroom and curriculum. Learning about diverse cultures will also provide an opportunity to enhance communication skills. One aspect of middle school reform is to implement teacher advisory programs. These programs have often faltered because of inadequate staff development. Successful advisor/advisee programs depend on good communication skills and a facilitative teaching style (Myrick & Myrick, 1990; Wittmer & Myrick, 1989). These same skills are needed for enhancing communication with parents. Training in communication and conferencing skills would enable advisory teachers to become the point of contact between home and school. If each advisor scheduled twice-yearly conferences with their advisees and their families, communications and parent involvement at the middle grades level would be greatly enhanced. Thus, if middle schools focused on strengthening their advisory periods, they are also likely to find that home/school communication is strengthened.

Another area for potential staff development is in designing quality homework and homelearning activities. The development of such materials lend themselves to an action research approach which Sagor (1991) has found useful in building faculty efficacy and enthusiasm. For example, interdisciplinary teams could develop and test different types of homework or homelearning activities to see which approach engages students and their families most effectively and which leads to desired outcomes. Teacher exploration, experimentation, and sharing of results is a powerful staff development model (Davies, 1991).

Areas for Further Research in Developing Middle Grades Home School Partnerships

While there is a fairly significant body of research and studies regarding parent involvement at the elementary level, especially in the pre-primary and primary grades, little work has been done to research parent involvement at the middle grades level. Each of the roles presented above suggest areas for further research. For example, more work needs to be done in understanding how best to communicate with the parents of middle grades students. What do parents most need to know about the school and to share with teachers? What methods of communication best meet parents needs? Could video and telephone message systems be effective tools of communication? How can communications be made more two-way and less unidirectional from school to the home? A recent large survey of parents in an elementary school district revealed that although parents felt teachers were communicating with them, they expressed a strong need for more communication, especially face-to-face communication (Chrispeels & Daugherty, 1992). Do middle grades parents feel the same way?

In the area of co-supporters, additional questions present themselves. As middle schools move to establish houses or villages or other types of smaller configurations for grouping students, are these smaller units being used to build parent support and create a sense of community? What strategies work best? Given the significant social, emotional, health, and welfare needs of many students, how can middle schools build partnerships with community agencies to better meet student and family needs? How extensive do the partnerships and interagency collaboration need to be, and how can resources be best utilized without overburdening already overworked school and agency staff?

The third area needing research is that of co-learners and co-teachers. These two areas are closely interrelated. As parents and school staff enhance their own learning, the capacity to teach also is likely to increase. What do parents and school staff need to know if they are to work more effectively together to support student school success? Some of the areas for possible teacher staff development were outlined above. However, little research has actually been done to show which types of staff development and what content is most helpful to teachers in strengthening their working relations with students and their families.

In determining their learning needs, parents need to be active partners with school staff in deciding which topics would be most helpful to them. The format and frequency of workshops also need to be investigated. Are workshops in which family members and students are learning together more effective than if parents attend alone? Can parents play a more active teaching role if more curriculum-oriented workshops are held? Can curriculum-learning opportunities such as Family Math, Family Science, or Parents Sharing Books, strengthen family communications and interaction as well as workshops which focus just on parent/child communications? When families attend such workshops do teachers form more positive opinions about parents and their ability to help their child? The school survey cited above indicated that parents felt able to help their children with homework, although they also indicated they would like to have more guidance from teachers in how to help. Teachers, on the other hand, overwhelmingly felt that the largely Hispanic parent population of this district was unable to help. Do teachers hold similar views in regard to parents of middle grades students? Do these attitudes vary depending upon the ethnic and economic makeup of the community? If views and perceptions do vary, do teachers give less homework and expect less assistance from parents based on their presumptions of parent ability to help?

If greater parental support is desired with homework and home learning activities, there are a number of areas that would profit from further research. Cooper (1989) has conducted a thorough review of the research on homework, and some useful information is known that needs to be used by teachers to guide them in developing appropriate homework. However, most of the research examines traditional types of homework, such as math problems to solve. If teachers move toward a more meaning-centered curriculum and a project and problem-solving approach to learning, what kinds of homework assignments are appropriate and have the greatest impact on student learning? How can homework and home learning assignments be designed so they will not penalize students whose home learning environments have fewer resources than students from middle or upper-middle class families? How can parents and students be meaningfully and actively involved in evaluating student work and how does such involvement affect student and parent learning?

In relation to the typology of home/school partnership roles presented above, one last area for further research is in the area of co-decision-makers. advocates and advisors. A central issue for further research is: how can parents, students, and school staff work more effectively together on school decision-making bodies? What skills are needed and how can these be quickly acquired when there is often rapid turnover in committee membership? These are just a few of the many areas that can be identified as possible areas for further research. Existing research can help to guide parents and school staff as they work together to form stronger partnerships. It is important as schools work to build partnerships that data be collected and analyzed and action research projects used as a way to form the most viable partnerships in schools serving middle grades students and their families.

References

Ammon, M. S. (1992). *Report to the University of California/California Department of Education Joint Committee on Parent Involvement*. Sacramento, CA: California Department of Education.

Ammon, M. S., Ammon, P., Delgado-Gaitan, C, Evans-Schilling, D., & Levin, P. (1992a, October) *Helping teachers design and use curricula that foster partnerships with families*. Paper presented at the Association for Constructivist Teaching, Berkeley, CA.

Ammon, M. S., D'Emido-Caston, M. A., Evans-Schilling, D., Peretti, D., & Winkelman, P. (1992b, October). *Preparing teachers to work with families of culturally diverse and special needs children*. Paper presented at the Association for Constructivist Teaching, Berkeley, CA.

California State Department of Education. (1987). *Caught in the middle: Educational reform for young adolescents in California public schools.* Sacramento, CA: Author.

California State Department of Education. (1992). *Second to none: The report of the California high school task force.* Sacramento, CA: Author.

Carnegie Council on Adolescent Development. (1989). *Turning points: Preparing American youth for the 21st century.* New York: Carnegie Corporation.

Chavkin, N. F.,& Williams D. L. (1988). Critical issues for teacher training for parent involvement. *Educational Horizons, 66*(2), 87-89.

Chrispeels, J. H. (1987). The family as an educational resource. *Community Education Journal, 14*(3),10-17.

Chrispeels, J. H. (1991). District leadership in parent involvement: Policies and actions in San Diego. *Phi Delta Kappan, 72,* 367-71.

Chrispeels, J. H. (1992). *Purposeful restructuring: Creating a climate for learning and achievement in elementary schools.* London: Falmer.

Chrispeels, J. H., & Daugherty, M. (1992). *Report to the National School District Board of Education on the results of the parent involvement survey.* National City, CA: National School District.

Copper, H. (1989). *Homework.* New York: Longman.

Davies, D. (1991). Schools reaching out: Family, school, and community partnerships for student success. *Phi Delta Kappan, 72,* 372-82.

Epstein, J. L. (1987a). What principals should know about parent involvement. *Principal, 66*(8), 4-9.

Epstein, J. L. (1987b). *Teacher's manual: Teachers involve parents in schoolwork* (TIPS. Report P 61). Baltimore, MD: The Johns Hopkins University.

Epstein, J. L., & Becker, H. J. (1982). Teacher practice of parent involvement: Problems and possibilities. *Elementary School Journal, 83,* 103-113.

Epstein, J. L., & Dauber, S. L. (1989). *Evaluation of students' knowledge and attitudes in the Teachers Involve Parents in Schoolwork (TIPS) social studies and art program.* (CREMS Report No. 41). Baltimore, MD: The Johns Hopkins University.

Epstein, J. L., & Herrick, S. C. (1991a). *Two reports: Implementation and effects of summer home learning packets in the middle grades* (Report No. 21). Baltimore, MD: The Johns Hopkins University.

Epstein, J. L., & Herrick S. C. (1991b). *Improving school and family partnerships in urban middle grades schools: Orientation days and school newsletters.* Baltimore MD: The Johns Hopkins University.

Epstein, J. L. & Mac Iver, D. J. (1990). *Education in the middle grades: National practices and trends.* Columbus, OH: National Middle School Association.

Gardner, Howard. (1989). *To open minds.* New York: Basic Books.

George, P. S., & Oldaker, L. L. (1985). A national survey of middle school effectiveness. *Educational Leadership, 42,* 85-86.

George, P. S., Stevenson, C., Thomason, J, & Beane, J. (1992). *The middle school—and beyond.* Alexandria, VA: Association for Supervision and Curriculum Development.

Johnson, S. L., Brookover, W. G., & Farrell, Jr., W. C. (1989, March). *School perceptions of parents' roles, interests, and expectations for their childrens' education and student achievement.* Paper presented at the annual meeting of the American Educational Research Association, San Francisco, CA.

Liontos, L. B. (1992). *At-risk families and schools: Becoming partners.* Eugene, OR: ERIC Clearinghouse on Educational Management.

Lipsitz, J. (1984). *Successful schools for young, adolescents.* New Brunswick, NJ: Transaction.

Lyons, P., Robbins, A., & Smith, A. (1983). *Involving parents: A handbook for participation in schools.* Santa Monica, CA: Systems Development Corporation.

Marshall, H. H. (1992, April). *Reconceptualizing learning for restructured schools.* Paper presented at the annual meeting of the American Educational Research Association, San Francisco, CA.

McGlip, E. J. (1992, April). *Parental involvement in children's artistic learning.* Paper presented at the International Roundtable of the Center for Families, Communities, Schools, and Children's Learning. San Francisco, CA.

Myrick, R. D., Myrick, L. S., & Contributors. (1990). *The teacher advisor program: An innovative approach to school guidance.* Ann Arbor, Ml: ERIC Counseling and Personnel Services Clearinghouse, The University of Michigan.

National Association of Secondary School Principals. (1985). *An agenda for excellence at the middle level.* Reston, VA: Author.

Pizarro, R. S. (1992, April). *School + home = experimental synthesis for successful students.* Paper presented at the annual meeting of the American Educational Research Association, San Francisco, CA.

Purnell, R. G., & Gotts, E. E. (1983,). *An approach for improving parent involvement through more effective school-home communications.* Paper presented at the meeting of Southern Association of Colleges and Schools, New Orleans, LA. (ERIC Document Reproduction Service No ED 245 842)

Smith, L. (1993). *Parents sharing books: Report of project implementation.* Bloomington, IN: Indiana University.

Sagor, Richard. (1991). What Project LEARN reveals about collaborative action research. *Educational Leadership*, *48*(6), 6-10.

U.S. Department of Education. (1983). *A nation at risk.* Washington, DC: Author.

Wittmer, J., & Myrick, R. D. (1989). *The teacher as facilitator.* Minneapolis, MN. Educational Media Corporation.

Chapter 3

School and Family Partnerships in the Middle Grades

Joyce L. Epstein
Lori J. Connors

Introduction

Early adolescence has been called the time in a child's life when parents are the most difficult! In early adolescence—the years between 10-14—youngsters experience simultaneous social, emotional, intellectual, and physical changes and challenges. Most early adolescents and their families successfully negotiate this period of development and move on to new challenges in late adolescence, high school, and young adulthood (Offer, Ostror, Howard, & Atkinson, 1988). Some youngsters, however, have serious problems that appear or increase in the middle grades, creating turmoil during these pivotal years, and preventing some students from measuring up to their full potential. As students enter adolescence, many parents begin to lose touch with their children's schools and, therefore, with their children as students. Middle grades schools need to think about how to connect and communicate with families in order to maximize support for student learning and development.

What must be done to develop and maintain family and school connections when students become early adolescents? When middle grades schools become more complex? When families become more confused about how their children are developing and about their continuing influence on their children's education? We address these questions with a brief overview of middle grades students, families, and schools; a theory and framework to help build successful partnerships; a summary of research on partnerships at this level; and a discussion of issues for educators and researchers to consider as they work to improve practice and increase knowledge about school and family partnerships in the middle grades.

The Concept of "Partnership"

What do we mean by "parent involvement" in the middle grades? We suggest that the term "school and family partnerships" better expresses the shared interests, responsibilities, investments, and overlapping influences of families and schools in children's education through adolescence. There are several reasons for this. The broader term emphasizes that the two institutions share major responsibilities for children's education and that both are needed to support children as "students." In addition to recognizing the school as equals in partnership, the broader term recognizes the importance and potential influence of all family members, not only parents,

139

and all family structures, not only those that include natural parents. Moreover, the term allows students to join the partnership as communicators with and for their schools and families. The term makes room, too, for community groups, individuals, agencies, and organizations to work with schools and families and to invest in the education of children whose futures affect the quality of life of the community.

When some say "parent involvement" they mean things that some parents do on their own by their own invention. The "know-how" may be social-class-based or experience-based, relying on parents' skills to locate information they want and need. Other terms are sometimes used to describe the connections of families and schools. The term "home/school relations" sounds informal and conversational, rather than planned and comprehensive. By contrast, "partnership" expresses a formal alliance and contractual agreement to work actively toward shared goals and to share the profits or benefits of mutual investments.

School and family partnerships recognize that leadership is needed from schools to help all families obtain useful information that is not available from other sources. In the middle grades, school-generated information may be the only equitable way to enable all families to become more knowledgeable about their early adolescents and their schools. Partnerships also recognize that in order to design more effective and responsive practices, schools need to obtain information from families about their children, their goals, and the connections they want with their middle grades schools.

Much like partners in business, partners in education must work hard to clarify their mutual interests in the children they share. All of the parties in a partnership must work to develop trust, organize their responsibilities, and appreciate each others' investments and contributions. Strong partnerships develop over time, as partners exchange information and work together to assess their strengths and needs, set goals, plan projects, implement practices, evaluate results, celebrate successes, and revise activities to assist their children to succeed in school. These interactions should result in better school, family, and community programs and practices.

There are no shortcuts to the process of developing partnerships and improving programs. Experience shows that three to five years are needed to build strong partnerships in schools with all families, and even more time is needed to assure a lasting structure of successful practices to involve families (Comer, 1980; Epstein & Dauber, 1991).

Although one should not get sidetracked by semantics, the words we choose are important if they influence the understanding of responsibilities and the design and conduct of interactions. The terms "parent involvement" and "home-school relations" should be considered shorthand for the broader, more inclusive concept of school, family, and community partnerships.

Theoretical Model—Overlapping Spheres of Influence

Overlapping spheres of influence. The term "partnership" is represented in a theoretical model of "overlapping spheres of influence" (Epstein, 1987a). The spheres of influence on children's learning and development include the family and the school, or, in full form, four spheres of influence of the family, school, community, and peer group (Epstein, 1988a). The spheres can, by design, be pushed together to overlap to create an area for partnership activities or pulled apart to separate the family and school based on forces that operate in each environment. The **external model** of the spheres of influence shows that the extent of overlap is affected by the forces of (a) time—to account for changes in the ages and grade levels of students and the influence of historic changes, and (b) behavior—to account for the backgrounds, philosophies, and practices in each environment. The external model recognizes pictorially that there are some practices that schools and families (and the other spheres) conduct separately and others jointly, and that those that overlap are potentially important influences on students.

The **internal model** of the spheres of influence recognizes the complex and essential interpersonal relations and influence patterns that occur between and among individuals at home and at school (and also, more fully, in the community and peer groups) in practices that concern students' education and development. There are two levels of interpersonal relations—one at the institutional level of schools and families, as when schools invite all families to events or send the same communications to all families, and the other at the individual level, as when a parent, teacher, and student meet in conference to discuss an individual student's progress or problem, or when a teacher telephones or writes to a parent for an individual communication. These levels of interpersonal relations also can intersect as when teachers give the whole class interactive homework assignments but only some students conduct the exchanges with a parent.

The central role of the student. Students are at the center of the model of overlapping spheres of influence for school and family partnerships. The model assumes that student learning, development, and success, broadly defined, are the main reasons for home and school partnerships. Productive connections of schools and families, and pertinent individual interactions of parents, teachers, and students are conducted in order to help students increase their academic skills, self-esteem, positive attitudes toward learning, independence, other achievements, accomplishments, and other desired behaviors that are characteristic of successful students.

Students are not passive in their educational growth and change, but are the main actors in their own success in school. School and family partnerships do not "produce" successful students. Rather, the partnership activities that include teachers, parents, and students engage and guide students so that they produce their own success.

As they mature, children face many competing demands and options for their time in school and out. Most middle grades students choose to invest their time, energy, and identity in those activities that motivate and reward them, increase their self-esteem, increase their social status among peers, and provide challenges and opportunities for success. When schools and families work in partnership, students hear that school is important from parents and teachers, and see that influential people in both environments are investing time and resources to work together to help them become successful students. The students' own work is legitimized by this process of mutual support.

The central role of the student in school and family partnerships occurs across the grades but is especially important beginning in the middle grades when students become even more instrumental in helping to conduct and interpret school communications with their families. Also, with the more complex curriculum in the middle grades, students must work harder to convert support from their schools and families into individual achievements. Programs of school and family connections in the middle grades will fail unless the early adolescents understand, accept, and participate in the partnerships designed to assist them to be more successful in school.

The full model of overlapping spheres of influence recognizes the interlocking histories of institutions that motivate, socialize, and educate children and the changing interactions and accumulating skills of the educators, family members, and students. These are the bases for implementing and for studying connections that benefit students, families, and schools in the middle grades.

Middle Grades Schools, Students, and Families

The model of overlapping spheres of influence highlights the importance of time as one of the forces that influence partnership practices. That is, the extent of overlap and the practices of partnership change from year to year, as students move from one teacher to the next who use different practices to inform and involve families, and from one level of schooling to the next, such as from the elementary to the middle grades, or from middle grades to high school. The different levels of schooling have different histories of partnerships with families. For example, preschool and elementary schools have been working at developing partnerships longer and more seriously than middle grades schools up to now. In other words, school and family partnerships are developmental, accounting for and responsive to the changes that occur in the characteristics of the middle grades students, families, and schools.

The children are changing. In early adolescence—the years between 10-14—youngsters experience simultaneous social, emotional, physical, and intellectual changes and challenges. The rate of student development varies widely, across and within grades, making it difficult to identify an "average" early adolescent. Early adolescents need opportunities to develop their independence and to take more responsibility for themselves, even as they continue to need adults to guide and support them. They deepen their relationships with peers as they seek the comfort of conformity in their age group, but at the same time, they increase their self-confidence as they identify their unique talents and skills. Even as peers become more important influences for each other, adults—parents, teachers, coaches, mentors, and others—continue to be important influences. They need to be available and supportive as knowledgeable partners about education.

Middle grades students are often the main source of information for parents about their schools. Because of their increasing maturity and new relationships with their families and teachers, students play important roles—more powerful than in the earlier grades—in three-way partnerships.

School and family partnerships need to help parents understand early adolescent development, peer relations, and middle grades schools, and help children understand that their school recognizes the continuing importance and influence of their families in their lives.

The families are changing. Compared to parents of elementary school children, the parents of middle grades youngsters are, themselves, older. They may live further from the middle grades school; be busy with younger children in the elementary grades; or working full-time and balancing their careers with family responsibilities.

Parents of early adolescents often wonder what happened to the young child they thought they knew. They may be confused about their early adolescents' development and worried about the problems that teens face today. Parents may be unsure of how they can foster student independence and still take a role in guiding their youngsters in important behaviors and decisions about school and about other aspects of life.

School and family partnerships in the middle grades need to be designed and implemented so that they fit the needs and realities of family life, working parents, varied family structures, and other factors that affect families. The connections need to help families understand their sons and daughters who also are middle grades students.

The schools are changing. Middle grades schools are differently organized and staffed from most elementary schools. They are usually larger, fully departmentalized, with more teachers certified for the secondary grades, educated as subject-matter experts, and unprepared to work with families. The schools vary in grade span, staffing, middle grades practices such as interdisciplinary teams or advisory programs, and other aspects of instruction. They offer students more complex and demanding subjects than in the younger grades. The content of the curriculum—expanded from the time that parents went to school—becomes more difficult for parents to understand, keep track of, or talk about easily with their children. Counselors and other school administrators work with students on attendance, behavior, health, course choices, academic program and track placements, career planning, college preparation, and other issues that also concern families. Often, however, the families are not informed about these topics nor about how to reinforce or extend the school programs to benefit their children.

School and family partnerships need to be organized to make the best use of the various adults who have important roles in middle grades schools, assist teachers to understand their students' families and how to mobilize family support to assist student learning, and alert families to the programs and practices that are new in the middle grades.

Summary of Research on Effective Partnerships in the Middle Grades

A major message of many early and some continuing studies of family environments and influence is simply that families are important for children's learning, development, and school success across the grades, including the middle grades. This line of research suggests that students at all grade levels do better in their academic work as well as have more positive school attitudes, higher aspirations, and other positive behaviors, if they happen to have parents who are aware, knowledgeable, encouraging, and involved. The influence on students is stronger if family support is continuous and consistent.

Most studies do not differentiate between schools and teachers that use practices to help all families participate in their children's education, and those that leave parents on their own to become involved. Without a formal program to provide information, parents are left to draw from their own resources and information, but some families have access to more resources than others. More recent research examines the impact on families, students, and teaching practice of specific school and classroom practices to inform and involve all families equally. The main question in these studies is: If family support is important for students, how can all schools maximize the number of families who are informed and involved in their children's education across the grades? (For full reviews and references of research on school and family connections at all levels see Epstein, 1992; and at the middle level see Rutherford, Billig, & Kettering, 1994).

Overview of selected results from research on partnerships at the middle level. Research is accumulating that shows that middle grades schools can take leadership in developing and implementing practices of partnership that enable more parents to become and remain involved in their children's education. Here we highlight a few of the general results from studies of middle grades families and teacher practices of involvement. The broad conclusions are synthesized from more than one study from the research of Bauch (1988), Benson (1991), Dauber & Epstein (1993), Dolan & Caroselli (1982), Dornbusch & Ritter (1988), Epstein (1986), Epstein & Dauber (1991), Epstein, Herrick, and Coates (in press), Epstein & Herrick (1991),

Epstein & Lee (1992), Johns & Panofsky (1987), Leitch & Tangri (1988), Marockie & Jones (1987), Stevenson & Baker (1987), Useem (1992), and Youniss & Smollar (1989). Although a few of these studies focus on middle or high school organizations, they include samples of parents or students from the middle grades (grades 5-9) in useful ways.

From these references we draw the following conclusions that support the systematic development by middle grades schools of comprehensive and equitable programs to inform and involve all families in the education of their early adolescents.

- Schools' practices of partnership with families decline with each grade level and decrease dramatically at the point of transition to the middle grades. Coincidentally, with each year in school, more families report that they are unable to understand the schools or assist their children. This pattern changes when middle schools add practices to inform and involve families.

- Most parents do not participate at the school building as volunteers or in decision-making or leadership roles. Many do not have the time, working full or part-time during the school day. Many do not want to; others do not know that they are welcome. In many middle grades schools, there are no procedures for recruiting, training, and scheduling volunteers or for including parents on committees or decision making teams. Many middle grades schools have no parent organization to develop leadership or to promote family participation.

- By contrast, most parents, including up to 90% in the middle grades, want to know how to help their own children at home in order to help their children succeed at school. Studies confirm that families need and want more information and guidance from the schools to monitor and support the education of their early adolescents. Presently, only some families—indeed, relatively few—have information about the schools, courses, choices, grading procedures, and many other topics that change at the middle level. Research on the implementation and effects of practices for the middle level show that parents of early adolescents, including those in inner city schools, want to assist and interact with their children about school subjects, schoolwork, and homework in helpful ways. They want to do so during the school year and during the summer, but they are given little guidance by the schools.

- Families of middle grades students have many questions about the schools that go unanswered. They also have many suggestions to offer about improving school programs, events, and partnerships that go unheard by the school. Few schools have two-way communications processes and practices that allow an easy flow of information to and from schools and families.

- Families have high hopes for their middle grades children, with large percentages expecting their children to attend and complete college. Many lack information that would help translate their values and goals into behaviors to guide their children toward college or other post-secondary education.

- Even as peers become increasingly important in early adolescence, families remain important to students.

- Social, academic, and personal problems of students that begin to increase in early adolescence require attention from all who share interest and investments in children. The efforts of schools, families, and communities to prevent problems from occurring or to treat problems that occur have not been well-organized to date. Each institution usually works separately with children, often without knowledge of or communication with the other. The disorganized delivery of services to teens and families has contributed to the unacceptable statistics on school failure, retentions in grade, drug and alcohol abuse, delinquency, teen pregnancy, and other problems that prevent students from reaching their potential. Services must be more successfully integrated in new programs of school, community and family partnerships.

Overall, evidence is accumulating from local, regional, and national studies that indicates that when middle grades schools take steps to involve all families, more parents appreciate the assistance, become successful partners, and more students benefit in achievements, attitudes, and behaviors.

Framework and Application of Six Types of Involvement

In applying the theory of overlapping spheres of influence, we ask: *What practices fall within the area of overlap as shared responsibilities of schools and families?* and *How can schools think about, organize, and implement practices to create a comprehensive program of partnership with families and with the community?*

Results from many studies lead to the formulation of a framework of six major types of involvement that describes a comprehensive program of school and family partnerships in the middle grades (Epstein, 1987b, 1992). Many practices can be selected by schools to operationalize each type of involvement (Brandt, 1989; Epstein, 1987b, 1991; Davies, Burch & Johnson, 1992). The practices must be "tailored" in the middle grades to respond to the changing characteristics and needs of students, school organization and families discussed above (Epstein & Connors, 1992). Each type of involvement in the framework includes practices that are likely to lead to different outcomes or results for students, for parents, for teaching practice, and for school climate. The connection of each type of involvement with particular practices and specific outcomes corrects the simplistic assumption that any involvement of parents will quickly or dramatically increase student achievement. Studies are beginning to show that different important outcomes for students, parents, and for teaching practice will result from the varied types of involvement.

In this section we outline the six major types of involvement and give a few examples of practices that continue across the grades and other practices that may be particularly important for accommodating the characteristics and needs of early adolescents, their families, and their schools. We note some of the challenges of implementation and the kinds of results (or outcomes) that have been found or that can be expected from each type of involvement in the middle grades.

Type 1

Basic obligations of families refer to schools providing information that families need about adolescent's health and safety, supervision, nutrition, discipline and guidance, and other parenting skills and child-rearing approaches. Middle grades schools also need to provide families with information about building positive home conditions that support learning at each grade level. Some schools help parents with their basic obligations through workshops at the school or in other locations, and in other forms of parent education, training, and information sharing.

Families continue to teach their early adolescents many attitudes, behaviors, beliefs, customs, and skills that are unique to and valued by the family, apart from the school curriculum. Schools are enriched by understanding the backgrounds and cultures of the families of their students. This two-way exchange—information to help families understand child and adolescent development and information to help schools understand family life and students' needs, interests, and talents—is at the heart of Type 1 activities.

In the middle grades, Type 1 practices may help families understand early and later adolescence, support early adolescent health and mental health, and prevent key problems in adolescent development. Families may want information (and may want to give the school information) on how to meet early adolescents' simultaneous needs for increased independence and continued guidance from families; on understanding the importance of peers and the risks of peer pressure; and on other topics. Families may want more information about setting appropriate family rules, providing decision-making opportunities to early adolescents, and changing discipline practices to support student development. With good information from and to their child's middle-grades school, families can continue to promote home conditions to help students balance their studying, homework, part-time jobs, and home chores.

Other Type 1 practices that have been implemented by middle grades schools include courses for parents in adult education, GED, and English language; home visits; parent rooms for workshops for parents on difficult topics to discuss at home such as teen sexuality and drug abuse; workshops for parents and teens to attend together; and sessions for parents to talk with each other about child development and parenting.

Challenges. One challenge of successful Type 1 activities is to get information to all families who want it and who need it, and not just to the few who can attend workshops at the school. This may be done with videos, tape recordings, summaries, newsletters. cable broadcasts, and other ways. Another challenge is to arrange and maintain the channels for two-way communication that allow important information from families to come to the schools.

Outcomes. These activities should help reach goals and produce results to increase families' understanding of their early adolescents, students' awareness of the continuing role that parents play in their education, and educators' understanding of their students' families.

Type 2

Basic obligations of schools refer to communications from schools to families about school programs and students' progress. This includes notices, memos, phone calls, newsletters, report cards, conferences, open-house nights or other visiting opportunities, and other more innovative communications. This also includes information to help families to choose or change schools, if such policies are used in a district. Middle grades schools vary the forms, frequency, and content of communications and greatly affect whether and how families receive information and whether the information sent home can be understood by all families.

In the middle grades, Type 2 communications also help families help students select curricula, courses, special programs, and other activities each year.

Families need information at important transition points from elementary to middle grades and from middle to high school. Useful orientations at these times recognize that families make transitions with their children, and that if they are informed, can help students adjust to their new schools.

At entry to the middle grades, some structures and procedures change that families need to know about. For example, report cards often change in form and in content. Information explaining report card grading systems and interim reports should help families monitor how their adolescents are doing in school and how to help students improve their grades from one marking period to the next. Conferences may be reconfigured in the middle grades as parent/student/teacher conferences to assure that students understand the connection between their teachers' and parents' communications and their own control over their motivation and learning. Conferences in the middle grades also must allow connections of families with many teachers of different subjects or with teams of teachers if the school organizes its work in these ways.

Other topics that begin to be important to middle grades families include how they can help students plan for college and work; begin financial savings for education and training; learn of scholarships, loans, and grants; and plan for the tests students need to take to step toward their futures.

Other Type 2 practices that have been implemented by middle grades schools include giving families advance notice about special schedules, costs, and other requirements; conferences at home with parents who have no transportation to get to the school, or providing transportation by school bus or parent-taxi-carpools so that they can come; providing native-language translations of written or verbal communications; using local cable TV for a homework hotline, and other communications. To improve contacts, some schools have organized class parents, block parents, telephone trees, or the equivalent of a "welcome wagon" for education to provide a contact person and information to families who transfer to a middle grades school any time during the school year. (For other examples see Chrispeels, Bourta & Daugherty, 1988).

Challenges. One challenge of successful Type 2 activities is to make communications clear and understandable for all families, including parents who have less formal education, so that all can respond to the information they receive. Other challenges are to know which families are and are not receiving the communications in order to include those who are harder to reach in each school; to extend two-way channels so that families can initiate and respond to communications; and to help middle grades students become good partners by delivering communications home and discussing schoolwork and school decisions with their families.

Outcomes. These activities should help reach goals and produce results to increase families' and teachers' interactions; increase families' understanding and use of their school and classrooms programs and their children's progress; increase families' attendance at meetings, conferences, and events; and improve students' decisions about their schoolwork and courses with input from home. With targeted communications via tape recordings, video cassettes, summaries, newsletters, telephone answering machines or computerized messages, and other print and nonprint forms to middle grades families, student attendance, lateness, behavior, and other outcomes may improve.

Type 3

Involvement at school refers to parent and other volunteers at the middle-grades school or in classrooms, and to families who come to school to support student performances, sports, or other events. In addition to Type 2 communications that inform families about opportunities and events, schools increase the number of families and community members who come to the school building by varying schedules so that more are able to participate as volunteers and as audiences at different times of the day and evening, weekends, summer, or holidays.

In the middle grades, volunteers can be put to better use if there is a coordinator who matches volunteers' times and skills with the needs of teachers, administrators, and students. Programs that tap parents' and community members' talents, occupations, and interests can enrich students' subject classes and improve career explorations. Mentoring, coaching, and tutoring activities may be particularly helpful as students' skills, interests, and talents become increasingly diverse in the middle grades. Some parents may want to volunteer to work with other parents of middle grades students, perform language translations, monitor attendance, and other activities.

Other Type 3 practices that middle grades schools have implemented include volunteers working in a parent room or parent center; volunteers making cassette tapes for students to read along when their science or social studies books are at a reading level that is beyond their current reading skills; and curriculum-linked volunteers who integrate art activities into social studies classes. (See for example, Epstein & Salinas, TIPS Volunteers in Social Studies and Art, 1991.)

Challenges. One challenge of successful Type 3 activities is to recruit volunteers widely, make hours flexible for parents and other volunteers who work during the school day, and to enable volunteers to contribute productively to the school and to the curriculum. Volunteers are more likely to be productive if their tasks are clear and their training is focused. As one veteran of a volunteer program said of how to increase productive volunteers, "Ask people to do something specific and keep asking!" When volunteers are organized to productively contribute to the middle grades program (as when parents enrich or extend a curricular goal), teachers of different subjects are more likely to think about how to include volunteers in their work.

Another challenge of Type 3 involvement is to change the definition of "volunteer" to mean any one, any time, any place who supports school goals or students' learning. This opens up possibilities for more parents and others in the community to be volunteers in middle grades schools, or at home, or in other locations in the community. A related challenge is to help early adolescents understand that it is o.k. for a parent to be involved in ways that help middle grades school, students, or other families.

Outcomes. These activities should help reach goals and produce results to increase the contributions made by many families to support school programs; increase families' comfort and familiarity with the school and staff; vary students' communications with adults; increase teachers' readiness to involve families in other ways at home and at school; and improve teachers' awareness of parents' and other community members' abilities to contribute substantively to the school. Other outcomes may include fewer discipline problems due to lower ratios of students to adults, stronger school offerings and more student awareness of opportunities in life due to varied programs offered by volunteers with diverse talents, work, and interests.

Type 4

Involvement in learning activities at home refers to requests and guidance from middle grades teachers for parents to monitor, assist, and interact with their own children at home on learning activities that are coordinated with students' classwork or that contribute to success in school. It also includes parent-initiated, student-initiated, and teacher-directed discussions and interactions about homework or school subjects. Type 4 practices assist families to become more knowledgeable partners about the teachers' curricula and instructional methods; the academic and other skills required to pass each grade, the work their children are doing in class; how to support, monitor, discuss, and help with homework; and how to help students practice and study for tests.

In middle grades schools, information on the skills needed to pass each course and how families can help at home must come from several teachers of different subjects. It must be clear that the school does not expect families to "teach" school subjects but to encourage, listen, react, praise, guide, monitor, and discuss the work the students bring home. This may be done with interactive homework, student/teacher/family "contracts," long-term projects, or other interactive strategies that keep students and families talking about schoolwork at home.

Other Type 4 practices that middle grades schools have implemented to keep schoolwork on the agenda at home include videotapes to demonstrate how to motivate early adolescent learners, videos of sample class lessons to discuss at home, pre-unit introductory activities and discussions, summer home learning packets, student demonstrations of newly mastered math skills, and others. (See, for example, Epstein, Jackson & Salinas, TIPS Interactive Homework in the Middle Grades in Language Arts and Science, 1992.)

Challenges. One challenge of successful Type 4 activities is to design and organize a regular schedule of interactive work that enables students to take the leadership role in discussing important and interesting things they are learning, interviewing family members, recording reactions, and sharing written work. This approach helps middle grades students understand that the school wants their families to know what they are learning in school, and wants students to talk over ideas and school decisions at home. A regular weekly or biweekly schedule of interactive homework helps keep families aware of the depth of the curriculum and their children's progress throughout the year. The interactions about homework must be the students' responsibilities, however, without requiring parents to read, write, or teach school subjects. The emphasis is on helping families interact with early adolescents in ways that also help students become more independent learners.

Another challenge is to design homework activities or projects which are responsive to the needs and time available of students and families without putting undue pressure on either. The methods to encourage interaction must not be unduly burdensome on middle grades teachers who often have many students to teach and many families to reach. Interactive homework should enable parents to send reactions or observations back to the school, maintaining two-way communications on involvement about learning activities, as in the other types.

A general challenge is to design ways to increase the amount of useful information all families receive that will help them continue conversations with their early adolescents about the curriculum, classwork, and positive achievements.

Outcomes. It is this type of involvement that may be most likely to increase student curricular achievements. The interactions and support from family members should help students to improve their homework completion, report card grades, test scores, and other subject-specific attitudes and achievements. Students' feelings of competence may increase if they regularly lead enjoyable interactions with their families to demonstrate what they are learning. They also should be more aware that their family knows about the important part of school life—the learning activities. Teachers' recognition of the part parents play in encouraging students' classroom learning also should increase, and teachers' attention to the design and content of homework should improve. These activities should help reach goals and produce results to increase families' understanding of the school curriculum and how to help at home. More families should be able to support their children by coordinating home and community activities with things their children are learning in school.

Type 5

Involvement in decision-making, governance, and advocacy refers to parents and others in the community in participatory roles in parent/teacher/student organizations, school advisory councils, school-site decision-making or improvement teams, Chapter 1, and other school committees. It also refers to parents as activists in independent education advocacy groups in the community. Middle grades schools strengthen parent participation in school decisions by encouraging the organization of parent groups and committees and by training parents and students in leadership and decision-making skills. Schools assist advocacy groups by providing them with information that will bolster community support for middle grades school improvement.

In addition to the continuation of active parent organizations, parent representatives on committees are important in middle grades schools on a wide array of topics that affect the quality of school programs. These include committees on curriculum. safety, supplies and equipment, family involvement, career development, and other topics for school improvement.

Other Type 5 activities that middle grades schools have implemented to involve families in school decision-making and advocacy include guidelines developed by parent groups that outline how and how much parents are told about middle grades grouping policies, course selection, placement, and appeals processes. Some practices link types of involvement as when the coordinator of volunteers or parent leaders on specific committees are appointed or elected council members of the PTA/PTO. Parent associations have run clothing exchanges, school stores, fairs, "gold card" discount programs with local merchants, and many other activities. (For other examples of school-based management structures see Comer, 1980, 1988.)

Challenges. One challenge of successful Type 5 activities is to include parent leaders from all of the racial and ethnic groups, socioeconomic groups, and geographic communities that are present in the middle grades school. This is a more difficult task in middle and junior high schools that typically draw from a wider and more diverse community than elementary schools. A related challenge is to help parents who are leaders to act as true representatives of the families they serve, with good two-way communications among parents, and between the school and the parent organizations or committees. A third challenge is to include middle grades student representatives in decision-making groups and leadership positions. An ongoing challenge is to assist school committee members to listen to each other, treat each other with respect, and take each other's ideas seriously as they work toward common goals for school improvement.

Outcomes. These activities should help reach goals and produce results to increase families' input on decisions that affect the quality of education for their children, students' awareness that families and students have a say in school policies, and teachers' understanding of family perspectives on policies and programs for improving the school.

Type 6

Collaborations and exchanges with the community refer to connections by schools, families, and students with agencies, businesses, religious organizations, cultural, and other groups in the community that share responsibility for children's education and interest in their futures. This includes middle grades schools' efforts to provide or coordinate students' and families' access to community and support services such as after-school recreation, tutorial programs, health services, cultural events, and other programs.

Middle grades schools vary in how much they draw on community resources to link to and strengthen work in the other types of involvement, and how much they inform families about these programs. Community resources may be tapped, for example, to provide parent education on adolescent development, as when local mental health groups run workshops in schools (Type 1); to improve schools' communications with families, as when local radio or cable TV stations assist with public service announcements or when churches, clinics, supermarkets, and laundromats assist with important communications from school to home (Type 2); to increase the number of volunteers at the school from the community or enlist business support for workers who are parents to volunteer or attend activities or conferences at the school (Type 3); to enhance and enrich the curriculum and other experiences of students, as when museums or business link their programs and services to school curricula for use in the schools or in the community sites (Type 4); and to extend participation on school committees to business and community representatives (Type 5). Thus, in addition to Type 6 being identifiable as a discrete connection to assist families and schools, community resources also can strengthen the other types of involvement (Epstein and Scott-Jones, in press).

As students enter adolescence their boundaries for exploration and education extend beyond home and school to the neighborhood and wider community. Many students take lessons outside of school, belong to organizations in the community, work or volunteer in the community, or participate in other community activities which have the potential to support and extend school-based learning. Community programs and resources can provide important experiences for students in and out of the school building. Middle grades schools can work to get the surrounding community to open opportunities to middle grades students and can help their students obtain equal access to these opportunities.

Other Type 6 activities implemented by middle grades schools to establish viable collaborations and exchanges with the community include a) small grants for demonstration projects to improve parent/adolescent communications; b) community organizations' "educational parties" for families in the homes of middle grades students to increase parental involvement in their children's education and to empower parents with advocacy skills, or community agency fairs to introduce families to local services; c) state legislation or community-developed policies that ask or require employers to allow employees who are parents to attend conferences with their children's teachers and other activities at the schools (including middle grades schools); d) state support and coordination of education, health, recreation, job training, and other services for 13-19 year-olds including sites at middle schools (see Center for the Future of Children, 1992); e) business partnerships for improving school programs, students' career explorations and opportunities, teacher internships, mentoring or tutoring programs for direct help to youngsters, mock job interviews, and for other reasons; f) school-sponsored telephone referral systems to community services for teens and families; and g) work-site seminars for workshops for parents who cannot come to the school.

Challenges. One challenge of successful Type 6 activities is to solve the problems often associated with community/school collaborations, such as poor communications about the multiple goals of the school, "turf" problems of who is in charge of collaborative activities, and whose funds are used for what purposes. Another challenge is for middle grades schools to find ways to link students' valuable learning experiences in the community to the school curricula and to recognize students' skills and talents that are developed in their community experiences.

Outcomes. These activities should help reach goals and produce results to increase the knowledge of families, students, and schools about the resources they can tap in their community to help them reach individual and common goals. Also, good coordination of school, family, and community resources should help more students solve some of the problems that arise in early adolescence before they become too serious. Type 6 activities also should support and enrich school curricula and extra-curricular programs.

Topics of Special Importance for Practices of Partnership in the Middle Grades

The framework of six types of involvement permits the selection of many different practices of school, family, and community partnerships in the middle grades. The practices selected also will be influenced by local, state, or national guidelines for school improvement and by emerging new directions for middle grades reform.

There are many topics concerning the characteristics of early adolescents, the features of middle grades schools, and teaching practices that influence the design of practices to inform families at this level of schooling. We have selected a few to introduce some issues that may be particularly important to families. They include early adolescent development, transitions to the middle grades, and specific practices such as interdisciplinary teams, untracking, student assessments, report cards, conferences, and school/community connections. Many other topics and examples are given in the discussion about the six types of involvement on the previous pages. With each topic we raise some questions for debate and discussion that may guide the design of new practices or may suggest questions for new research.

Features of middle grades schools. Middle grades practices to involve families will vary from those in the early grades because of many factors—such as the geographic location of the school, size of school and grade levels, and other organizational features. For example, the organization of programs and some practices of partnership in small K-12, rural schools with about 50 students per grade level will differ from those in large 7-9 junior high schools with over 500 students per grade level. Partnership practices also will change across the middle grades as developmental changes take early adolescents toward adolescence and young adulthood. That is, the connections with families need to change to reflect the characteristics of sixth graders, the uniqueness of seventh graders, and the status of eighth graders, or the features of students at any grade level in a middle grades school.

Here we discuss a few features of early adolescence and middle grades schools (i.e., the transition from the elementary grades and to high school; interdisciplinary teams; tracking or untracking) that are particularly relevant to the design and content of partnerships with families. There are many other topics about middle grades schools that may be similarly studied for how they affect school and family partnerships.

Early adolescent development. The most important aspect of middle grades schools is that they serve early adolescents. There are many characteristics of students at this age, but one worthy of attention is the simultaneous need for greater independence and continued guidance and supervision. This seeming conflict has serious implications for school and family partnerships.

As early adolescents struggle to gain or increase their independence, they may be resistant to family involvement in their middle grades schools. Recent studies indicate that young adolescents want their families involved as knowledgeable partners at home, but they may not want their peers to know that they still need their families' guidance. Students may not be sure where they fit in school and family partnerships, if neither teachers nor parents acknowledge and explain the students' roles. Data suggest that early adolescents want their families to support them in learning activities at home and accept their assistance in school, but in different roles than were common in the elementary grades (Epstein & Dauber, in press; Epstein & Herrick 1991; Montandon & Perrenoud, 1987).

Families and schools also may be initially resistant to practices of family involvement because they may see adolescents in the middle grades as bigger and older and, therefore, less in need of adult "help." There may be a tendency to reduce involvement and interaction if it is viewed as interfering with the development of student independence. The fact is, however, that students become more independent if their families and other adults remain age-appropriately informed and involved in their education (Epstein, 1983).

In research and in practice we need to discuss and study:

- What methods are effective in reducing resistance and increasing acceptance of students, families, and teachers of new school/family partnership practices in the middle grades?

- How can middle grades students be given a central role in the design and implementation of family/school partnership practices so that they understand how such practices meet their needs for independence and for guidance?

- What are the benefits to students, parents, and teachers from various practices to inform and involve families in the middle grades? Which practices have the most benefits for families, without threatening students' development of independence or diminishing their sense of self or feelings of competence?

Transitions from elementary grades and to the high school grades. One of the defining features of the middle grades is that students usually experience two transitions—from the elementary to the middle grades school and from the middle grades to the high school. Although most schools take time to assist students with these transitions, few schools systematically include families. Yet, each time a student changes schools, the family makes the transition with the child. At each point of transition, families need good information from schools in order to communicate knowledgeably with their children during these important, exciting, but potentially stressful times. Elementary, middle, and high schools need ways to work separately and together as "feeder" and "receiver" sites to inform and involve families so that they can interact with and assist their children to make successful adjustments to new situations. This includes the orientation to the middle grades and to new settings and relationships, and the preparations for high school course work and plans for the future.

Only about 40% of the middle grades schools in the country have programs that involve the families at key transition points (Epstein & Mac Iver, 1990). In those that do, the elementary school may start the process by orienting families to the schools their children will attend, first with activities and information at the elementary school, moving on to visits with middle grades representatives at the elementary and then at the middle grades school. The middle grades school may pick up the process of transition with mailings, contacts, and other visits in the summer and into the fall after the transition is made. Similar patterns of pre-transition and post-transition information, interactions, and visits are conducted by some feeder and receiver schools as students and their families move on to high school. The activities familiarize students and families with the buildings, programs, and changes in courses, expectations, and opportunities that they will meet in their new school.

The data also indicate that middle grades schools that involve families before the transition are more likely to continue other parent involvement practices through the middle grades. Thus, family involvement at points of transition also helps families continue their involvement with the schools.

In research and in practice we need to discuss and study:

- How can families be prepared to understand the transitions their children will make and to understand the kinds of support that will be helpful to their children?

- What is the most useful schedule, form, and content of articulation activities for families and students to be scheduled while students are still in the elementary grades, after the transition to the middle grades, and before moving on to high school?

- What are the benefits to students, parents, and teachers from practices that include families in the transitions experienced by middle grades students?

Interdisciplinary teams. One of the common complaints of middle grades teachers when asked about family involvement is, "I have too many students to pay attention to their families!" Interdisciplinary teams are groups of 4 or 5 teachers of different disciplines who work together in a team or cluster and share responsibility for a common group of about 125-150 students. Teams, created to reduce student anonymity and teacher isolation, may improve family/school partnerships in the middle grades. Teachers can work together to inform families about the new forms of teachers' teams, as parents may be unfamiliar with the construct. The teachers on a team may work together to develop effective practices to involve families. One of the most common uses for team planning time is for meetings with parents and students. Conferences are often a team activity, saving parents and teachers time. Teachers who share students can share some of the other activities that require contacting families, can mobilize family support more cohesively, and can coordinate homework assignments that require students to seek family involvement in order to balance demands for family time.

Also, in addition to their contacts with teachers, students and their families on a team have more opportunities to get to know one another, support each other in learning activities, and develop a sense of community through their shared experiences at school.

In research and in practice we need to discuss and study:

- In what ways can interdisciplinary teams offer new opportunities for parents to become better informed about middle grades programs and features (e.g., courses, grading, opportunities available to their children), and about how to help their early adolescents succeed in the middle grades?

- How can interdisciplinary teams of teachers "share the load" of designing and implementing family involvement practices for their team?

- What are the benefits to students, parents, and teachers from various practices that teachers on interdisciplinary teams use to inform and involve families?

Untracking. Many middle grades schools involved in restructuring efforts are changing their practices of tracking students by ability to "untracking" students in mixed-ability classes. Families need to know about the policies and practices that schools use to group their children in various ways, and why the practices have been chosen. In a national study of middle schools that were untracking their classes, principals reported that parents could make or break their efforts to reduce or eliminate tracking, and emphasized the need to involve families early in the process of planning and implementing heterogeneous groups (Wheelock, 1992). Families may be included through informational workshops, observations in classrooms, talking with families in other schools who have experienced successful untracking, giving parents and students choices of placements in some or all heterogeneous or homogeneous classes, discussions through the year about the curriculum, grouping practices, and student progress, and other ways.

In research and in practice we need to discuss and study:

- What kinds of information, and in what forms, do parents need about tracking or untracking in order for them to understand the issues, contribute ideas and suggestions to the school, and support their children in the placements that result?

- What is the student's role in the school's placement policies? How can schools help students and their families if the decision is to move from tracked to "untracked" courses?

- What are the benefits to students, parents, and teachers from contrasting strategies to inform and involve families about grouping strategies?

Student assessment. Alternative assessment strategies are being explored in many states and districts, such as the use of portfolios (e.g., Vermont, Rhode Island), other performance-based assessments, and new standardized tests of higher level skills (e.g., Connecticut, California, Maryland). How should families be informed about new national, state, and local standards on which their children will be judged? What should families know about the changes in assessment goals, forms, and content, and about what the new assessments mean for their children's progress and work in school? As one example, "The Portfolio Project," funded by the Rockefeller Foundation, is testing the use of portfolios in eight urban and two rural middle schools, however the role of parents and other family members is not given systematic attention. New standards, tests, and other evaluations can be confusing to families. They need good information about the assessments and about their results in order to support their children as they experience new evaluations, and as they help their children work to improve skills to meet higher standards and to make plans for the future.

In research and in practice we need to discuss and study:

- What information do parents need in order to support a school's adoption of new assessment strategies? In order to support their children's participation in new types of tests?

- In what ways should families be involved in designing, implementing, or evaluating alternative assessment strategies? In helping other parents under-

159

stand confusing aspects of tests or other components of middle grades assessment programs?

- What are the benefits to students, parents, and schools when connections are made with families about new standards and new assessments?

Report cards. While parents generally report satisfaction with the information they receive on report cards, most parents would like more information (Olhausen & Powell, 1992). Parents are rarely asked for input into the design of reporting systems (Reid, 1984). As traditional grading systems are replaced or supplemented with the introduction of alternative assessment strategies, other methods for reporting student progress will be needed and may supplement or replace current report card forms. In the middle grades, the form and content of report cards often change from those used in the earlier grades, and the components that determine grades also change. Families are usually not informed about these changes, or about how to interpret the grades, or how to guide their early adolescents toward better performance.

In research and in practice we need to discuss and study:

- What information do parents need and want about student achievements, report cards, and progress?

- What roles can students play in developing new methods of reporting progress, making self-assessments, sharing their progress or problems with their families, and working on improving their work and behavior with their teachers and families?

- What are the benefits to students, parents, and teachers when connections are made with families about various forms and contents of report cards?

Parent/teacher/student conferences. Some suggest that all parent/teacher conferences in the middle grades should include the student (Deborah Meier, personal communication, 1992), and that all communications between school and family should also be shared with and involve the student. In other words, there should be no parent/teacher conspiracies during early adolescence when the student's skills in self-direction and self-regulation are rapidly developing. Others suggest that there are times when parents and teachers may meet to get to know one another and talk informally, even if the student is not present. Schools need to think about these questions and related practices as they build their connections with families.

In some middle grades schools that are organized with teacher teams, conferences with parents (or with parents and students) are conducted as a team activity allowing parents to meet with all teachers at one time instead of requiring four or five conferences. Also, in some middle grades schools, portfolio conferences and other performance-based demonstrations of student achievement may replace traditional parent/teacher conferences. Other schools are devising procedures for a series of three or four conferences a year, akin to the individualized educational plan meetings that have been used in special education, but for all students (as in some Utah demonstration sites). These reformations must be explained to families so that they can participate comfortably. One challenge to educators is to design conference procedures that inform parents of their student's achievements and allow families to share their own perspectives on their child's education and development. (Also see Chrispeels, 1988; Epstein, 1988b; and Swap, 1992.) Another challenge is to create an integrated system of student assessments, including report card forms and conferences, to give parents, teachers, and students several opportunities to come together to share ideas with each other about how to help students make the greatest progress in their learning and development.

In research and in practice we need to discuss and study:

- What are the purposes of parent/teacher(/student) conferences?

- Are there other methods that enable teachers, students, and families to share information, concerns, and achievements?

- Can students take more active roles in conferences to reflect the student-centered philosophy of middle grades education and new assessments?

- What are the benefits to students, parents, and teachers from contrasting conferencing strategies?

School/community partnerships. Collaborations or partnerships between schools and universities, businesses, health organizations, and other institutions and associations in the community provide opportunities for schools to offer services to students that the school system alone could not afford to provide. A major challenge to middle grades schools is to structure these partnerships so that the resources from the community support the school's overall goals for programs, students, and connections with families. For example, mentoring and tutoring programs, school-based health clinics, homework clubs or after school centers, and school/business partnerships rarely include programmatic components to facilitate family involvement. There is a danger that families feel left out or, in some settings, that they are being replaced by well-intentioned but insensitive adults. Families need to be informed of their student's participation in these activities, given information so that they can support their child in the program and discuss their activities.

In research and in practice we need to discuss and study:

- What strategies should be implemented to inform and include families in school/family/community partnerships?

- What roles should families play in school-business partnerships, mentoring programs, and other activities that link their children with members of the community?

- How should schools organize and structure partnership activities so that all families and students have equal access to services and opportunities offered by school/community partnerships?

- What are the benefits to students, parents, and teachers from alternative ways of organizing community connections?

Comprehensive School and Family Partnerships

A comprehensive program of partnership includes practices from all six types of involvement that have been selected to help produce specific outcomes of importance to students, to families, and to teachers. Schools develop their programs by providing "the basics" in each of the six types, and adding at least one new practice from each type of involvement each year to reach more and more families. Another way to develop a more comprehensive program is to recognize and work on the challenges associated with each type of involvement in order to improve practices each year. Or, schools may be assisted in program development by considering the components of middle grades education that families need to understand (the transition to a new school; new rules about attendance; new approaches such as teaming, grouping, grading; and others), and by creating practices to communicate with families about these features that affect their children's success in school.

Comprehensive programs of partnership in the middle grades can be developed if committees of teachers, parents, students, and others worked together to design or select, implement, and assess practices to accomplish the goals they set together for improving school practices to involve families. A coordinator or lead teacher is needed to oversee and advise the organization and implementation of new activities, or to help solve problems that arise as new practices are tried and tested. Each year, or more frequently, progress should be shared on each of the six types of involvement; practices should be reviewed, continued or improved, dropped or added; and excellent work by teachers, families, students, or others in the community should be recognized. Over time, these investments, efforts, and collaborations should lead to more comprehensive programs of partnership to benefit middle grades students.

Conclusion

The main goals of family and school connections in the years of early adolescence are to help youngsters maintain good health, develop positive attitudes toward learning, continue to succeed in school, and set high expectations, plans, and strategies for high school and for the future. More students will meet these goals if schools, families, and communities join in partnership to work to encourage and assist the children they share.

Families need the school staff to give them information about critical issues facing teens which will help families make decisions with their adolescents. Schools need information from families on their goals, values, expectations, interests, and needs to fully understand the children they serve and to help plan school programs that will engage all students. Middle grades students need to know that their families, teachers, and others at school and in the community are available to support them as students and to help them deal with the inevitable challenges of adolescence.

We have summarized a research-based theory, a framework for action, and examples of practices that may help middle grades schools move beyond rhetoric about parent involvement into productive family/school/community partnerships.

Three themes underlie the design of comprehensive programs of partnerships in the middle grades: equity, development, and quality. The following questions on each theme may help to guide the selection and implementation of practices.

Questions of equity ask: Are all families included and informed so that they can be involved with their own children at home in productive activities to boost student motivation and learning? Are programs and opportunities designed and implemented so that all families feel welcome to participate at school?

Questions of development ask: Do practices of partnership reflect the changes that occur from the elementary to the middle grades in the characteristics of students, families. and schools? Do practices of partnership also account for the diversity at each middle grade level in the characteristics and needs of students, families, and teachers?

Questions of quality ask: Are practices to involve families in their children's education well designed? Are the practices worthy of the time of teachers, parents, and students? Are evaluations conducted to determine if practices are successfully implemented and if they have the effects or results that they were selected to produce?

Middle grades schools have lagged behind preschools and elementary schools in developing comprehensive programs to involve families. In most middle grades improvement plans, "parent involvement" is on the list of important components, but is often ignored or treated casually. With the heightened awareness of the importance of the shared responsibilities of schools and families in the education and development of early adolescents, and with advances in theories, research, policies, and practices of partnership, the time is right for middle grades educators and researchers who study early adolescents and their schools to join the agenda.

References

Bauch, P.A. (1988). Is parent involvement different in private schools? *Educational Horizons*, 66(2), 78-82.

Benson, P. (1991). *The troubled journey: A portrait of 6th-12th grade youth*. Minneapolis, MN: Search Institute.

Brandt, R. (1989). On parents and schools: A conversation with Joyce Epstein. *Educational Leadership*, 17(2), 24-27.

Center for the Future of Children. (1992). School linked services. *The Future of Children*, 2(1), 4-144.

Chrispeels, J., Bourta, M., & Daugherty, M. (1988). *Communicating with parents*. San Diego, CA: San Diego Public Schools.

Chrispeels, J. (1988). Building collaboration through parent-teacher conferencing. *Educational Horizons*, 66(2), 84-86.

Comer, J.P. (1980). *School power: Implications of an intervention project*. New York: Free Press.

Comer, J.P. (1988). Educating poor minority children. *Scientific American*, 259(5), 42-48.

Dauber, S.L., & Epstein, J.L. (1993). Parents' attitudes and practices of involvement in inner-city elementary and middle schools. In N. Chavkin (Ed.). *Families and schools in a pluralistic society*, (pp. 53-71). Albany, NY: State University of New York Press.

Davies, D., Burch, P., & Johnson, V. (1992). *A portrait of schools reaching out: Report of a survey on practices and policies of family-community-school collaboration*. (Report 1). Baltimore, MD: John Hopkins University, Center on Families, Communities, Schools and Childrens Learning.

Dolan, L., & Caroselli, M. (1982). Parent involvement as a means to improve writing skills in secondary schools. *Research in the Teaching of English*, 16, 288-294.

Dornbusch, S.M., & Ritter, P.L. (1988). Parents of high school students: A neglected resource. *Educational Horizons*, 66(2), 75-77.

Epstein, J.L. (1983). Longitudinal effects of family-school person interactions on student outcomes. In A. Kerckhoff (Ed.), *Research in sociology of education and socialization*, Vol. 4. (pp. 101-128), Greenwich, CT: JAI Press.

Epstein, J.L. (1986). Parents' reactions to teacher practices of parent involvement. *The Elementary School Journal*, 86, 277-294.

Epstein, J.L. (1987a). Toward a theory of family-school connections: Teacher practices and parent involvement. In K. Hurrelmann, F. Kaufmann, & F. Losel (Eds.), *Social intervention: Potential and constraints*, (pp. 121-136). New York: DeGruyter.

Epstein, J.L. (1987b). What principals should know about parent involvement. *Principal*, 66(3), 6-9.

Epstein, J.L. (1988a). *Schools in the center: School, family, peer, and community connections for more effective middle grades schools and students*. Baltimore, MD: The Johns Hopkins University.

Epstein, J.L. (1988b). Parent-teacher conferences. In R. Gorton, G. Schneider, & J. Fisher (Eds.) *Encyclopedia of school administration and supervision* (pp. 189-191). Phoenix, AZ: Oryx.

Epstein, J.L. (1991). Effects on student achievement of teacher practices of parent involvement. In S. Silvern (Ed.), *Literacy through family, community, and school interaction*, (pp. 261-276). Greenwich, CT: JAI Press.

Epstein, J.L. (1992). School and family partnerships. In M. Alkin (Ed.), *Encyclopedia of educational research*, 6th Edition, (pp. 1139-1151). New York: MacMillan.

Epstein, J.L. & Connors, L.J. (1992). Schools and family partnerships in middle grades and high schools. *Practitioner*, 18(4), 1-8.

Epstein, J.L., & Dauber, S.L. (in press). Effects on students of an interdisciplinary program linking social studies, art, and family volunteers in the middle grades. *Journal of Early Adolescence*.

Epstein, J.L., & Dauber, S.L. (1991). School programs and teacher practices of parent involvement in inner-city elementary and middle schools. *Elementary School Journal, 91,* 289-303.

Epstein, J.L., Herrick, S.C., & Coates, L. (in press). Effects of summer home learning pockets on student achievement in language arts in the middle grades. *School Effectiveness and School Improvement.*

Epstein, J.L., & Herrick, S.C., (1991). *Improving school and family partnerships in urban middle grades schools: Orientation days and school newsletters.* (Report 20). Baltimore, MD: The Johns Hopkins University.

Epstein, J.L., Jackson, V., & Salinas, K.C. (1992). *Manual for teachers: Teachers involve parents in schoolwork (TIPS) language arts and science/health interactive homework in the middle grades.* Baltimore, MD: The Johns Hopkins University.

Epstein, J.L., & Lee, S. (1992, March). *National patterns of school and family connections in the middle grades.* Paper presented at the annual meeting of the Society for Research on Adolescence, Washington, DC.

Epstein, J.L., & Mac Iver, D.J. (1990). *Education in the middle grades: National practices and trends.* Columbus, OH: National Middle School Association.

Epstein, J.L., & Salinas, K.C. (1991). *TIPS social studies and art manual and prototype activities.* Baltimore, MD: The Johns Hopkins University Center on Families, Communities, Schools, and Children's Learning.

Johns, J., & Panofsky, C. (1987). *The Homestart Program evaluation report.* Albuquerque, NM: Albuquerque Public Schools.

Leitch, M.L., & Tangri, S.S. (1988). Barriers to home-school collaboration. *Educational Horizons,* 66(2), 70-74.

Marockie, H., & Jones, H.L. (1987). Reducing dropout rates through home-school communication. *Education and Urban Society,* 19, 200-205.

Meier, D. (1992. Personal Communication.

Montandon, C., & Perrenoud, P. (1987). *Entre parents et ensignants un diologue impossible?* Berne, Switzerland: P. Lang.

Offer, D., Ostrov, D., Howard, K.I., & Atkinson, R. (1988). *Teenage world: Adolescent self image in ten countries.* New York: Putnam.

Olhausen, M., & Powell, R. (1992, April). *Parents: What do they think about traditional and alternative reporting systems?* Paper presented at the annual meeting of the American Educational Research Association, San Francisco.

Reid, M. (1984). School reports to parents: A study of policy and practice in the secondary school. *Educational Research,* 26(2), 82-86.

Rutherford, B., Billig, S., & Kettering, J. (1994). *Creating family/school partnerships: A review of the research and literature on parent and community involvement related to the middle grades.* Denver, CO: RMC Research Corporation.

Stevenson, D., & Baker, D. (1987). The family-school relation and the child's school performance. *Child Development,* 58, 1348-1357.

Swap, S.M. (1992). *Developing home-school partnerships: From concepts to practice.* New York: Teachers College Press.

Useem, E.L. (1992). Middle schools and math groups: Parents' involvement in children's placement. *Sociology of Education,* 65, 263-279.

Youniss, J., & Smollar, J. (1989). *Adolescent relations with mothers, fathers, and friends.* Chicago, IL: University of Chicago Press.

Chapter 4

Activities in the Home That Support School Learning in the
Middle Grades

Diane Scott-Jones

Researchers and practitioners now widely acknowledge the importance of under-standing the social contexts of students' education and learning. Families and communities, in addition to schools, are recognized as important contexts in which students learn and are educated. Considerable attention has been directed toward the interactions of parents and young children and the activities in the home that support learning and school achievement. Because researchers and practitioners have focused on young children, however, gaps exist in our knowledge of the social con-texts of education in early adolescence. Findings from research with young children may not be generalizable to adolescents because of the many developmental differ-ences between the two age groups and the changes in the structure and content of schooling from elementary to middle schools. Parental involvement in learning activities in the home and in school activities declines precipitously after the early elementary grades (Dauber & Epstein, 1992; Epstein, 1986; Stevenson & Baker, 1987). In addition, young adolescents may begin a downward spiral in the middle grades, with a decline in letter grades and in motivation (Eccles, Midgley, Wigfield, Buchanan, Flanagan, & Mac Iver, 1993). Because of these declines, it is necessary to understand what remains important in home activities through the middle grades and how positive home learning activities can be fostered for middle grades students.

What are the specific activities in homes that support school learning in the mid-dle grades? With young children, these activities are closely related to children's play and to their toys (see Levenstein, 1988; Scott-Jones, 1987). Home learning activities for young children are "fun"; many toys and games are constructed in a manner that helps children acquire basic concepts and skills. Parents' reading to and with chil-dren is an activity that supports the acquisition of early reading skills (Mason & Kerr, 1992) but is also quite enjoyable to most parents and children. In the middle grades, much of home learning activities centers around homework. The change in activities in the home that support school learning is aptly denoted by the use of the word "work." No longer clearly in the realm of fun and play, "homework" is a serious enterprise, to be completed before turning to more pleasant, less structured activities.

Homework is emphasized in this paper as the focus of home learning activities in the middle grades because of its relationship to later achievement. Keith, Reimers, Fehrmann, Pottebaum, and Aubey (1986), using the national High School and Beyond survey, found that time spent on homework had a strong positive effect on reading and mathematics achievement. The parental variables assessed in the study (parents' monitoring of students' school performance, knowledge of students' whereabouts, and influence on students' post-high school plans) had no direct effect on achievement. Television viewing had a small negative effect on achievement. Parents, however, can attempt to influence middle grades students' homework and other related activities in the home.

Some parents may be able to help directly with the skills middle grades students are mastering as they do homework. Many parents, however, may themselves lack some of the skills the students are learning. In addition, some parents who have the needed skills may not be able to sustain positive interactions as they try to teach their young adolescents. Therefore, it is necessary to augment the notion of "parent as teacher," which was developed from work with young children, to include other ways parents influence young adolescents.

Four levels of parental involvement are hypothesized for homework[1]. These levels are valuing, monitoring, helping, and doing. Parental helping focuses on the acquisition of basic skills such as skills in mathematics or reading. Valuing and monitoring are conceptualized as interactions in families affecting students' motivation and engagement in the processes of learning and schooling, even when those interactions are not directly focused on teaching children specific cognitive skills. Finally, we hypothesize a fourth level, doing, in which parents are overly involved in their students' school work—to the extent of actually doing the work for the students.

Underlying the hypothesized four levels of parental involvement is the lifespan human development perspective. The next section provides a brief overview of this broad theoretical perspective as it relates to learning activities in the homes of middle grades students. The following four sections describe the hypothesized levels of parental involvement in learning activities in the home: valuing, monitoring, helping, and doing. Although the focus is on homework, other aspects of home learning activities are included. The final section of the paper summarizes and suggests future directions for research and practice in home learning in the middle grades.

Life-Span Perspective

The broad theoretical perspective underlying this work is a life span human development perspective, which emphasizes human development in sociocultural and sociohistorical context. The contexts of development—families, communities, and schools—are interconnected and are embedded in the larger economic, institutional, and ideological patterns of society (Bronfenbrenner, 1979, 1986; Epstein, 1987; Epstein & Scott-Jones, in press). Diversity—in socioeconomic status, ethnicity, and family structure—is an important element of developmental contexts. The life span developmental perspective emphasizes the possibility of change throughout the life span (Lerner, 1986). This perspective is in sharp contrast to the view that children's basic capacity to learn is fixed early in life. The developmental view leads to optimism regarding intervention: Although change may be easier to effect in the preschool or early school years, students' capacity for improvement is not lost as they advance through the middle grades. Continuous attention throughout infancy, childhood, and adolescence is necessary for maximum educational productivity (Stipek, Valentine, & Zigler, 1979). In addition, parents as well as children change over time, and the family's role in education and schooling changes substantially as children progress through the school grades (Scott-Jones, 1988).

During the middle school years, children experience many developmental changes. Most notably, children may reach puberty during this time period; girls are, on average, two years ahead of boys in this aspect of their development. The physical changes of adolescence are more rapid and more dramatic than at any other time during the life span, with the exception of infancy. Adolescence is an important period in students' lives. As children enter adolescence, they view themselves as gaining in responsibility and independence (Pipp, Shaver, Jennings, Lamborn, & Fischer, 1985). Many young adolescents make decisions and engage in behaviors that have lasting effects on their adult lives. The middle grades may be important to students' later career aspirations and goals. For example, Clewell and Anderson (1992) concluded that the middle grades are a crucial time when female students are in the greatest danger of leaving the science track. Continued engagement in school during the middle grades is critical for later educational success and for the prevention of social problems, such as drug abuse and unplanned pregnancy, that currently plague American youth.

In addition to changes within the individual, the structure of schools changes in the middle grades. Students make an important transition from elementary school to middle school. Middle schools may diminish the teacher-student relationship (August, 1988). The typical elementary school organization, in which one teacher remains with students for the entire school day, is replaced by departmentalized instruction, with different teachers responsible for different subjects (McPartland, 1987; McPartland, Coldiron, & Braddock, 1987). There is a relatively high rate of teacher turnover (August, 1988) and teachers' sense of their own efficacy may diminish (Eccles et al., 1993). In addition, African-American and other minority students may not be taught by minority teachers. Although the proportion of minorities in the student population has increased, the proportion of minorities in the teaching force has declined sharply. In 1971, almost 12% of teachers were minorities; by the year 2000, that proportion is expected to drop below 5% (Nicklos & Brown, 1989).

The structure of middle schools may diminish the sense of belongingness among students and their parents that might have been present in the elementary years. Many academic and adjustment problems, which may have had their origins in the earlier grades, become apparent or are exacerbated (August, 1988). Middle school programs and practices often do not encourage parental involvement; parents and teachers may have negative views of one another. Extensive interviews of teachers and parents in two junior high schools serving low-income African-American populations indicated that teachers tend to blame parents for their children's problems. Parents located some problems within themselves and their circumstances but also cited teachers' attitudes and behavior as problems (Leitch & Tangri, 1988; Tangri & Leitch, 1982).

Change also is occurring for the parents of adolescents (see Demick, Bursik, & Dibiase, 1993, for broad discussion of parental development). Adolescents' parents will be of different ages and at different points in their own development. For some adolescents, other relatives such as grandparents may act as parents. Typically, adolescents' parents, compared to the parents of younger children, are facing greater economic pressures, more job responsibilities, more marital dissatisfaction, and more health problems. These various aspects of parents' lives will affect their engagement in learning activities with their young adolescents in the home. Parents must strive to maintain a balance between control and responsiveness as their young adolescents become increasingly independent.

Because of the extensive and sometimes abrupt changes that occur in students, schools, and parents in the middle grades, many barriers to positive learning activities in the home may exist. Adolescents, however, greatly need assistance and support in the family. Adolescents need to maintain a sense of connectedness to the family at the same time they begin to establish an individual identity and a sense of independence (Cooper, Grotevant, & Condon, 1983).

Valuing

We hypothesize that an important component of the academic socialization of middle grades students is the direct and indirect communication of the value of education. Parents' valuing of learning, education, and schooling is part of parents' belief system which in turn serves as a cognitive mediator of parents' interactions with their children (see Scott-Jones, 1984, for review). Communication regarding the prestige and authority of the teacher (Ginsburg, Bembechat & Chung, 1992) is important as is communication regarding respect for the school as an institution. Much of what children learn about the value of education may result, not from direct teaching by parents, but from children's observation of parents in their everyday lives (Nickerson, 1992). Parental beliefs about effort and ability, and messages they convey to children about the value of effort and ability, may be important. Bempechat (1992) suggests that Asian and Asian-American parents' strong belief in the value of effort is related to their children's high achievement. Placing a high value on the role of personal effort in achievement, and a correspondingly low value on the role of innate abilities, is thought to lead to children's being disciplined and persistent even when their school work is difficult.

In addition to conveying the value of education and schooling generally, parents need to convey the value of specific subjects such as mathematics (Marshall, 1992). Parents and students should believe that mathematical knowledge gives them personal power in their lives. Marshall (1992) gives examples of ways parents can establish the value of mathematics by working with students on projects, such as building a stereo cabinet or deciding on and purchasing items for a party, that require some knowledge of and use of mathematics. Marshall's examples, however, are of activities more likely to occur in middle and upper income homes than in poor homes. Researchers and practitioners need to direct more attention toward activities that would be feasible for a broad range of families and students.

Nickerson (1992) argues that the transmission of values, beliefs, and attitudes that motivate the development of cognitive skills, and the humane use of those skills, is more important than the transmission of the skills. Without denying the importance of skills, Nickerson asserts that a higher priority should be placed on parents' transmitting to their children a sense of inquisitiveness, love of learning, awareness of their own intellectual potential, and a commitment to fair-mindedness. In spite of the importance of family values regarding education, Ginsburg et al. (1992) suggest that programs cannot teach parents to convey these values to their children. These authors assert that values develop in a complex manner and cannot be taught in relatively brief training sessions. Further, according to these authors, social and economic conditions in society may weaken parental valuing of education, particularly in low-income and minority groups. Ginsburg et al. (1992) suggest that programs may provide experiences that influence parents' construction of their values and beliefs related to education. Further, Eccles and Harold (1993) suggest that involving middle grades parents in school governance is important for learning activities in the home. Eccles and Harold suggest that if parents help to develop school goals, they are more likely to agree with them, to become invested in them, and to foster them at home.

Monitoring

Parents' monitoring includes establishing rules regarding homework, establishing a routine and schedule for students' studying and completing homework, and checking that homework is completed. Also important is monitoring activities that might interfere with schoolwork such as television viewing. Monitoring is enhanced when parents are aware of the kinds of courses students take and how students are performing in those courses. Parental awareness of students' courses and performance levels appears to vary according to socioeconomic status. Baker and Stevenson (1986) interviewed mothers of eighth graders who were making the transition from middle school to high school. Mothers with high educational levels were more likely than other mothers to be able to identify the student's best and worst subjects.

Another aspect of parental monitoring is helping the middle grades student to develop self-monitoring or self-management skills. Students need experience in planning. For example, students need to learn to plan the amount of time to be spent on homework. For long-term projects, they need to plan the timing and sequence of work from beginning to deadline. Non-school tasks, including chores, hobbies, and household and family management, are hypothesized to support school learning indirectly through the middle grades students' acquisition of self-management skills and learning strategies: planning, persistence, practice, flexibility, and confidence. Parents can help their middle grades students acquire these self-management skills and learning strategies as they perform non-school tasks.

Parental monitoring of middle grades students is complicated by the young adolescents' needs to establish some level of autonomy while still benefitting from the protection and guidance of parents. Adolescence is no longer characterized as a time when young people necessarily break away from or reject their parents (Cooper et al., 1983). Instead, the relationship with parents becomes transformed during this time. Adolescents establish their independence and individuality but also maintain a connectedness to their families.

Adolescents perceive their parents as gradually exerting less control (Dornbusch, Ritter, Leiderman, Roberts & Fraleigh, 1987; Steinberg, 1987). Parental influence may become more indirect as adolescents internalize parental values and use those values when they have opportunities for independent decision-making. Parental control is not relinquished entirely, however. Parental control appears to become increasingly domain specific. For example, middle-class white 12 to 19 year-olds gradually gain control over their style of dress but believe their parents retain the right to set standards for their school performance (Youniss & Smollar, 1985). Parents still may establish rules and monitor the adolescents' behavior. Parents also may communicate with adolescents regarding important aspects of their behavior and development, encourage adolescents to express their own opinions and feelings, and respond to input from adolescents in setting and enforcing rules.

Students' school performance is positively associated with parents' exerting firm control, through clear standards for behavior, but also responding to adolescents' needs and desires, allowing them input into decisions, and maintaining open communication (Dornbusch et al., 1987). In a long-standing typology, this parenting style, consisting of appropriately high levels of both control and responsiveness, is labeled authoritative (Baumrind, 1966; 1991). In contrast, authoritarian parents are high on control and low on responsiveness; permissive parents are low on control and high on responsiveness.

Ethnic and socioeconomic status differences may exist in these parenting styles (Baumrind, 1972). According to Dornbusch et al. (1987), Asian, Black, and Hispanic adolescents reported higher levels of authoritarian parenting than did whites. Adolescents from lower socioeconomic status families rated their parents higher on the indicators of authoritarian parenting than did middle socioeconomic status adolescents. Further, the positive relationship between authoritative parenting and school performance was greatest for white students. Baumrind's typology was developed from studies of middle income white children and families. Comparisons with other groups may be misleading (Baumrind, 1972). Careful study of various family contexts may be needed to clarify parents' use of control and responsiveness.

Clark (1983) provided case study descriptions of high and low achieving Black high school seniors, all from low income single or two parent families. Although Clark did not use Baumrind's typology, the dimension of control figured prominently in the homes of high achievers. Parents of high achievers appeared to exert control over their children and supervise them closely but not excessively. These parents believed that education was a means of social mobility; they monitored homework and interacted positively with the school. In contrast, low achieving students' families appeared to be in a state of great despair. With fewer social and material resources than the families of high achievers, the families of low achievers had struggled unsuccessfully for many years and appeared resigned to their economic conditions.

Monitoring of young adolescents may be more difficult when there is limited parental time or only one parent in the home but the actual effect of family structure may have been exaggerated. Recent structural changes in families, particularly the rise in single parent households and in employment of mothers outside the home, have been cited as reasons for the problems adolescents experience. These changes in families are interpreted by some as representative of a decline in parental commitment to their children. To test this hypothesis, Furstenberg and Condran (1988) analyzed data on family structure and on measures of adolescent well-being for African-Americans and whites from 1940 to 1980. The researchers concluded that the empirical evidence does not support a link between family change and change in adolescent behavior during this time period. For example, the percentage of 18 to 24 year old African-Americans who graduated from high school increased as their family conditions were deteriorating. Further, the correspondence between family change and change in adolescent well-being is lower for African-Americans than for whites.

The community or neighborhood in which the family lives may affect parents' use of control with adolescents. Parents who live in neighborhoods where high achievement in school is not the norm, and where drugs and violence may pull young adolescents from their focus on school, may find it necessary to use strict controlling strategies and to monitor students closely. These parents may exert high levels of control, in comparison to parents who live in safer neighborhoods, but the control and monitoring may be appropriate for the context. Similarly, adolescents' behavior may affect parents' use of control. Adolescents who do not follow rules may lead parents to exert more control than is beneficial.

The potential negative outcomes of parental control may be offset by the responsiveness of parents to their children. A responsive parent is informed about and sensitive to the young adolescents' developing skills and behavior and thus is able to provide appropriate control. Responsiveness incorporates the affective component of the parent-adolescent relationship. Parents may monitor and control adolescents' behavior effectively in the context of a responsive and caring relationship.

The role parental monitoring can play is illustrated in Dr. Benjamin S. Carson's description of his school and family experiences ("Scientist at Work", 1993). Dr. Carson, a noted pediatric neurosurgeon, is African-American and grew up in a low-income urban area in a single-parent home. Recalling that he was considered the "class dummy" in fifth grade, he indicated that he began to excel because of his mother's requirements. She restricted him and his brother to two or three television programs per week and required them to read and write reports for her on two books per week from the public library. His performance turned around; he finished high school third in his class and went to Yale on an academic scholarship. Years later, Dr. Carson discovered that his mother could not read those book reports. Thus, parental monitoring can be beneficial even in the absence of parental academic skills.

Helping

To help directly with school skills, parents of middle grades students must themselves possess the skills and must be able to gauge when they have given an appropriate amount of help—not too much and not too little. Parents' helping their children may follow the model of expert-novice or apprenticeship learning. In this model, parents are knowledgeable about the topic students are learning and, if the interactions have the appropriate emotional tone, can provide invaluable assistance. Parents help only as needed and gradually move the child to higher levels of independent performance (see Rogoff, 1990, for discussion of this model developed mainly for young children). Alternatively, parents' helping may follow the model of learning together. In this model, parents may learn about a subject along with the student. Finally, when parents have exhausted their resources for helping, they may contribute by identifying other sources of help for the young adolescent. Each of these three models is discussed below in relation to middle grades students and their parents.

Expert-novice. One aspect of parents' helping with homework that may change as children progress from elementary to middle schools is the parents' own mastery of the specific content of various subjects middle grades students are learning. An adequate level of literacy is required for parents to help with students' learning activities at home. Middle grades students' academic work is more difficult than that of elementary school students. Unlike the preschool and early elementary years, when many parents can help children acquire basic concepts, such as shape and number, and can read simple stories, in the middle grades students must acquire increasingly complex and abstract knowledge and skills. Parents who provided appropriate learning activities for their young children may have more difficulty when their children are in the middle grades. Parents' helping with homework is a radically different enterprise for a parent of a sixth-grader than for the parent of a second-grader. Older students may have closed the knowledge gap between themselves and their parents in some subject areas; in addition, older students in general do not value close parental teaching interactions as much as do young children.

Parents' skills may not be adequate for the level of work required in the middle grades. In addition, parents may feel themselves unable to provide assistance, or students may perceive their parents as lacking in requisite skills. Any of the these possibilities — the actual lack of parental academic skills, or the parents' or students' perception of a lack of parental skills — could lead to less parental help with homework in middle than in elementary schools.

Parents may have difficulty helping with schoolwork even before students reach the middle grades. Parents of third through fifth graders who participated in a family mathematics intervention program reported problems in providing guidance with homework (Sloane, 1990). Parents were concerned about their own lack of knowledge beyond simple arithmetic and about possible differences between the methods they used to help their children and the methods teachers used. In addition to these concerns about cognitive skills and teaching strategies, parents also were concerned about the affective quality of helping interactions; parents or children sometimes felt frustrated and unhappy during homework help sessions. These concerns occurred in this sample even though the participating mothers far exceeded the level of formal education one would expect to be necessary to help third through fifth graders; 53% of Caucasian, 21% of African-American, 17% of Native American, and 6% of Hispanic mothers had completed college and some had taken graduate level courses.

Parents cannot teach children skills they do not themselves possess and exercise regularly in their own lives (Chipman, 1992; Scott-Jones, 1987). When parents are highly skilled in the subjects middle grades students are learning, however, parents can act as tutors. One-on-one tutoring has great advantages over the group instruction of classrooms (Chipman, 1992). In these interactions, parents are "experts" giving individual attention and instruction to the "novice" or "apprentice."

Mathematics and science have been the focus of some home learning intervention programs, because American children lag behind children in other countries in these subject areas. In addition, within the United States, African-American and Hispanic students lag behind white students in mathematics and science achievement and are underrepresented in careers related to mathematics and science (Clewell, Anderson, & Thorpe, 1992). Family Math (Shields & David, 1988; Stenmark, Thompson, & Cossey, 1986) is a program developed to improve the mathematics achievement of students from kindergarten through twelfth grade. Family Math emphasizes increasing the involvement of females and ethnic minorities in mathematics and increasing the involvement of families in their children's mathematics education. The focus of the program is on problem solving and everyday uses of mathematics. Trainers demonstrate activities and teaching styles to be used by parents at home. An example of the tasks used in Family Math is playing with dice to learn the concept of probability (Stenmark et al., 1986).

Recruitment of parents into programs such as Family Math may be a problem. Thompson reported that 7 to 15 parents participated in Family Math sites. Although recruitment may be a problem, the implementation of Family Math has been undertaken with families described as hard to reach (Shields & David, 1988). Family Math programs initially were offered through schools and reached suburban communities. Through community agencies, Family Math was established in poor and minority communities. Shields and David (1988) report on five sites, including Hispanic, African-American, and Native American Indian communities. Family Math classes were held in libraries, homes, and schools. Shields and David conclude that Family Math can be as effective in low-income minority communities as in more affluent communities. No evaluations of these implementations are reported, however.

Two evaluations of Family Math are reported in Clewell et al. (1992). Both evaluations focused on parents' attitudes and behaviors following participation in the program. The majority of parents reported positive changes in their attitudes toward mathematics, their knowledge of mathematics, and their assistance with their children's mathematics homework. In addition, more than half of the parent participants later conducted or assisted in Family Math classes or pursued more mathematics education for themselves. Clewell et al. (1992) do not report any evaluation of students' mathematics achievement following participation in Family Math (Stenmark et al., 1986).

The evaluation of Family Math with third to fifth graders and their families reported by Weisbaum (1990) also indicated that parents, who usually were mothers, became more positive about mathematics and about helping their children with mathematics homework. Overall, however, parents did not consider mathematics one of their favorite subjects. Although all parents held a deep commitment to their children's education, the majority did not use Family Math activities in the home. Parents used the teaching strategies learned in Family Math to help children with their homework. Direct assessment of children's mathematics achievement was not included in this evaluation and few parents reported improved mathematics grades for their children.

Elementary students enrolled in a Saturday Family Math and Science program showed achievement gains after one year. Sessions, including field trips and sessions at the schools, were held once each month during the school year. Participants showed a 1.1 grade-equivalent increase in mathematics and a 1.3 grade-equivalent increase in science on the Metropolitan Achievement Tests, compared to a .7 grade-equivalent increase for non-participants in both subjects.

An additional troublesome aspect of reports of such programs is that the complexity and abstract nature of mathematics may not be adequately recognized. For example, Shields and David's (1988) report of Family Math indicates that practical activities such as estimating a grocery bill put parents on equal footing with teachers. When older children are learning more advanced mathematical concepts, however, parents' practical knowledge may not be equivalent to teachers' or students knowledge. Interventions such as Family Math need to address the skill levels required of parents at different grade levels.

The attitude of teachers toward parents' providing learning activities at home is important. Ginsburg et al. (1992) suggest that teachers, because they want to control the process of learning, may be threatened by parents' providing "uncontrolled" learning experiences at home. Teachers are actively involved in the intervention developed by Joyce Epstein. Based on her research linking teachers' practices of parental involvement with students' achievement, Epstein developed a program called Teachers Involve Parents in Schoolwork (TIPS). TIPS includes activities to involve parents in students' homework. The homework assignments require the student to interact with an adult at home regarding an interesting topic from current class work. The interactive homework is expected to convey to the student that parents believe schoolwork is important. TIPS mathematics and language assignments are scheduled once each week; science activities are scheduled twice each month. TIPS activities involve active learning, rather than memorization, and are designed so that parents cannot simply do the homework for the student. Although TIPS activities are designed to be enjoyable, the assignments are graded.

A variation of TIPS is the development of summer home learning packets for seventh and eighth graders, to provide opportunities for continued learning of mathematics and language over the summer (Epstein & Herrick, 1991). The reactions of parents and students to the summer home learning packets were assessed via surveys. Almost one-third of the students indicated that a parent or other adult worked with them at least some of the time. Approximately one-third of parents and students stated they needed more instructions in the use of the packets.

Survey results were used to improve the TIPS packets. Epstein and Herrick (1991) then implemented the TIPS summer home learning program with African-American seventh graders. Students' spring English grades and standardized reading and language test scores were used as pretest scores; posttests administered in the fall assessed the skills targeted in the summer TIPS packets. Almost one-fourth of the students worked on most or all of the TIPS activities with a parent; 41% of the students did not work on any activities with a parent. Pretest scores were not related to amount of work on the TIPS activities but school attendance was related to completion of TIPS activities. Females were more likely than males to complete TIPS activities, even after attendance was controlled. Analyses of posttest scores indicated that the greater the number of TIPS activities completed, the higher the posttest scores. Pretest scores also were correlated with posttest scores, and controlling for pretest scores resulted in no significant independent effect of TIPS use. Further analyses, however, indicated that, although good students remained good students regardless of TIPS use, for "fair" students, high TIPS users had higher posttest scores than low TIPS users.

Epstein and Herrick (1991) also report the results of an evaluation of two newsletters, a general newsletter from the principal and a newsletter on school workshops on helping students at home, distributed in an urban middle school. A telephone survey was conducted with a representative sample of families of sixth, seventh, and eighth graders. The majority of respondents were mothers; almost one-third had completed high school and an additional 28% had completed some college. Almost one-half of the families were not aware of either newsletter. The majority of parents, however, said they wanted more information about helping their children at home.

Learning together. Any effort to encourage learning activities at home must take into account the current status of literacy among American adults. Only a small percentage of adults is completely illiterate, that is, lacking the rudimentary literacy skills of reading and writing. A larger percentage lacks functional literacy skills needed to negotiate everyday life in a technological society. An even larger percentage of adults may lack "empowering" literacy skills, the advanced literacy skills enabling individuals to comprehend complex ideas and phenomena and to engage in discourse on complex issues. It is this aspect of literacy—reading to master complex subjects—that poses the greatest problem in the United States today (Athey & Singer, 1987).

Programs to support learning activities in the home for middle grades must recognize and make accommodations for variations in literacy levels among parents. For young children and their parents, intergenerational literacy programs have been developed in which both parents and children learn to read. This model of learning together could be adapted for some middle grades home learning activities for situations in which parents lack some specific skills but have the requisite basic skills. Although parents contribute to children's academic performance in other ways, such as by encouraging and rewarding achievement, direct help with specific school skills is limited for many parents. In addition, parents may be able to provide help with some subjects but not others.

Related to parents' literacy levels is their proficiency in English. Parents with limited English proficiency may have great difficulty helping their middle grades students with school work. In some instances, students' English proficiency may surpass that of their parents and students may be in a position to help their parents.

An example of the influence parents can have when they must learn along with their children comes from a university professor's description of his childhood and his father in Nigeria. Although this example is from a culture different from the United States, similar relationships undoubtedly exist in many cultural groups. The father was barely literate but the son credits his father with fostering the son's mental development.

> My father was the type of semi-literate villager who would buy a newspaper during a visit to the nearby township and then spend a whole week spelling his way through it. When I learned to read, he made me read newspapers or the Local Government Ordinance to him, first in English and then translated into Igbo, a test of the education I was supposed to be getting...
> My father was my mentor, trainer... (Echewa, 1993, p. D7)

Identifying sources of help. When parents are not able to help directly, they may be able to identify sources of help, if such help is available. The concept of social support as an important buttress to parenting (Slaughter-Defoe, 1992) should be included in efforts to increase learning activities in the home. Siblings or other adults in the home may be able to provide help to students in the middle grades. In addition, parents might harness and channel peer relations, which are becoming important in the middle grades, by encouraging joint out-of-school projects in the home with middle grades students and their friends.

Parents also can help by identifying sources of support in the school and community. Homework hotlines may be provided by schools or community agencies. Individual tutors may also be available. Communities may provide programs that focus on school skills. Of the community after-school programs studied by the Center for Early Adolescence (Davidson & Koppenhaver, 1988), some were sponsored by community agencies such as churches, businesses, and social-service agencies. Few programs were for early adolescents and, in most of these, young adolescents were the oldest eligible participants in programs designed for elementary school children. Examples of after-school community literacy programs from Davidson and Koppenhaver's (1988) study include an East Harlem community literacy center for all ages and levels of readers, including adults, operated from a combination library-bookstore; an individual tutoring program developed in Chicago in 1965 by a corporation and a housing project; and a program in which college and high-school students tutor younger Native American students. Davidson and Koppenhaver (1988) found that public libraries were unlikely to sponsor programs for adolescents, which is surprising given that libraries have provided literacy programs for children and for adults. Davidson and Koppenhaver (1988) also found community-based literacy programs that were part of comprehensive services to families and children. One program, the Philadelphia Federation of Settlement Houses, includes among its activities after-school, summer school, and summer camp programs to enhance the literacy skills of young adolescents. The summer day camp program provides literacy enhancement activities along with the usual swimming and arts and crafts. A summer residential camp that provides literacy instruction is being developed.

The community or neighborhood also can affect the focus of activities in the home. Characteristics of the neighborhood can direct parents and middle grades students away from enriching activities to those focused on safety, avoiding trouble, and eventually escaping from the neighborhood. The many problems of poor urban neighborhoods are widely acknowledged. Illegal drugs and associated violence create an unsafe atmosphere for families in these neighborhoods. Families may be in physical danger and developing adolescents may be exposed to lifestyles that are not conducive to high educational achievement. The family's provision of home learning activities is made more difficult when the neighborhood has few elements that value or require high educational achievement. An ongoing study of young adolescents' neighborhoods (Eccles & Harold, 1993) finds that parents from less risky neighborhoods are able to take advantage of available neighborhood resources whereas parents in high-risk, low-resource neighborhoods must rely on what they can do in the home; the latter group of parents emphasizes protecting their young adolescents from outside dangers. According to Garbarino and Sherman (1980), the neighborhood provides the ecological niche that "makes or breaks" low-income families.

Urban African-American communities are often discussed in terms of potential negative effects on adolescents. African-American communities, however, continue to be important in augmenting the efforts of families to socialize their children toward achievement (Billingsley, 1968, 1992). Community members, in formal roles as teachers and ministers, as well as in informal roles, provide models and direct help for African-American youth. Billingsley (1968, 1992) singled out the Black church as having an especially positive impact. The church may not necessarily be in the physical neighborhood in which a family resides. "Community," then, can be defined by organizations chosen by families. The "church community" or the "church family" may be important in some adolescents' achievement.

Doing

Parents with low literacy skills may have difficulty helping their middle grades students. Another problem arises when parents are highly skilled and find it more efficient and more effective to do school work for children, instead of helping and guiding their children. Parents' motivation to help may lead to overinvolvement in young adolescents' schoolwork. Overinvolved parents may complete projects that young adolescents should do for themselves. Parents' goal should be to help young adolescents acquire or practice skills. Parents must judge when and how much to help and must encourage children to take responsibility for their own work.

Parents should foster an active role on the part of the student. The student's decisions to seek help from parents or from other sources should be monitored by parents. When parents do provide help, they must not dominate the helping interaction.

The affective relationship between parent and adolescent is important. Successful instruction occurs in contexts that have positive social meanings (Reder, 1992). Parents' helping adolescents with homework needs to be a positive social interaction rather than a negative or coercive interaction. Students in middle grades are moving toward increased independence and need a supportive environment in which to realize their achievement strivings. Eccles et al. (1993) suggest that there is a mismatch between young adolescents' needs for autonomy and both the home environment and the school environment. The lack of fit between young adolescents' needs and their experiences in home and school can lead to conflict. According to Eccles et al., young adolescents perceive their opportunities for decision-making to be less than they want and need.

Summary and Future Directions

Activities in the home that support school learning are affected by a complex array of factors: characteristics of the middle grades student; characteristics of parents; siblings; other adults in the household; peers; resources in the community; and characteristics of the school. The content and impact of home learning activities are affected by the interaction of these variables. Programs to support learning activities in the home must take into account these interacting variables.

Program developers also should bear in mind that parental involvement in learning activities in the home is only one of several important connections between families and schools. Epstein and Connors (1993) outlined six types of connections between home and school; Epstein's earlier work outlined five types. The six are: basic obligations of families to provide for children; basic obligations of schools to communicate with parents; parental involvement at school; parental involvement in learning activities in the home; parental involvement in school governance and decision-making; and collaborations and exchanges with the community.

Program developers must give careful attention to the characteristics of the school and teacher practices. In addition to variations in quality of education provided, schools may differ in the extent to which they support and encourage home learning. Teachers assign homework. A school or district may have specific policies and practices related to homework. Families' role in homework, therefore, is necessarily constrained by the schools' or teachers' decisions regarding homework. In addition, in the middle grades, where teaching is departmentalized, homework in each subject may be assigned by a different teacher.

In spite of the general consensus that parental influence is strong, Nickerson

(1992) cautions us that the details of how parents influence children's thinking have not been empirically established. Nickerson further asserts that the research community has not communicated well with parents, and that books for parents typically are written in ways that oversimplify or distort what we know. Similarly, Slaughter-Defoe (1992) questions whether our knowledge base is sufficient to support the development and implementation of effective programs for parents. Thus, interventions must be cautious and carefully evaluated. Typically, programs have limited funds that are used to provide services rather than to set up evaluations. Program developers often must rely upon anecdotal evidence of their programs' success.

Programs to enhance learning activities in the home must take into account the pervasive poverty in American society. These programs cannot have a far-reaching impact unless other reforms take place in the quality of schooling and the structure of the economy (Ginsburg et al., 1992). Approximately one-fifth of children under 18 years of age live below the poverty level (Bane & Ellwood, 1989; Children's Defense Fund, 1990). The proportion of adolescents living in poverty has increased steadily since the mid-1970s (Furstenberg & Condran, 1988). Although poverty is wide-ranging, affecting many white and two-parent working families (Bane & Ellwood, 1989), a disproportionate number of African-American, Hispanic children, and children in single-parent families live in poverty. According to the Children's Defense Fund (1990), 44% of Black, 36% of Hispanic, and 15% of white children live in poverty.

Although poverty is associated with low achievement, some children from poor families perform well in school and some middle-income children have difficulties. In the National Longitudinal Survey of Young Americans, the majority of 14- and 15-year-olds who had inadequate basic skills were poor. Poor students with good basic skills, however, were no more likely to drop out of high school two years later than were their more affluent counterparts (August, 1988).

The framework developed in this paper is one that allows the development of a set of activities that would be appropriate for the broad range of families and students we hope to reach in our educational system. Many parents engage in learning activities in the home and could use their experiences to contribute to program development. The hypothesized four levels of parental involvement in learning activities at home are listed below, with some proposed guidelines for each.

Valuing

1. Parents need to reflect on, formulate, or reformulate broad educational values. Schools can assist by allowing parents to be involved in school governance, in the setting of or commenting on school goals and values. Schools can provide parents the opportunity to reflect on and discuss their educational values. Schools' educational values and goals for all middle grades

students should be clear and should be conveyed clearly to parents.

2. Parents need to communicate the general educational values to their middle grades students. Specific expectations for the individual student also should be conveyed. Parents need to convey these values and expectations both directly in their conversations and indirectly through their behavior and everyday interactions with middle grades students.

3. Parents need to emphasize the importance of students' effort and avoid making negative attributions to students' ability.

4. Parents need to emphasize the importance of specific subjects, such as mathematics, and their relationship to everyday life and later careers.

Monitoring

1. Parents need information from the school about the amount of homework to expect in various subjects, and students' performance and skills, so that they have realistic and appropriate expectations.

2. Parents need to exercise firm control by setting and enforcing rules and checking on adolescents' compliance in homework and related activities. Because young adolescents need to develop a sense of autonomy, parental control must be tempered by an appropriate degree of responsiveness to adolescents' feelings, needs, and wants.

Helping

1. Parents who are highly skilled in a subject can help to teach the middle grades student in an expert-novice or apprenticeship model. As middle grades students become proficient in their academic subjects, they may close the "knowledge gap" between themselves and their parents in some subjects. Parents may be unable to help directly.

2. Parents' helping may follow the model of learning together. Some parents help by learning along with the student. Parents acquire skills and knowledge in order to help their students, and students may, in turn, help their parents.

3. When parents have exhausted their own resources for helping, they may contribute by identifying sources of help. Resources in the community, the school, other family members, and even the adolescents' peer group can serve as an important buttress to parenting.

Doing

1. Parents must set appropriate limits on helping. Parents must judge carefully how much help to give so that the middle grades student increases in responsibility, autonomy, and competence.

2. Parents must establish an appropriate emotional tone and avoid conflict in attempting to help their middle grades students. Parents must avoid a mismatch between the adolescents' need for autonomy and the parents' desire to control interactions with the adolescent.

Footnotes

1. This conceptualization is from the author's ongoing study of parental involvement, which is part of the national Center on Families, Communities, Schools, and Children's Learning, funded under the Educational Research and Development Center Program (Agreement No. R117Q00031) as administered by the Office of Educational Research and Improvement, U.S. Department of Education.

References

Athey, I., & Singer, H. (1987). Developing the nation's reading potential for a technological era. *Harvard Educational Review, 57*(1), 84-93.

August, D. (1988). *Making the middle grades work*. Washington, DC: Children's Defense Fund.

Baker, D.P., & Stevenson, D.L. (1986). Mothers' strategies for children's school achievement: Managing the transition to high school. *Sociology of Education, 59*, 156-166.

Bane, M.J., & Ellwood, D.T. (1989). One-fifth of the nation's children: Why are they poor? *Science, 245*, 1047-1053.

Baumrind, D. (1966). Effects of authoritative parental control on child behavior. *Child Development, 37*, 887-907.

Baumrind, D. (1972). An exploratory study of socialization effects on Black children: Some Black-White comparisons. *Child Development, 43*, 261-267.

Baumrind, D. (1991). Effective parenting during the early adolescent transition. In P.A. Cowan & M. Hetherington (Eds.), *Family transitions* (pp. 111-163). Hillsdale, NJ: Erlbaum.

Bempechat, J. (1992). The intergenerational transfer of motivational skills. In T.G. Sticht, B.A. McDonald, & M.J. Beeler (Eds.), *The intergenerational transfer of cognitive skills.* Vol. II (pp. 41-48). Norwood, NJ: Ablex.

Billingsley, A. (1968). *Black families in White America*. Englewood Cliffs, NJ: Prentice-Hall.

Billingsley, A. (1992). *Climbing Jacob's ladder: The enduring legacy of African-American families.* New York: Simon & Schuster.

Bronfenbrenner, U. (1979). *The ecology of human development*. Cambridge, MA: Harvard University Press.

Bronfenbrenner, U. (1986). Ecology of the family as a context for human development: Research perspectives. *Developmental Psychology, 22*, 723-742.

Children's Defense Fund (November, 1990). U.S. fails to reduce child poverty. *Children's Defense Fund Reports, 12*(3), 1, 10.

Chipman, S.F. (1992). The higher-order cognitive skills: What they are and how they might be transmitted. In T.G. Sticht, B.A. McDonald, & M.J. Beeler (Eds.), *The intergenerational transfer of cognitive skills*. Vol. II (pp. 128-158). Norwood, NJ: Ablex.

Clark, R. (1983). *Family life and school achievement: Why poor Black children succeed or fail.* Chicago, IL: University of Chicago Press.

Clewell, B.C., & Anderson, B. (1992). *Women of color.* Washington, DC: Center for Women Policy Studies.

Clewell, B.C., Anderson, B., & Thorpe, M.E. (1992). *Breaking the barriers: Helping female and minority students succeed in mathematics and science.* San Francisco, CA: Jossey-Bass.

Cooper, C.R., Grotevant, H.D., & Condon, S.M. (1983). Individuality and connectedness in the family as a context for adolescent identity formation and role-taking skill. *New Directions for Child Development, 22,* 43-59.

Davidson, J., & Koppenhaver, D. (1988). *Adolescent literacy: What works and why.* New York: Garland.

Dauber, S., & Epstein, J. (1992). Parents' attitudes and practices of involvement in inner-city elementary and middle schools. In N. Chavkin (Ed.). *Minority parent involvement in education* (pp. 53-72). Albany, NY: State University of New York Press.

Demick, J., Bursik, K., & Dibiase, R. (1993). *Parental development.* Hillsdale, NJ: Erlbaum.

Dornbusch, S. M., Ritter, P. L., Leiderman, P. H., Roberts, D. F., & Fraleigh, M. J. (1987). The relation of parenting style to adolescent school performance. *Child Development, 58,* 1244-1257.

Eccles, J., & Harold, R. (1993). Parent-school involvement in the early adolescent years. *Teachers' College Record, 94,* 568-587.

Eccles, J., Midgley, C., Wigfield, A., Buchanan, D., Flanagan, C., & Mac Iver, D. (1993). Development during adolescence: The impact of stage-environment fit on young adolescents' experiences in schools and families. *American Psychologist, 48*(2), 90-101.

Echewa, T.O. (1993, June 20). The son a carbon copy of the father who raised him in Nigeria. *The Philadelphia Inquirer,* D7.

Epstein, J.L. (1986). Parents' reactions to teacher practices of parent involvement. *The Elementary School Journal, 86,* 277-294.

Epstein, J.L. (1987). Toward a theory of family-school connections: Teacher practices and parent involvement. In K. Hurrelman, F. Kaufmann, & F. Losel (Eds.), *Social intervention: Potential and constraints* (pp. 121-136). New York: DeGruyter.

Epstein, J. L. & Connors, L. J. (1993). *School and family partnerships in the middle grades.* (Contract No RR-91-1720.08). Denver, CO: RMC Research Corporation.

Epstein, J., & Herrick, S. (1991). *Two reports: Implementation and effects of summer home learning packets in the middle grades* (Report No. 21). Baltimore, MD: Johns Hopkins University.

Epstein, J.L., & Scott-Jones, D. (in press). *School-family-community connections for accelerating student progress in the elementary and middle grades.*

Furstenberg, F.F., & Condran, G.A. (1988). Family change and adolescent well-being: A reexamination of U.S. trends. In A.J. Cherlin (Ed.), *The changing American family and public policy* (pp. 117-155). Washington, DC: The Urban Institute Press.

Garbarino, J., & Sherman, D. (1980). High-risk neighborhoods and high-risk families: The human ecology of child maltreatment. *Child Development, 51,* 188-198.

Ginsburg, H.P., Bempechat, J., & Chung, Y.E. (1992). Parent influences on children's mathematics. In T.G. Sticht, B.A. McDonald, & M.J. Beeler (Eds.), *The intergenerational transfer of cognitive skills*. Vol. II (pp. 91-121). Norwood, NJ: Ablex.

Keith, T.Z., Reimers, T.M., Fehrmann, P.G., Pottebaum, S.M., & Aubey, L.W. (1986). Parental involvement, homework, and TV time: Direct and indirect effects on high school achievement. *Journal of Educational Psychology, 78,* 373-380.

Leitch, M.L., & Tangri, S.S. (1988). Barriers to home-school collaboration. *Educational Horizons, 66*(2), 70-74.

Lerner, R.M. (1986). Plasticity in development: Concepts and issues for intervention. *Journal of Applied Developmental Psychology, 7*, 139-152.

Levenstein, P. (1988). *Messages from home: The mother-child home program and the prevention of school disadvantage.* Columbus, OH: Ohio State University Press.

Mason, J.M., & Kerr, B.M. (1992). Literacy transfer from parents to children in the preschool years. In T.G. Sticht, B.A. McDonald, & M.J. Beeler (Eds.), *The intergenerational transfer of cognitive skills,* Vol. 2 (pp. 49- 68), Norwood, NJ: Ablex.

Marshall, S.P. (1992). What mathematical cognitive skills do parents offer children? In T.G. Sticht, B.A. McDonald, & M.J. Beeler (Eds.), *The intergenerational transfer of cognitive skills,* Vol. 2 (pp. 122-127), Norwood, NJ: Ablex.

McPartland, J. M. (1987). *Balancing high quality subject-matter instruction with positive teacher-student relations in the middle grades: Effects of departmentalization, tracking, and block scheduling on learning environments.* (Tech. Rep. No. 15). Baltimore, MD: The Johns Hopkins University.

McPartland, J. M., Coldiron, J.R., & Braddock, J.M. (1987). *School structures and classroom practices in elementary, middle, and secondary schools.* (Tech. Rep. No. 14). Baltimore, MD: The Johns Hopkins University.

Nickerson, R.S. (1992). On the intergenerational transfer of higher-order skills. In T.G. Sticht, B.A. McDonald, & M.J. Beeler (Eds.), *The intergenerational transfer of cognitive skills,* Vol. 2 (pp. 159-171), Norwood, NJ: Ablex.

Nicklos, L.B., & Brown, W.S. (1989). Recruiting minorities into the teaching profession: An educational imperative. *Educational Horizons, 67*, 145-149.

Pipp, S., Shaver, P., Jennings, S., Lamborn, S., & Fischer, K.W., (1985). Adolescents' theories about the development of their relationships with parents. *Journal of Personality and Social Psychology, 48*, 991-1001.

Reder, S. (1992). Getting the message across: Cultural factors in the intergenerational transfer of cognitive skills. In T.G. Sticht, B.A. McDonald, & M.J. Beeler (Eds.), *The intergenerational transfer of cognitive skills,* Vol. II (pp. 202-228).

Rogoff, B. (1990). *Apprenticeship in thinking: Cognitive development in social context.* New York: Oxford University.

Scientist at work: Benjamin S. Carson (1993, June 8). *The New York Times,* pp. C1, C12.

Scott-Jones, D. (1984). Family influences on cognitive development and school achievement. *Review of Research in Education, 11*, 259-304.

Scott-Jones, D. (1987). Mother-as-teacher in the families of high- and low-achieving low-income Black first-graders. *Journal of Negro Education, 56*, 21-34.

Scott-Jones, D. (1988). Families as educators: The transition from informal to formal school learning. *Educational Horizons, 66*, 66-69.

Shields, P.M., & David, J.L. (1988). *The implementation of Family Math in five community agencies.* Berkeley, CA: University of California Lawrence Hall of Science.

Slaughter-Defoe, D.T. (1992). Forward to the past: Black and White American families, literacy, and policy lag. In T.G. Sticht, B.A. McDonald, & M.J. Beeler (Eds.), *The intergenerational transfer of cognitive skills,* Vol. 2 (pp. 69-83), Norwood, NJ: Ablex.

Sloane, K. (1990). *The families of Family Math research project.* Berkeley, CA: University of California Lawrence Hall of Science.

Steinberg, L.D. (1987). Impact of puberty on family relations: Effects of pubertal status and pubertal timing. *Developmental Psychology, 23*, 451-460.

Stenmark, J., Thompson, V., & Cossey, R. (1986). *Family Math.* Berkeley, CA: University of

California Lawrence Hall of Science.

Stevenson, D., & Baker, D. (1987). The family-school relation and the child's school performance. *Child Development, 58*, 1348-1357.

Stipek, D.J., Valentine, J., & Zigler, E. (1979). Project Head Start: A critique of theory and practice. In E. Zigler & J. Valentine (Eds.), *Project Head Start: A legacy of the war on poverty* (pp. 291-314), New York: The Free Press.

Tangri, S.S., & Leitch, M.L. (1982). *Barriers to home-school collaboration: Two case studies in junior high schools.* Washington, DC: National Institute of Education, Final Report.

Weisbaum, K. S. (1990). *Families in family math research project.* (Final Report). Berkeley, CA: University of California Lawrence Hall of Science.

Youniss, J., & Smollar, J. (1989). *Adolescent reations with mothers, fathers, and friends.* Chicago: University of Chicago Press.

Chapter 5

Bringing Schools and Communities Together in Preparation for the 21st Century: Implications of the Current Educational Reform Movement for Family and Community Involvement Policies

Patrick M. Shields

Overview

Current efforts to improve the nation's schools depart radically from previous reform movements in their willingness to question the basic structures of the system of educating our children. Unlike earlier efforts that sought to extend the benefits of the current system to excluded groups or that worked to increase the quantity of education received by all children, today's reforms seek to redesign schools from the bottom up in order to create new institutions for the 21st Century.

Underlying this reform movement are a number of assumptions that are very different from those guiding the reforms of the late 1960's, the 1970's, and the early to mid-1980's. First, we have come to understand that teaching and learning have to focus on the acquisition of critical thinking skills for all students. Second, we recognize that the school, not the statehouse or Washington, is the appropriate locus for decisions about how to improve teaching and learning. Third, changing the teaching and learning environment while giving school staff more responsibility for designing that environment will require much more from teachers and administrators. Fourth, in return for the increased responsibilities, schools must be held more accountable for their outcomes. Finally, districts, states, and the federal government will have to assume new roles to provide the resources and assistance necessary to enable school staff to take on these new challenges.

This vision of school improvement compels us to create a new conception of the appropriate relationship between the school and its community, parents, and families. Pedagogically, as we have come to know the importance of rooting learning in children's real lives, we can no longer tolerate the artificial boundaries between the classroom and the home. Politically, as we move the authority for decision-making down to those closest to children, we cannot afford to exclude parents and community members from the process of crafting new schools. Nor can we avoid being held more directly accountable to the immediate community constituency for decisions made at the school site. Practically, schools have no chance of enacting the fundamental changes on the reform agenda in the absence of wholehearted support from their entire community (parents, citizens, and business).

The idea that schools can best succeed by isolating themselves and their students from the community has been discredited. As we move toward the next century, the improvement of our schools will have to be accompanied by closer connections between schools and their communities, teachers, and families.

In this paper, I explore the implications of the current reform agenda for governmental policies concerning the involvement of communities and families. The underlying questions I will try to address are: (1) What are the most appropriate roles for parents and communities in the current efforts to improve schooling?; and (2) What policies should federal, state, or local decision-makers put in place to support this involvement? Where relevant, I focus special attention on policies related to the middle grades (4-8).

In the following section, I provide a brief review of the history of educational reform and parent involvement policies over the past few decades. I then describe how the current wave of reform differs from previous efforts and discuss the implications for parent and community participation in the schools. Based on this discussion, I outline a set of policy recommendation for decision-makers at all levels of the educational system. Finally, I point to some promising directions for future research.

A Brief History of Educational Reform and Policies on Parent Involvement

The modern history of educational reform begins with the Great Society legislation designed to address the needs of "disadvantaged" populations. The legislation began with Head Start in the 1964 Economic Opportunity Act and the Elementary and Secondary Education Act (1965), continued with Follow Through (1967), The Bilingual Education Act, the Migrant Education Act, and perhaps ended with the Education for All Handicapped Children Act (1975).

This set of laws was based on the premise that although we know how to educate children, certain subsets of children are excluded, by the lack of ability or will on the part of state and local officials, from equal opportunities for quality education. Each program then sought to increase children's opportunities by providing funds to local governments (or community agencies) and requiring that the funds be spent on specific categories of activities (e.g., basic reading skills, health services) and for specific types of children (poor, limited English-speaking, etc.)

These programs reflected federal policymakers' beliefs that in the absence of categorical requirements state and local educators would not ensure that special populations received equal educational opportunities. Based on this same belief, these pieces of legislation included a requirement for some form of parent or community involvement, typically in the decision-making process through some form of council. The rationale for the community participation mandate was summed up well by Robert Kennedy in his testimony in favor of Head Start:

> The institutions which affect the poor—education, welfare, recreation, business, labor—are huge complex structures operating outside their control...(We) must basically change these organizations by building into these programs real representation for the poor in the planning and implementation of the programs: giving them a real voice in their institutions (cited in Piven and Cloward, 1971, p. 20).

Title I of the Elementary and Secondary Education Act of 1965 (now Chapter 1) provides a telling example of the evolution of federal policy on the involvement of parents. Following the logic expressed by Robert F. Kennedy, the original Title I legislation called for "community participation" in the compensatory program. In response to numerous allegations that funds were being misspent (e.g., Martin and McClure, 1969), however, policymakers repeatedly strengthened the participation requirement. By 1970, the U.S. Commissioner of Education required district-level parent councils in all local agencies receiving Title I funds. In 1974, a requirement for school-level councils was added to ensure parents a voice in the program. In 1978, when Congress again reauthorized the legislation, the parent involvement requirements were further strengthened to include specific areas of responsibility for parents and to outline the steps districts and schools had to take to support the involvement of parents (Shields, 1989).

This trend toward stricter requirements for parent involvement in education programs shifted in the early 1980s as the federal government began to favor more state and local control of programs. For example, the 1981 reauthorization of Title I deleted the formal requirement for parents, replacing it with a simple call for "consultation with parents." Subsequent reauthorizations and regulations, while clarifying congressional intent that parents be involved in the program, have never reinstated the formal requirements of the earlier legislation.

In fact, during the 1980's, as the earlier concern with bringing excluded groups into the political process of educational decision-making waned, policy-makers showed a renewed interest in involving parents more directly in their children's education, especially in support roles at home. Policies promoting support roles for parents also go back to the early Head Start legislation and are based on the simple fact that parents are children's first and primary teachers, for even school-age children spend just over a tenth of their time in formal institutions of learning (Walberg, 1984). Thus, throughout the 1980s, programs such as Parents As Tutors (PAT) gained increasing prominence and were adopted in many local communities.

Importantly, research has shown the effectiveness of home support programs in promoting gains in student achievement. Even parents with minimal formal education can be taught a variety of techniques (e.g., reading aloud to their children, tutoring them in different subject areas, or simply listening to their children read) that lead to increased school achievement (Clarke-Sterwart, 1983; Lazar & Darlington, 1978). Although much of this research has been done with very young children, studies have also shown that parents can be trained to offer middle grades students instructionally related support at home that results in higher achievement (Barth, 1979).

A key assumption of earlier educational reform movements was a belief that the educational system was working well for some students. The reforms of the Great Society era and the 1970s, by and large, focused on extending opportunities to excluded groups. Even the reforms of the early 1980s, while recognizing some of the shortcomings of the entire educational system, still sought primarily to extend current services to more students for greater periods of time. Thus, for example, during the mid-1980s the most prominent reform efforts involved increasing graduation requirements, extending the school day, and requiring students to take more academic courses (Smith & O'Day, 1991).

Policies promoting the involvement of parents reflected these same priorities. One stream of policies focused on extending opportunities to the parents of excluded groups. A second stream sought to increase the support at home for what was taking place in the school classroom. Both sets of policies brought parents into supporting roles into the system as it then existed. The next wave of reform in which we are currently makes very different assumptions about the value of the entire system of schooling, and in doing so requires a different set of roles for parents and community members.

The Current School Reform Agenda: Creating New Relationships with Families, Parents, and Communities

The current movement to improve the nation's schooling begins with the radically different assumption that our schools are not working very well for any students, so that the entire system needs fundamental changes if we are to prepare youngsters to be productive citizens and workers for the next century. This perspective calls for fundamental shifts in our conceptions of the classroom, of the school, of governance and authority relationships, and of organizational structures supporting schooling.

In turn, these changes require a new series of relationships between the classroom and home, between educators and families, and between schools and their broader community. In this section of the paper, I review the major components of the new vision of educational reform and discuss their implications for the involvement of parents and community members in the schooling process.

New Ways of Teaching and Learning: Breaking Down the Barriers between Home and Classroom. At the heart of the current wave of reform is a vision of how teachers and students interact and the content of that interaction. No longer can we be satisfied with wholly teacher-directed instruction focused on the linear acquisition of basic skills structured by a rigid curriculum. Rather, all students must be provided sufficient opportunity to direct their own learning and to become engaged in stimulating, real-world-based, critical problem solving (Knapp & Shields, 1990).

Central to this view is the idea that instruction must be built on students' out-of-school experience and so teachers need to allow students to use these experiences as the starting points for learning. Effective teachers encourage students to use their personal experiences to make sense of classroom content (Diaz, Moll, & Mehan, 1986; Lipson, 1983; Schreck, 1981). To be able to build on their personal experience, teachers must then allow students opportunities to actively direct their own learning (Cohen, 1988; Slavin, 1986). Moreover, helping students to build on their knowledge base is facilitated when teachers learn more about students' home cultures and adapt their teaching approach to incorporate students' cultural characteristics (Heath, 1983; Shields & Wilson, 1992; Tharp, 1989).

Making school relevant to students' real lives is especially important in the middle grades, for it is during these years that students begin to make conscious decisions about the value and appropriateness of specific subject matter and school in general. In short, this is when students turn on or off to school (Carnegie Council on Adolescent Development, 1989; Estrada, 1992).

For teaching and learning to change in these ways clearly requires the razing of the artificial barriers between the classroom and the home. Students need to understand the value of out-of-school experiences and feel free to bring those experiences into the classroom. Parents cannot remain ignorant of what takes place in classrooms if they are to facilitate their children's learning. Teachers and administrators cannot remain ignorant of students' home lives if they are to structure appropriate learning experiences.

The destruction of these barriers will require a new openness to communicate, to create opportunities for families to spend more time in the school, and for school staff to spend more time in the community. This is not easily accomplished, but is far from impossible, as evidenced in the following vignette of just such a learning activity in an elementary school in a small Appalachian town.

Tapping the community's expertise: A visit to the pumpkin patch

It's a misty, cold morning in South Bernstone, a small coal and farming community in the foothills of the Appalachian Mountains, and a group of fourth graders are sitting cross-legged in their sweaters and boots engrossed in the "lecture" being given by Mr. McCormick, a local farmer and parent to one of the school's sixth graders. Mr. McCormick is simply describing the process of fertilizing, weeding, and harvesting in this field of pumpkins. Mr. McCormick calls on children in turn who are interested in why bugs do not eat up all the pumpkins and how much money he will make when he brings them to market.

This is the class' third visit to the farm—they witnessed some of the seeding and came back to see the new plants sprouting their first fruits. As with their previous visits, the students will go back to school and write essays in small groups for their science class. This time, however, they will also get to bring a pumpkin home, some of which will be cooked in the school kitchen.

This little story illustrates a number of interesting pedagogical techniques: integration of disciplines, writing across the curriculum, real-world-based learning, and cooperative learning. It also provides a wonderful example of a teacher asking community members to share their expertise with students. Here, the community is viewed as a resource to be used to help students learn important concepts—in ways that send students and parents alike a positive message about the value of schooling and the work of the community.

A New Vision of the School House: Forging New Relationships with the Community. A second major theme of the current educational reform movement, which builds on the idea of real-world-based, student-directed learning, involves a vision of the school as an active learning community structured exclusively to enhance student learning. In such "restructured" institutions, the day's schedule, the organization of staff and student time, and the roles and responsibilities of teachers and administrators are designed explicitly to help students learn (Elmore & Associates, 1990) .

Thus, for example, the length of class periods or the assignment of staff to teaching responsibilities are not seen as "givens" that must structure each day. Rather, teachers in these schools might teach only two or three subjects per day, each class involving teams of teachers working with the same group of students for a length of time, depending on the subject to be covered. In the same vein, "teachers" may play several different roles in such a school, acting as instructors, curriculum developers, and decision-makers (David & Shields, 1991).

Following this logic, the school building is not viewed as the only location teaching and learning can take place. Based partly on the argument that students need to learn critical thinking within a real-world context, as we discussed above, teachers in such learning communities are likely to design learning experiences that take place outside of the formal school building. Science projects carried out in nearby parks, mathematics projects requiring the timing of bus routes, and writing assignments based on field experiences are examples of appropriate out-of-school learning experiences for children in the middle grades.

Rethinking the basic structure and routines of the school also leads to consideration of the need to provide other services to students. More and more schools are recognizing that their students' ability to learn is contingent on their physical and mental well-being and the well-being of their families. Consequently, schools are experimenting with new ways of providing more integrated services to their communities, wherein the traditional educational function of the school is extended to include specific health and social services (Reisner, Chimerine, Morrill, & Marks, 1991). Schools embarking on integrated service delivery vary considerably in the extent to which they actually provide versus coordinate such services, but the underlying logic remains the same: the structure of the "school" should be defined not by tradition but by the needs of the specific student body.

The implications of such shifts in the traditional structure of schools for bridging the gap between the school and the community are clear. Staff of such schools are open to leaving the school building to promote educational activities for their students in their own communities. Such steps increase the opportunity for community members to become acquainted with the schools as well as for school staff to know the community better. At the same time, by structuring schools to meet the broader needs of the students' families through the provision of noneducational services, teachers and administrators are opening their doors to the broader community and explicitly expressing their desire to help community members. Thus, restructuring in these ways can both bring the school to the community and attract the community to the school.

Again, breaking down the long-standing barriers between school and community and asking teachers, parents, and even students to assume new roles is no easy task. The following vignette shows how the traditional lines between school and home, teacher and parent can be crossed in ways that promote student learning and increase communication and understanding. In this story, we see how parents, trained in giving classes in mathematics, can attract and interest other parents in coming to school after hours to take part in interesting learning experiences with their fifth and sixth grade children.

Parents as teachers of parents: Family math in a California bordertown

In the front of the room is a Venn diagram on the blackboard; toward the back of the room is a table with various-sized jars filled with beans and M & M's for estimation exercises. A group of 15 parents and their children are sitting around uncomfortably: parents not accustomed to sitting in chairs designed for ten-year-olds, students not used to having their parents at school with them.

At the front of the room, four local parent-leaders and one classroom teacher make last-minute preparations for the class. One parent-leader quiets the crowd and quickly launches into the first activity of the evening. Scissors and paper are handed out and parent-child teams are asked to form a series of shapes. It's not difficult, the children enjoy cutting and everyone can make a couple of shapes from the pieces, while the best can form dozens. Slowly the tension in the room dissipates as all are playing a fun game. The parent-leaders come around to help everyone clean up and to make sure that everyone has some shapes and paper to take home to continue the "geometry lesson."

The next exercise involves measurement. Everyone is given a string and asked to cut it to match the partner's height (each adult is paired with a child). The parent-leaders then ask the class to estimate how many times the string will wrap around a partner's wrist, head, and waist. Glancing around the room, one notices that families, which an hour earlier appeared afraid of the experience, are standing on tables, wrapping strings around one another, pinching each other's fat, laughing—and being introduced to concepts of estimation, measurement, and spatial reasoning. (Shields & David, 1988, p. 29-30)

School-Based Governance: New Opportunities for Parent and Community Participation. A third theme of the current reform movement is school-based governance, based on the argument that if schools are to structure themselves to become true learning environments, the individuals closest to the students must have the authority to make fundamental decisions about how best to serve students (David, 1989). The establishment of true authority at the school site has implications both for the direct involvement of community members in the decision-making process and for accountability to the immediate community for the school outcomes.

The ideas underlying school-based governance can be traced back to the research on effective schools and the findings that well-functioning schools had staff that were consciously assessing their schools' needs and developing coherent plans to address those needs (Purkey & Smith, 1983). The resulting effective schools movement sought to organize such self-reflective activities in a formal committee structure. Some states, such as California, formalized such councils in state-funded school improvement initiatives.

Unlike these effective schools councils or other forms of parent, teacher, and community advisory councils, school-based governance involves the formal transfer of power from a higher level of government to the school. In school-based governance, individuals at the school site do not just advise superiors, they possess the authority to make key instructional, organizational, and budgetary decisions, within legal guidelines.

Along with this new authority come a host of new responsibilities. First, school staff must decide how decisions will be made at the school site. The common strategy is to create steering committees made up of representatives of the key groups in the school community: administrators, teachers, and parents. Educators realize that the logic of having decisions made by those "closest to the children" compels them to include parents in school-based governance.

A second domain of responsibility involves accountability. Having assumed authority for making key decisions, schools should be held accountable for their results. Partly, this accountability is to the higher levels of the system from whom the school received the authority. Thus, for example, in Kentucky's new educational reform law, schools are provided more power over their own operations, but every two years they must meet a state-established standard based on their students' performance on a state-developed test. If schools fare poorly enough, they can be taken over by "distinguished educators" appointed by the state.

At the same time, this "authority for accountability" swap creates a new relationship between the school and the immediate community of families. If schools have responsibility for creating the learning environment, then they are also accountable for their results to their most immediate constituents and consumers: local community members. Not surprisingly, Kentucky's reform law includes a provision that allows parents to transfer their students from failing neighborhood schools at no cost to themselves.

Thus, school-based governance, a centerpiece of current reforms, reshapes the relationship between the community and the school in two fundamental ways. First, it creates the opportunities for parents and community members to have more direct input into the decision-making process than was typically possible under any earlier governance arrangements. Here, parents can sit on, elect representatives to, and attend the meetings of the decision-making bodies of the school. Second, this same structure therefore makes the schools more readily accountable to the community. In certain renditions of school-based governance, this accountability is strengthened by a parental-choice provision.

In sum, moving authority down to the school site through school-based governance can work to democratize the educational decision-making process and create meaningful opportunities for parents to influence the outcomes of that process. Under these circumstances, the provision of school choice to parents can further strengthen their political power in local schools.

The following story is an example of how parents can play an active role in the decision-making process of a school. This example is taken from a large urban school system that has implemented both school-based decision-making and a controlled-choice program, which allows parents some opportunity to choose among the schools their children attend. Here, the staff and parents of two poorly performing schools, a middle school and a high school that share the same campus, are working on rebuilding the schools from the bottom up.

Designing a new school from the bottom up: Parents, teachers, and community members working together

A group of eleven teachers, four parents, and two administrators are sitting around a large conference table in Mohawk Middle School's administrative offices. The design team, as they are called, is trying to rethink the structure of the middle school and the high school, which share a common campus. The two Mohawk schools have been at the bottom of the district's ranking on every conceivable indicator of success (attendance, achievement, dropout rate, etc.). At the urging of a couple of active teachers and parents, the district has handed over considerable responsibility to the school to redesign its educational program. The design team, elected by peers, has the task of making the tough decisions.

At the heart of the discussion today is a proposal to form teams of teachers who will have collective responsibility for the education of a small set of students (around 100). One teacher notes, "I like the idea—but it's not feasible unless the team of teachers and students are all located on one wing of the building. In my case, I would have to move—and I have spent 15 years creating a wonderful learning environment in my classroom. I don't want to have to move." A parent responds, "Are you forgetting what our job here is? We're trying to create a school that works for children—not trying to make teachers' jobs easier. If you need help moving, I'll get some other parents to come in on Saturday and we'll give you a hand." There was a moment of silence and then the discussion returned to the educational issues involved in restructuring the school.

New Requirements for the System Supporting Schooling. A final theme of the current reform agenda concerns the support system around the school, including the district, the state, the federal government, and the local community. In calling for the transformation of the classroom, of the schoolhouse, of relations between home and school, and of the authority structures governing each of these, we are asking much of teachers and school-level administrators. If we expect school staff to assume their new roles of teacher/facilitators, administrator/coordinators, decision-makers, and curriculum developers, they will need significant levels of support.

Such support comes first in the form of technical assistance and staff development—helping school staff to understand and prepare for their new roles. In one study, we have found teachers spending over 160 hours per year on additional formal training to gain the skills they need to change their classrooms and schools (Shields, Anderson, Banburg, Hawkins, Knapp, Ruskus, Wechsler & Wilson, 1994). Thus, a second type of support school staff need is time—time to broaden their teaching repertoires, time to plan with other teachers, and time to participate in the decision-making process.

Such assistance represents an extremely large financial investment —for example, if schools were to provide all staff with an additional 80 hours of staff development (half what is needed in the schools I am currently studying), schools' annual budgets could easily rise by five percent.

Another type of support needed by school staff results from teachers' and administrators' need to craft a school program built on real-world experience and needs. If schools are expected to prepare the next generation of workers, for example, they need to know the required skills for the workplace. Thus, they need ongoing access to and feedback from the business community—not in written reports but through direct communication. Similarly, if we expect teachers to constantly reconsider their activities, they need access to new ideas in the field of pedagogy and in specific subject areas. Again, this access has to be ongoing and fairly easy.

Taken together, these requirements for more technical assistance, time, and access to business and research require a new definition of schools' relationship with their broader communities. Here community is not limited to individual parents and community members in the schools' immediate neighborhoods. Rather I am referring to the larger community of a metropolitan area or region, including those active in business and research. Connections to this broader community are necessary not only because of the need for concrete knowledge, but also to garner the necessary political will to support the massive effort that will be required to change our schools and to keep them improving.

In short, the project of creating self-reflective, constantly improving schools will never take place if the school community tries to do so in isolation. Only with the financial and political resources of the full community will school staff ever have a chance of meeting the challenging goals set forth in the current reform agenda.

Policy Recommendations

As the above discussion makes clear, current efforts to reform schooling force us to reconsider both the basic structures and routines of the school and the traditional relationships between the home, community, and schools. Thus, the first set of recommendations to policymakers and practitioners alike concerns the need to reconceptualize "parent involvement," so that:

- **Parent involvement comes to mean parent, family, neighborhood, and community involvement.** Those with stakes in local schools go beyond the immediate guardians of a school's student body.

- **Family and community involvement is no longer seen as "us against them,"** with the community as the outsider fighting against the professional school staff, or the staff trying to protect the school from the community.

Rather, we need to consider families, communities, and professional staff as members of the same team working toward the same general purposes.

- **Family and community involvement involves a wide range of activities,** necessarily going beyond support for learning in the home.

- **There is no "correct" form of family and community involvement.** Participation will naturally vary from place to place; such variation should be respected.

Working from these basic premises, we can develop a set of more specific recommendations regarding state, district, and federal policies to support family and community involvement. Policymakers should:

- **Provide schools significant flexibility.** Avoid overly prescriptive requirements—for example, defining the specific areas parents have to be involved in and outlining how many times a certain activity has to take place.

- **Develop policies within the context of a broader reform agenda.** Family and community involvement should not be viewed as a project to be accomplished or a program to be implemented, nor should it be considered as separate from more sweeping attempts to change schools. One clear lesson of the research on educational change over the past few years is that shifts in the relationship between the home and school form an integral part of shifts in instruction, governance policies, and accountability mechanisms. So, for example, we should not think restructuring leads to changes in parent involvement, nor do changes in parent involvement lead to restructuring. Rather restructuring involves changes in all structures and relationships, including those involving the community.

- **Utilize the power of the bully pulpit.** Changing schools from the bottom up and creating new relationship between schools and their communities are extremely difficult tasks. Educators need to be convinced that such changes are essential; the public needs to be convinced of the importance of supporting these changes. High-level leaders (federal and state policymakers, district superintendents and school board members) can exercise significant influence by identifying themselves with the needed changes, "selling" them, and building the necessary political coalitions.

- **Assist schools in developing the capacity to involve families and communities.** Asking school staff and community members to assume new roles vis-à-vis one another requires skills that many do not possess. One of the most effective roles played by higher-level policymakers is helping locals develop their own capacity to create these new relationships. Such capacity building involves the provision of staff and parent development, the dissemination of effective models, and expenditure of the funds necessary to release school staff from other responsibilities and to reimburse some community members for their time.

- **Give policies enough time to work.** Again, the tasks we are expecting schools and communities to accomplish are formidable ones. One clear mistake policymakers have made in the past is to expect change to happen quickly and then to shift policy in midcourse before schools have had time to really change.

- **Include policies that provide the community a decision-making voice at the school site.** As districts and states provide schools more authority over key instructional, budgetary, and personnel decisions, parents and community members have to be given a voice in that process.

- **Hold schools accountable to their communities.** Schools must be accountable to their immediate constituents. Policymakers need to ensure that families and communities are kept informed of the progress of their schools and that, after a certain period of time, parents should be provided a no-cost option of choosing other schools if their current schools are not working.

Recommendations for Further Research

These policy recommendations suggest a number of directions for further research in the area of family and community involvement. **First, researchers always should look at the issue of family and community involvement within the whole school environment.** That is, we will learn less by studying the involvement of parents in the school in isolation than we will by asking, "What are the goals and the trajectory of this school, and how does family and community involvement fit into this pattern?"

Second, researchers should examine all types of parent involvement at one time, not isolating one from another. For example, if a school develops a new home tutoring program, we should look at this program alongside other opportunities (or lack thereof) for families and community members to participate at the school site.

Third, researchers need to develop more complex theoretical models of the effects of parent involvement. Too often, we find ourselves searching for effects (did test scores go up with more participation of parents on the school council?) that we cannot reasonably expect to tie directly to the participation of families and community members. Given a more coherent theoretical model, we could make a more convincing case for the impact of family and parent communication on various aspects of the schooling process, which in turn might lead to certain student-level outcomes.

Finally, researchers have to provide examples of effective practice to the practitioners who go out of their way to open their schools and classrooms to us. Good models of how to involve families and communities in meaningful ways are not readily available to many teachers and administrators. Given the privilege of researchers' access, we should be prepared to return to practitioners concrete evidence of our findings.

References

Barth, R. (1979). Home-based reinforcement of school behavior: A review and analysis. *Review of Educational Research, 49*, 436-458.

Carnegie Council on Adolescent Development. (1989). *Turning points: Preparing American youth for the 21st century.* New York: Carnegie Corporation.

Clarke-Stewart, A.K. (1983). Exploring the assumptions of parent education. In R. Haskins & D. Adams (Eds.), *Parent education and public policy* (pp. 257-276). Norwood, NJ: Ablex.

Cohen, E.G. (1988). *On the sociology of the classroom.* Stanford, CA: Center for Educational Research.

David, J.L. (1989). Synthesis of research on school-based management. *Educational Leadership, 46*(8), 45-53.

David, J.L. & Shields, P.M. (1991). *From effective schools to restructuring A literature review.* Washington, DC: U.S. Department of Education.

Diaz, S., Moll, L.C., & Mehan, H. (1986). Sociocultural resources in instruction: A context-specific approach. In California State Department of Education, *Beyond language: Social and cultural factors in schooling language minority children* (pp. 187-230). Los Angeles, CA: California State University, Evaluation, Dissemination and Assessment Center.

Elmore, R.F., & Associates. (1990). *Restructuring schools: The next generation of education reform.* San Francisco, CA: Jossey-Bass.

Estrada, P. (1992, April). *Social-emotional and educational functioning in poor urban youth during the transition to middle school: The role of social support and the contexts of family, schools, and peers.* Paper presented at the annual meeting of the American Educational Research Association, San Francisco, CA.

Heath, S.B. (1983). *Ways with words.* New York: Cambridge University Press.

Knapp, M.S., & Shields, P.M. (1990). Reconceiving academic instruction for the children of poverty. *Phi Delta Kappan, 71*, 752-758.

Lazar, L., & Darlington, R. (1978). *Lasting effects after preschool.* Ithaca, NY: Cornell University.

Lipson, M.Y. (1983). The influence of religious affiliation on children's memory for text information. *Reading Research Quarterly, 18*(4), 448-457.

Martin, R., & McClure, P. (1969). *Title I of ESEA: Is it helping poor children?* Washington, DC: NAACP Legal Defense and Education Fund.

Piven, F.F., & Cloward, R.A. (1971). *Regulating the poor.* New York: Vintage Books.

Purkey, S.C., & Smith, M.S. (1983). Effective schools—A review. *Elementary School Journal, 83*, 427-452.

Reisner, E.R., Chimerine, C.B., Morrill, W.A., & Marks, E.L. (1991). *Collaborations that integrate services for children and families: A framework for research.* Washington, DC: Mathtech, Inc., & Policy Studies Associates, Inc.

Schreck, J. (1981). *The effects of contents schema on reading comprehension for Hispanic, black, and white cultural groups.* Unpublished doctoral dissertation, University of Illinois, Urbana, IL.

Shields, P.M. (1989). *Federal mandates for citizen participation: The case for parents and compensatory education.* Unpublished doctoral dissertation, Stanford University, Stanford, CA.

Shields, P.M., Anderson, L., Banburg, J.D., Hawkins, E.F., Knapp, M.S., Ruskus, J., Wechsler, M.,& Wilson, C.L. (1994). *Improving schools from the bottom up: From effective schools to restructuring.* Menlo Park, CA: SRI International.

Shields, P.M., & David, J. (1988). *The implementation of Family Math in five community agencies.* Menlo Park, CA: SRI International.

Shields, P.M., & Wilson, C.L. (1992, April). *The search for effective instruction for the children of poverty: A multicultural perspective: Accommodating particular student populations.* Paper presented at the annual meeting of the American Educational Research Association, San Francisco, CA.

Slavin, R.E. (1986). *Ability grouping and student achievement in elementary schools: A best evidence synthesis.* Baltimore, MD: The Johns Hopkins University.

Smith, M.S., & O'Day, J. (1991). Systemic school reform. In S.H. Fuhrman & B. Malen (Eds.) *Politics of Education Association yearbook 1990* (pp. 233-267) London: Taylor & Francis Ltd.

Tharp, R.G. (1989). Psychocultural variables and constants: Effects on teaching and learning in schools. *American Psychologist*, *44*, 349-359.

Walberg, H.S. (1984). Improving the productivity of America's schools. *Educational Leadership*, *44*(8), pp. 19-27.

Appendix

Annotated Bibiliography

Ascher, C. (1987). *Improving the home-school connection for poor and minority urban students* (ERIC/CUE Trends and Issues, 8). New York: Columbia University Teachers College. Eric Clearinghouse on Urban Education.

This article includes the definition of roles (i.e., decision-maker, supporter, advocate, teacher) parents can play in their children's education. A variety of research studies on the effects of parent involvement are cited. Some suggestions for making the involvement of low-income parents easier are included, as well as ways to convince parents to become involved. Particular attention is paid to parent involvement in home learning activities.

Becker, H.J., & Epstein, J.L. (1982). *Influence on teachers' use of parent involvement at home* (Report Number 324). Baltimore, MD: The Johns Hopkins University, Center for Social Organization of Schools.

This paper provides an analysis of different ways in which teachers use parental involvement strategies. Survey data from 3,698 teachers in 600 schools in Maryland examined the effects of techniques used, including most successful and least successful strategies. Techniques used depended upon teachers' attitudes and behavior, parental characteristics, and grade level, including separate discussion of fifth grade results. The 14 most commonly used strategies were examined. Attention was also given to obstacles to the use of parent involvement strategies. Most teachers who acknowledged benefits of parental involvement overcame these obstacles.

Bliss, B. (1986). Literacy and the limited English population: A national perspective. In C. Simich-Dudgeon (Ed.), *Issues of Parent Involvement and Literacy* (pp. 5-6). Proceedings of symposium held at Trinity College, Washington, DC.

Two myths often surround discussions of literacy in the United States: (1) that the current school reform movement benefits minority students; and (2) that a technological and information age has emerged that requires new, higher literacy levels. Neither is accurate, for there is no economic imperative for the improvement of literacy, only an urgent social imperative. The implications for enhancing parent involvement include: (1) having realistic expectations about the capabilities of the parents; (2) realizing that immigrant and refugee children often pick up English and become Americanized much more quickly than their parents; (3) understanding that the children who need help the most are those who do not have a parent available to become involved; (4) making educational programs part of a larger array of support systems and services; (5) being aware of a key distinction between immigrant populations and students born and raised in American language minority neighborhoods; (6) focusing our energy and programs at the junior high and middle school levels, where children are a captive audience and still exploring their options; and (7) working in partnership with the private sector in our communities.

Brantlinger, E. (1985a). Low income parents' opinions about the social class composition of schools. *American Journal of Education, 93*, 389-408.

Interviews with low income parents revealed that they were aware of the class character of local schools and believed that high-income schools were superior. Ninety-four percent favored social class school desegregation, believing that their children would thereby obtain a better education and better preparation for social interaction in adult life.

Brantlinger, E. (1985b). Low income parents' perceptions of favoritism in the schools. *Urban Education, 20*(1), 82-102.

Low income parents were interviewed regarding their perspective and feelings regarding class differences in the schools. Most parents felt that schools favor students of higher socioeconomic status. Though they showed interest and concern in their children's education, these parents felt powerless to alter the inequalities they perceived.

Cale, L. (1990). *Planning for parent involvement: A handbook for administrators, teachers, and parents*. Phoenix, AZ: Author.

An excellent resource of ideas and materials for teachers, parents and school administrators to be used for parent involvement planning. Topics include: benefits of parent involvement; how parents want to be involved; the changing American family; changing demographics; identifying obstacles and finding opportunities; principles of effective family-school partnerships; suggestions for successful parental involvement in education; types of parent involvement; and steps for developing successful parent involvement programs. Questionnaires, checklists, ideas, recent legislation, resources and references are also included.

Carnegie Council on Adolescent Development. (1989). *Turning points: Preparing American youth for the 21st century*. New York: Carnegie Corporation.

This report examines the condition of America's young adolescents and how well middle grade schools, health organizations, and community organizations serve them. The Task Force makes recommendations for new structures for middle grade education, which the Task Force believes will help to preserve a strong and vital America.

Chavkin, N.F., & Williams D.L. Jr., (1987). Enhancing parent involvement: Guidelines for access to an important resource for school administrators. *Education and Urban Society, 19*, 164-84.

This article poses a number of theories on parent involvement, such as: administrators must visualize a broader role for parents to participate in their children's education, yet administrators fail to capitalize on parents as an educational resource; parents fail to recognize administrators as access points to the increased involvement they deserve; Parent-administrator partnerships do not automatically reduce the tensions and value differences which exist. Two surveys were conducted - one given to administrators, who were asked their attitudes, current practices, and policies related to parent involvement in elementary school. Parents were given the survey with similar questions. Methods, analysis, and results of the survey are examined.

Chrispeels, J.A. (1987). The family as an educational resource. *Community Education Journal, 14*(3), 10-17.

This paper reports on a three-year project to find ways to strengthen home-school partnerships. Emphasizes the need for parents to have basic information about school goals, programs, and policies in order to support their children at school and home. Techniques for establishing two-way communication were developed emphasizing listening to parents. Schools must develop ways for parents to learn how to help their children, including workshops, and newsletters. Encouraging communication with parents also leads to their effective participation in school policy-making decisions.

Chrispeels, J.A. (1991). District leadership in parent involvement: Policies and actions in San Diego. *Phi Delta Kappan, 72*, 367-371.

Recent California state and district policy initiatives place emphasis on the multifaceted nature of parent involvement and the need for active support. Many district policies provide a clearer definition of parent involvement in the schools. The San Diego County Office of Education has supported the development of both policies and practices in the county's schools by serving as an information clearing house, by acting as a source of direct services to parents and by providing staff development and assistance planning to schools. The San Diego School Board has committed itself to involve parents as partners in school governance, establish effective two-way communication with parents, develop strategies and structures for active participation of parents in their children's education and to use the schools to connect families with community resources.

Clark, R.M. (1989). *The role of parents in ensuring education success in school restructuring efforts.* Washington, DC: Council of Chief State School Officers.

Reginald Clark offers suggestions on the role of parents in ensuring education success by first examining how successful and non-successful students spend their time. He reports that over 180 school days successful students spend more than 630 hours in literacy activities while non-achieving students spend only about 270 hours. Clark discusses the home and community curriculum that is necessary for school success. He examines the role of state education agencies in encouraging and supporting districts in four key areas: planning and implementing effective education programs; soliciting and maintaining parent involvement and community support; helping parents acquire parenting ideas and leadership strategies for helping their children achieve literacy skills; helping districts to directly help students become effectively connected to community-based programs. Clark includes the California policy and specific steps for helping schools develop a written school plan for comprehensive parent involvement activities.

Coleman, J.S. (1991). *Policy perspectives: Parent involvement in education.* Washington, DC: U.S. Department of Education, Office of Educational Research and Improvement.

This article shows how children learned and families functioned in the early years of our nation. It then goes on to show the transformation in homes, schools, and society up through the present day. The author stresses parents' essential role in inculcating values and promoting learning, and highlights the important role communities play as resources for children needing or seeking help or guidance.

Comer, J.P. (1986). Parent participation in the schools. *Phi Delta Kappan, 67*, 442-446.

The author states that, properly carried out, systematic programs of parent participation can benefit children's behavioral and academic development. Obstacles to parent participation in schools exist for many reasons, among them: (1) schools may not want parents present; (2) low-economic and less educated parents may feel they have nothing to contribute; and (3) teachers are not trained in working with parents. In response to those problems, the Yale Child Study Center team began to organize programs in 1968 in low-socioeconomic, under-achieving schools in New Haven, Connecticut. They found the key to improvement to be the organization of school management teams made up of staff, teachers, and parents. They developed a master plan which included building-level objectives, goals, and strategies in three areas: school climate, academics, and staff development.

Comer, J.P. (1988, November/December). School parent relationships that work: An interview with James Comer. *Harvard Education Letter*, pp. 4-6.

This interview with James Comer is an over of his school development program initiated in 1968 in New Haven, Connecticut schools having the lowest achievement and worst behavior problems in the city. Comer's approach to school change is the coming together of key stakeholders in the educational process—the principal, teachers, support staff, and parents. They are all represented in a governance and management group. This group develops a comprehensive school plan with a focus on creating a climate that will facilitate the social and academic growth of students. Comer explains the function of the program on the elementary level and how it had expanded into middle and high schools.

Davies, D. (1988). Low income parents and the schools: A research report and a plan for action. *Equity and Choice*, *4*, 51-57.

Parents from low-income and low-social status homes have the most to gain from parent involvement. Interviews of 150 low-income parents in Boston, Liverpool, and Portugal were conducted. Study examines reasons for social class barriers to participation and possible solutions. Results from interviews summarized that teachers and administrators are as much to blame as parents' unwillingness to participate. Examples given of three worldwide programs which promote involvement of low income families. Also cited is the Institute for Responsive Education (IRE) which has organized a demonstration project in two laboratory schools in Boston and New York to develop ways to overcome social class barriers to parent involvement. Proposed course of action outlined.

Davies, D. (1991). Schools reaching out: Family, school and community partnerships for students' success. *Phi Delta Kappan*, *72*, 376-382.

The article describe the Schools Reaching Out national project that includes three successful practices developed in the project's demonstration schools: (1) the parent centers that were staffed by paid coordinators set up grade-level breakfasts, served as escort and referral service to health and social agencies, operated clothing exchanges, toy/book libraries and school stores, and recruited parent volunteers for teachers; (2) home visitors provided information to families about school expectations, curriculum, rules, student materials, and encouraged participation in Raise a Reader program; (3) action research teams directly involved teachers in studying home/school/community relations and in developing action plans for improving the family and community involvement at their schools.

de Kanter, A., Ginsburg, A.L., & Milne, A.M. (1986, June). *Parent involvement strategies: A new emphasis on traditional parent roles.* Paper presented at the Conference on Effects of Alternative Designs in Compensatory Education, Washington, DC. (ERIC Document Reproduction Service No. ED 293 919)

This paper proposes a new emphasis on home-based parental involvement for parents of low-achieving children, one which takes into account realistic limitations of time and academic skills. This approach differs from federally-mandated programs for low-income parents of children served by Title I. Common characteristics of low-achievers are defined. This involvement approach is based on encouraging parents to use everyday activities in the home to develop in their children behavior and attitudes which will promote academic success.

Doherty, E.J., & Wilson, L.S. (1990). The making of a contract for education reform. *Phi Delta Kappan, 71*, 791-796.

The article describes Boston's efforts to abandon adversarial bargaining in favor of a reform-oriented contract establishing a shared decision-making model of school-based management. The model includes significant parent involvement, a mentoring program for new teachers, a voluntary peer-assistance program for veteran teachers, and collaborative accountability features.

Epstein, J.L. (1987). Toward a theory of family-school connections: Teacher practices and parent involvement. In K. Hurrelmann, F. Kaufmann, & F. Losel (Eds.), *Social intervention: Potential and constraints* (pp. 121-136). New York: DeGruyter.

This paper examines theories that seek to explain family and school connections, shows how data from families and schools about teacher practices of parent involvement support or refute the different theoretical perspectives, and integrates useful strands of multiple theories in a new model to explain and guide research on family and school connections and their effects on students, parents, and teachers.

Epstein, J.L. (1988). How do we improve programs for parent involvement? *Educational Horizons, 66*(2) 58-59.

Some schools have begun to move from telling parents what their involvement is to showing them, guiding and assisting them in appropriate ways to help their children's development and learning. Results from studies of variations in school parent involvement practices show (1) school and family connections must take a developmental course; (2) the changing structure of the family requires consideration; (3) that there is no one set program of parent involvement found even in like schools; (4) each program must be tailored to its own needs and resources; (5) all grade levels need at-home learning. A list of five types of parent involvement and their goals is given.

Epstein, J.L. (1989). Family structures and student motivation: A developmental perspective. In C. Ames & R. Ames (Eds.), *Research on motivation in education: Goals and cognitions* (pp. 259-295). San Diego, CA: Academic Press.

For many years, the Center has conducted research on the alternative variables of schools and classrooms—the structures that schools can change in order to promote more positive effects on student learning and development. This report refers to these structures as the TARGET structures—tasks, authority, rewards, grouping, evaluation, and time. Each of these structures can be changed by schools in ways that will promote student learning and development. The first paper in this report examines these TARGET structures as the basic building blocks of effective school and classroom organization, and relates the TARGET structures to the need to deal with student diversity and develop more effective students. The TARGET structures and their influence are not unique to schools, however, parallel structures exist in family relationships and, as in schools, the structures can be changed in families in ways that promote student motivation and thus improve student learning and development. The second paper examines the existence and influence of the TARGET structures in family relationships.

Epstein, J.L. (1991). Paths to partnerships: What we can learn from federal, state, district, and school initiatives. *Phi Delta Kappan, 72*, 344-349.

This article provides an overview of successful initiatives for connecting schools, families, and communities. On the national level, Chapter 1 programs, FIRST (Fund for the Improvement and Reform of Schools and Teaching) programs, Head Start, and the new Center on Families, Communities, Schools, and Children's Learning are discussed. Key themes across all of these initiatives are: parents and schools share common goals; programs must continue beyond early childhood; programs must include all families; programs make teachers' jobs easier; program development is not quick and easy; grants encourage participation; family/school coordinators are crucial; programs need rooms for parents; programs must reach out to parents without requiring parents to come to school; technology (radio, television, audio- and videotapes, computers) can help improve parent involvement; programs need to be evaluated. The possibilities discussed in this article offer concrete suggestions and may be adopted or revised by other educators.

Epstein, J.L., & Dauber, S.L. (1989). *Evaluation of students' knowledge and attitudes in the Teachers Involve Parents in Schoolwork (TIPS) social studies and art program.* (CREMS Report No. 41). Baltimore, MD: The Johns Hopkins University Center for Research on Elementary and Middle Schools.

This study evaluates the implementation and effects of the Teachers Involve Parents in Schoolwork (TIPS) Social Studies and Art Program in an urban middle school. The program links art appreciation, history, and criticism to middle school social studies curricula. The program involves parents in preparing (at home) or presenting (in school) lessons on well-known artwork. The evaluation found increased student awareness of artists and paintings, development of attitudes toward and preferences for different styles of art, and student capability and willingness to convey their likes and dislikes.

Garfunkel, F. (1986). *Parents and school: Partnerships or politics.* (IRE Report No. 11). Boston, MA: Institute for Responsive Education (ED 280 227)

The literature on parent-school relationships suggests that there have been two dominant trends in the field: the first, which advocates partnership, is consistent with keeping education and schools as they are; the second, which questions school practices, particularly as they relate to particular groups of students — handicapped, minority, poor — and advocates some form of an adversarial model, is focused on changing educational policies and practices. The experience of special education in setting up mechanisms for parents and students to question and oppose school policies and practices is presented as one way of responding to inequities in American schools.

Gotts, E.E., & Purnell, R.F. (1984, April). *Evaluation of home-school communication strategies.* Paper Presented at the Symposium on Parent Involvement in Education: Varieties and Outcomes, annual meeting of the American Education Research Association, New Orleans, LA. (ED 244 376)

The authors have developed a conceptual approach for evaluating the effectiveness of school-home communications. They suggest that researchers should link evaluation activities to the following six aspects of the school-home communications mix: (1) academic level of interaction; (2) locus of communication; (3) intended audience; (4) school-to-home versus home-to-school; (5) topic of communication; and (6) communication method or vehicle used. Subsequent evaluation of communication strategies can lead to improving school effectiveness.

Griswold, P.A. (1986). *Parent involvement in unusually successful compensatory education.* Portland, OR: Northwest Regional Educational Laboratory. (ED 279 428)

This paper evaluates the parent involvement element in 116 successful Chapter 1 projects. Parent and/or community involvement was one of three characteristics of success which appeared most often in those programs. A wide range of participation was reported. Serving on school advisory committees was the most common form followed by training parents as at-home instructors, parent-teacher meetings, classroom visitations, general awareness level workshops, social activities, volunteerism, and help with homework. The author concludes that parent involvement activities reported in pre-1982 Chapter 1 programs are only slightly different from those currently reported.

Harris, Louis and Associates, Inc. (1987). *The Metropolitan Life survey of the American teacher 1987: Strengthening links between home and school.* New York: Author.

This is the latest in a series of Metropolitan Life surveys of teachers in the United States and contains survey results gathered from both teachers and parents. The survey is based on interviews with 1,002 teachers and 2,011 parents. Tables and samples of questionnaires are included. Parents and teachers rate the quality of education and identify specific aspects of school they feel are more successful vs. less successful. The role of parents in education is critiqued and the frequency of contact, forms of involvement, and barriers are explored. New steps to strengthen ties between home and school are evaluated and parent choice in schools is explored. Parents and teachers view the problem of students dropping out of schools and indicate joint steps that can be taken to deal with the problem. Teachers' views of parent involvement are linked with job satisfaction.

Henderson, A.T. (1987). *The evidence continues to grow.* Columbia, MD: National Committee for Citizens in Education.

Annotated bibliography (49 works) covering parent-child, parent-school, and community approaches to parent involvement. From the studies summarized, the editor concludes that: (1) family provides the primary educational environment; (2) involving parents improves student achievement; (3) parent involvement is most effective when it is comprehensive, long-lasting, and well-planned; and (4) benefits of parent involvement are not confined to early childhood; there are strong effects from involving parents throughout high school.

Henderson, A.T. (1988). Parents are a school's best friend. *Phi Delta Kappan, 70,* 148-153.

In recent years, parent involvement in schools has been on the decline. During this same period, children have been falling behind and dropping out in record numbers. Research strongly suggests there is a connection. The author cites studies which conclude that involving parents can make a critical difference in school improvement efforts. These findings have resulted in major efforts to train teachers to work more closely with parents. Yet teacher resistance still exists, and the form parent involvement should take remains a debate. This paper examines: (1) improving parent/child relationships; (2) introducing parent involvement in the school; and (3) building a partnership between the home and the school.

Henderson, A.T., Marburger, C.L., & Ooms, T. (1986). *Beyond the bake sale: An educator's guide to working with parents.* Columbia, MD: The National Committee For Citizens in Education.

This book emphasizes that a child's education is vitally affected by the quality and character of the relationships between home and school. School reform and improvement implies that both home and school commit to a stronger and fuller communication effort, and teachers and administrators must assume the responsibility for initiating and encouraging parent involvement. Effective practices for enhancing parent involvement in schools can be replicated in virtually any school setting. Some constructive and encouraging advice is provided to help build trust and confidence between parents and educators, and to describe the different roles parents play in and around schools. Teachers and principals are provided with some compelling reasons to involve parents and with specific ways parents can be constructively involved. A checklist for gauging a school's current strengths and liabilities is provided along with suggested changes in district, state, and federal policies that will facilitate strong home-school collaboration. A synthesis of research about family-school partnerships is presented.

Henderson, P. (1987). *Parental Involvement (Los Padres Participan). Encouraging Parent Involvement Through ESL, Bilingual Parent-Teacher Workshops, Computer Literacy Classes, and the Bilingual Adult Evening School Program.* New York: New York City Board of Education Office of Bilingual Education. (ED 285 400)

Manual of the Bilingual Demonstration Project for the Parent Involvement Program - Los Padres Participan (New York City). The manual's purpose is to provide teachers and administrators with ideas and materials for working with a bilingual parent population in need of learning English. The materials included are: ESL dialog, parent-teacher workshop agenda, articles on parenting, cultural materials, handouts, and computer literacy teaching materials. This manual could be used in similar ESL parent programs.

McCormick, K. (1989). *An equal chance: Educating at-risk children to succeed.* Alexandria, VA: National School Boards Association.

This report describes a "third wave" of educational reform that focuses on improving academic achievement and preventing dropping out among disadvantaged children. It contains eight sections. The Executive Summary surveys the dimensions of the at-risk situation and strategies to confront it. "The Scope of the Problem" provides background on the issue and describe that is at stake for society as a whole. "Why Are Youth at Risk?" defines the problem in terms of poverty, transience and homelessness, and single-parent families. This section also describes demographic changes and discusses the following problems related to at-risk students: (1) dropping out; low academic achievement; (3) teenage parents; (4) emotional-physical health and related problems; (5) substance abuse; (6) youth unemployment; and (7) juvenile crime. "Research Related to Children at Risk" suggests the importance of parent involvement and early education. "Major Policy Statements" summarizes several papers issued recently by national organizations. In "Schools and the States Respond" the following responses to the problem are described: (1) school action; (2) local solutions; (3) state action; (4) a state action blueprint; and (5) results of a governors' report. In "Policy Implications for School Boards" the need for school restructuring is identified and 10 policy suggestions from experts on students at risk are highlighted. The final section is "A Call to Action." The report concludes with the following appendices: (1) descriptions of effective school programs; (2) descriptions of state programs; (3) an assessment instrument; and (4) a selected bibliography. Statistical data are presented in eight tables.

McLaughlin, M.W., & Shields, P.M. (1986, June). *Involving parents in the schools: Lessons for policy*. Paper presented at the Conference on Effects of Alternative Designs in Compensatory Education, Washington, DC. (ED 293 290)

Two different modes of parent involvement are examined: (1) advisory—associated with federal parent involvement mandates (i.e., Head Start); and (2) collaborative—parent cooperation using either school-based or home-based methods. This paper discusses these two methods and their rationale with emphasis on low-income, low-status parents. School-based methods (volunteers, aides) were the least successful, often pointing out obvious conflicts between low-status families and teachers. Home-based (tutoring) was found to be less confrontational with teachers, created stronger parent-child bond, and showed parents the importance of their participation. Considering the positive and negative attitudes of parents and teachers towards parent participation, what is the role of policy? Guidelines for parent involvement policies are presented.

McLaughlin, M.W., & Shields, P.M. (1987). Involving low-income parents in the schools: A role for policy? *Phi Delta Kappan, 69*, 156-60.

Three questions are addressed concerning a role for policy in parent involvement for low-income, poorly educated parents: (1) does parent involvement work; (2) should it be a policy priority; and (3) is it a feasible target for policy? The author concludes that before policy can play a role, teachers and administrators must first change their beliefs about low-income parents. This finding suggests a policy can modify beliefs, and that a policy approach to parent involvement an strategically combine both pressure and support. The author suggests ways in which norm-based pressure (those tied to incentives which influence behavior of school personnel) and support can be implemented to accomplish this change. Reference provided.

Moles, O.C. (1987). Who wants parent involvement? Interest, skills, and opportunities among parents and educators. *Education and Urban Society, 19*, 137-145.

The author reports on the strong interest of parents and educators in building more support for home-school collaboration. He cites studies and polls from the National Education Association, the Gallup Poll, the Parents and Teachers Association, and recent research. Despite this strong interest, the skills of parents and teachers are not well-developed. The author calls for more parent involvement efforts and more evaluation of promising programs and strategies.

Oakes, J., & Lipton, M. (1990). *Making the best of schools: A handbook for parents, teachers, and policymakers*. New Haven, CT: Yale University Press.

This handbook shows parents and policymakers how to cooperatively improve schools for all children by explaining effective educational practices and schools for all children by explaining effective educational practices and suggesting educational policy reforms. Schools and school policies are analyzed from the following perspectives: (1) culture; (2) learning; (3) the classroom; (4) valued-knowledge; (5) evaluation and sorting; (6) special needs; (7) parent involvement; and (8) school reform. Each perspective offers a broad understanding of the following issues: (1) how the overall organization and atmosphere of a school affect students' opportunities to learn; (2) how classroom environments affects students' self-esteem; (3) how various classroom techniques affect how students learn the most important subjects; and 94) how the home environment affects school success. Recommendations are made for educational policy reform, based on democratic values and educational research. Each chapter includes suggestions for further reading. An index is appended.

Rich, D. (1986, June). *The parent gap in compensatory education and how to bridge it.* Paper presented at the Conference on Effects of Alternative Designs in Compensatory Education, Washington, DC. (ED 293 921)

Emphasizes that parent involvement programs must acknowledge the difference in family structure today. Two major considerations: (1) the majority of working mothers; and (2) the increase of single-parent families. Parents are interested in ways to help their children. Most parents are better educated today and better equipped to have more direct involvement in their children's achievement. Appropriate involvement today provides learning strategies for families to use at home. This "parent-as-tutor" approach acknowledges new family involvement limitations but maximizes that which they can do, thus achieving greater benefits. The Home and School Institute (HSI) system provides parents with techniques to increase children's learning which does not duplicate school work. Ten recommendations presented to promote successful home-school program.

Rich, D., Mattox, B., & Van Dien, J. (n.d.) *Building on family strengths: The nondeficit involvement model for teaming home and school.* Washington, DC: Home-School Institute.

The author states that creating effective parent involvement should be based on the belief that parents are the most important teachers for their children. The family, no matter how poor, can provide the best practical support for children and for schools. The nondeficit model builds on the existing strengths and creativity of homes and schools. Three programs from which data can be reported are cited.

Slaughter, D.T., & Epps, E.G. (1987). The home environment and academic achievement of Black American children and youth: An overview. *Journal of Negro Education*, *86*(1), 3-20.

Parent involvement in their children's educational experiences enhances student achievement. Low socioeconomic status (SES) Black families often lack the human and material resources needed for a positive academic environment at home; however, positive learning environments do exist in some low-SES Black homes. More developmentally oriented, macrosocial studies are needed.

Sullivan, O.R. (1981). Meeting the needs of low income families with handicapped children. *Journal of the International Association of Pupil Personnel Workers*, *25*(1), 26-31.

Discusses the role of pupil personnel workers and educators in providing service for handicapped children of low-income families. Parents need to be aware of their children's rights and the services available in the community and the school. Parent involvement should be encouraged.

Walberg, H. J. (1984). Improving the productivity of America's schools. *Educational Leadership*, *41*, 19-27.

In his synthesis of 20 controlled studies if the past decade, Walberg found the 91 percent of the comparisons favored children in cooperative home-school programs. The effect was twice that

Appendix

of socioeconomic status, and some programs has effects ten times as large. The programs benefitted older as well as younger students. Walberg concludes that school parent programs to improve academic conditions in the home have an outstanding record of success in promoting achievement. He says that "the alterable curriculum of the home" is twice as predictive of academic learning as family socioeconomic status.

Whitten, C.P. (1986). Bilingual education policies: An overview. In C. Simich-Dudgeon (Ed.), *Issues of parent involvement and literacy* (pp. 3-4). Proceedings and Symposium held at Trinity College, Washington, DC.

Regulations issued in June 1986 for implementation of 1984 amendments to the Bilingual Education Act represent a major step in bringing about reform. They have three main focuses: the autonomy of the local education agencies in deciding the amount of native language instruction to be used, recognition of the importance of parental involvement in the bilingual programs, and the need for local agencies to outline plans for managing and financing the instructional program when Title VII funds are reduced or are no longer available. These reforms recognize the major role of the local community in bilingual education. It is the responsibility of those who deal with the parents of limited-English-proficient students to carry the message to them about their role in the reform's success.

Williams, D.L. (1984). *Parent involvement in education: What a survey reveals.* Austin, TX: Southwest Educational Development Laboratory. (ED 253 327)

The Parent Involvement in Education Project, a research project done by Southwestern Educational Development Laboratory, surveyed parents, teachers, principals, and school associated professionals on five different aspects of parent involvement in the elementary grades: (1) attitudes; (2) decisions; (3) roles; (4) activities; and (5) as part of teacher training. Results show parents have a high degree of interest in home-school participation. But how this is achieved shows that parents and educators have different views on certain aspects of parent involvement. Parent involvement interests extend beyond those areas designated as appropriate by the schools. In order for parent involvement to become more acceptable, viable and effective, a clear definition is necessary - one in which all can agree.

Zeldin, S. (1989). *Perspectives on parent education: Implications from research and an evaluation of new partnerships for student achievement.* Washington, DC: Policy Studies Associates.

This study examines issues in designing, implementing, and evaluating programs of parent education, which are designed to promote home-school partnerships and to enhance the skills of caretakers in supporting their children's academic performance. Included in this study was an evaluation of a set of parent education programs sponsored by the Home and School Institute (HSI), called New Partnerships for Student Achievement (NPSA). The study addressed three questions: (1) what do existing research and theory identify as the primary components of effective parent-education programs; (2) what are the strengths and weaknesses of the NPSA programs; and (3) what can be learned from the NPSA programs for the design, implementation, and evaluation of parent-education programs under Chapter 1.